# PRE
# INVESTIGATIONS

Christopher Seddon

M000201840

GLANVILLE PUBLICATIONS

First published in 2015 by Glanville Publications.

Copyright © 2015 Christopher Seddon.

The right of Christopher Seddon to be identified as the author
of this book has been asserted by him in accordance with the
Copyright, Designs and Patents Act 1988.

ISBN 978-0-9927620-6-3

# Contents

# Introduction

Imagine an iceberg where not ninety percent but all bar less than one tenth of one percent lies below the waterline. This tiny fraction represents what we term 'recorded history', or about six thousand years. The remaining six or seven million years is 'prehistory': a vast period of time that begins with the emergence of the first two-legged apes and ends with the rise of the first cities and states.

In my first book, *Humans: from the beginning*, I attempted to present a complete history of the human world up to the time of the first state-level societies. The result, inevitably, was a sizeable volume which although well received requires a significant commitment on the part of the reader, and might not appeal to somebody who wants to just dip their toes into the field of human prehistory. It is for such a reader that this much shorter work is intended. Here, the human past is presented in fifty short chapters. Although they are arranged in roughly chronological order, they are more or less self-contained and may be read out of sequence. I felt that this was a better approach than trying to produce an abridged version of the earlier book. Inevitably, there is some overlap between the two works (which are after all dedicated to the same subject), but I have also included a number of topics that were not covered in *Humans: from the beginning*.

Within my lifetime (which admittedly now spans sixty years), our knowledge the distant past has been greatly increased by modern science. The invention of radiocarbon dating in the 1950s essentially rewrote the prehistory of Europe. More recently, genetic techniques have demonstrated our close evolutionary relationship to chimpanzees, and the recent African origin of modern humans. It has confirmed that our ancestors interbred with Neanderthals and revealed the hitherto-unsuspected existence of the Denisovans, an archaic human species that also interbred with modern humans. Much vital albeit less headline-making work is carried out using methods that would not be practical without computers. We should remember, though, that the study of prehistory is a fairly recent discipline. That there was even such a thing as prehistory was not widely recognised until the mid-nineteenth century.

Human evolution and prehistory is now a fast-moving and dynamic field. Even in the short time since *Humans: from the beginning* was published, there have been a number of epochal discoveries. The date for the emergence of the first humans has been pushed back to 2.8 million years ago; we now have stone tools that were made by our even more distant, more apelike ancestors; we have fossil evidence that modern humans were in China 100,000 years ago, finally putting paid to the notion that modern humans did not leave Africa until around 60,000 years ago. Not least of all, there has been the dramatic announcement of *Homo naledi*, a primitive human species discovered in the depths of the Rising Star cave system in South Africa. *Homo naledi* wasn't even the only new species announced in 2015. These discoveries were widely reported in the media, reflecting the level of public interest in our origins and our past.

This book, like its much longer predecessor, is concerned with a grouping of two-legged apes known as the hominins, of which modern humans (*Homo sapiens*) are but the most recent. The first hominins emerged in Africa around seven to eight million years ago, when our distant ancestors diverged from those of our closest living ape relatives, the chimpanzees. Although we are now the only hominin species in existence, for most of that long period there were several. Even our species has shared the planet with Neanderthals and other archaic humans for much of its existence.

Not all of these hominins were our direct ancestors; many were evolutionary cul-de-sacs that died out completely. Rather than an orderly procession of ever-more 'advanced' species, leading inexorably towards *Homo sapiens*, the hominin family tree has been likened to a tangled bush. The exact number of hominin species within this 'bush' remains uncertain. The first and most obvious reason is that many hominin species almost certainly remain undiscovered. Less obviously, perhaps, palaeoanthropologists frequently disagree on just how many distinct species are represented by the fossil record. The two rival schools of thought are commonly known as 'lumping' and 'splitting': 'lumpers' try shoehorn as many fossils into a single species, while 'splitters' do the exact opposite and proclaim new species and even new genera for each new fossil discovery. For example, a 'splitter' is likely to see *Homo ergaster*, *Homo georgicus* and *Homo antecessor* as separate human species, but to a 'lumper' they are all regional varieties of *Homo erectus*.

What is becoming clear is that after the hominin line split off from the chimpanzees, it went through three main 'phases' of evolution. The first phase lasted from around seven up to 4.2 million years ago and the hominins of this period may be thought of as 'dual-purpose' apes. Their brains were no larger than those of chimpanzees, and they were adapted for both tree-climbing and two-legged walking. Fortunately, there is a remarkably-complete hominin skeleton from this period, belonging to the species *Ardipithecus ramidus*. The 4.4-million-year-old skeleton of a female, popularly known as 'Ardi', was discovered in Ethiopia in 1994, and has greatly increased our knowledge of this period of hominin evolution. Ardi retained tree-climbing adaptations including an opposable big toe and thumb; later hominins retained only the opposable thumb. Subsequent discoveries included an earlier *Ardipithecus* species, *Ardipithecus kadabba*, which lived from 5.8 to 5.2 million years ago; and two even earlier species, *Orrorin tugenensis* and *Sahelanthropus tchadensis*. The latter may push the hominin fossil record right back to the split with chimpanzees.

The hominins of the second phase – which lasted from around 4.2 to 2.0 million years ago – are known as australopithecines. Their brains were still no larger than those of chimpanzees, and they probably still spent time in the trees, but they were now better adapted to walking upright. The opposable big toe gave way to the modern in-line big toe; the foot was arched; and there were other adaptations to the striding gait of a modern human. The australopithecines are now known to have made stone tools not too dissimilar to those of the first humans. They were widely distributed in Africa, though lumpers and splitters argue over just how many species there were. It is generally accepted that the first humans evolved from australopithecines, though from which species and where remains disputed.

The third and final phase lasted from 2.0 million to around 200,000 years ago, and it was during this period that the first humans emerged. In this work, I use the term 'human' to refer to any hominin belonging to Genus *Homo*, not just *Homo sapiens*. When I am referring specifically to the latter, I use the term 'modern human' as a synonym. Just how many human species there have been is a field in which the lumpers and splitters have had a field day, but there are probably at least seven: *Homo habilis*, *Homo erectus*, *Homo heidelbergensis*, *Homo neanderthalensis* (the Neanderthals), *Homo floresiensis* (the diminutive 'hobbit people' from the island of Flores), the recently-announced *Homo naledi*, and *Homo sapiens* (modern humans). Non-modern humans are usually referred to as 'archaic humans'. The brains of the earliest humans were still far smaller than those of modern humans, and it not was not until around 600,000 years ago that brain size began to approach modern proportions. Humans are thought to have been the first hominins to leave Africa (though this is by no means certain), and by one million years ago, they were widely distributed throughout the Old World.

Our own species, *Homo sapiens*, is now believed to have emerged in Africa at the end of this third phase, before 'going global' and replacing the archaic human populations throughout the Old World. A rival point of view, now largely abandoned, is that the archaic humans were actually early forms of *Homo sapiens*, and that modern humans emerged gradually from regional populations in different parts of the world. The two theories are known respectively as the replacement (or Out of Africa) and multiregional continuity hypotheses. In fact, we now know that modern humans did interbreed with at least two archaic human species, so neither view should really be thought of as wholly right or wrong.

It is important to realise that these three phases of hominin evolution did not lead to 'new, improved models'; hominins living four or five million years ago were as well-adapted to their environment as any that came after them. It is easy to take the conceited, human-centric view that large-brained, two-legged humans were an improvement upon small-brained tree-climbing apes, but even if that were so, evolution does not 'plan ahead'. When the first hominins emerged, nobody was thinking in terms of what features might be included in the second or third generation models. Rather, hominin evolution was driven by competition from other species and changing environmental conditions, which are the same processes that have always shaped living organisms.

In the fifty chapters that now follow, I try to present each topic in the context of the overall big picture I presented in my previous book. The reader will gain an overview of the human past but more importantly, I hope they will gain a sense of the richness and wonders of prehistoric times.

# 1: Establishing the 'Antiquity of Man'

*Had Boucher de Perthes really found conclusive proof that Man existed long before Biblical times?*

The year 1859 is now chiefly remembered for the publication of Charles Darwin's *The Origin of Species*. Earlier that year, however, there was an event that was no less pivotal in our understanding of prehistory when Joseph Prestwich and John Evans travelled to France to investigate the claims of a man whose work Darwin had dismissed as 'rubbish'. Both were primarily businessmen rather than full-time scholars: Prestwich was a vintner and Evans worked in his uncle's papermaking business, John Dickinson Stationery Ltd. The pair nevertheless took an interest in scholarly matters and their interests included geology, antiquaries and coins from the Classical era.

In 1859, almost two centuries had passed since the publication of Newton's *Principia Mathematica*. The second half of the seventeenth century saw great advances in the fields of mathematics, physics and astronomy, but other sciences lagged behind. Most people continued to believe that the Earth and all life on it had been created from nothing by God. In 1650, Archbishop James Ussher of Armagh had deduced purely from Biblical sources that the Creation occurred on 23 October 4004 BC. It was widely held that the Bible and the works of Classical scholars contained everything there was to know about human origins. By definition, therefore, there was no such thing as prehistory.

It was not until the latter part of the eighteenth century that the creationist viewpoint began to face a serious challenge. The Scottish geologist James Hutton argued that the processes that shaped the surface of the Earth had remained constant throughout the planet's history. He suggested that these processes occurred gradually and were driven by volcanic action, deposition of sediment, and erosion by wind and rain. Hutton realised that it would have required far longer than 6,000 years to shape the Earth as we know it. The final volume of the three-part *An Investigation of the Principles of Knowledge and of the Progress of Reason, from Sense to Science and Philosophy* was published in 1794 but – as may be hinted by the title – it was not the most accessible of works, and it attracted little interest in Hutton's lifetime. It was not until the 1830s that his theories were popularised by fellow Scot Sir Charles Lyell. Hutton's approach, for which Lyell coined the term 'uniformitarian', is now considered to be the foundation of modern geology.

Another problem for creationism was the growing realisation that the fossil record contained evidence of lifeforms that no longer existed. In 1795, the French naturalist Georges Cuvier demonstrated that fossil mammoths did not correspond to any living species of elephant. Why would God create a species only to allow it to become extinct? Cuvier proposed that extinctions were caused by periodic global catastrophes. In an attempt to hold on to Biblical explanations, some argued that Noah's flood must have been the most recent of these catastrophes, and the only one where humans had been present. In each case, God had created new species to replace those that had been wiped out. No species contemporary with humans had ever become extinct, as breeding stock of all of these had been taken aboard Noah's Ark.

It was against this background, in which the Ussher chronology was yielding only slowly to the weight of evidence, that Jacques Boucher de Perthes, a customs official from Abbeville in northern France, began collecting stone implements recovered from gravel pits in the Somme valley. Crucially, he noted that these were sometimes associated with the remains of elephants and rhinoceros, long extinct in France. There was only one possible explanation – humans were already in existence at that time. Boucher de Perthes was making use of what archaeologists now refer to as 'context' to attest to the great antiquity of prehistoric artefacts. If artefacts and fossil remains are found in the same context, it simply means that they were buried at the same time and by implication are the same age.

It was a 'double whammy' for creationism. Not only had now-extinct animals existed well before 6,000 years ago, but humans had also lived in these far distant times. In 1847, Boucher de Perthes published his conclusions in a three-volume work entitled *Antiquités celtiques et antédiluviennes* (Antiquities of the Celtic and Antediluvian peoples). Antediluvian (literally 'before the Flood') refers to what we now term the Pleistocene – the geological epoch preceding the current Holocene. Unfortunately, the work's mystical speculations about reincarnation detracted from its more valuable findings, and it attracted little interest from French academia. Across the Channel, Darwin is reputed to have been equally unimpressed.

One critic was Dr Marcel-Jérôme Rigollot, who lived a short distance away in Amiens. He nevertheless began to explore the river gravels in the suburb of Saint-Acheul and soon began to discover similar artefacts. Rigollot had a rather more pragmatic approach to his work and his report, published in 1854, was straightforward and well-illustrated. The artefacts recovered by Boucher de Perthes and Rigollot included triangular hand-axes of a type now known as 'Acheulean', named for Saint-Acheul. Similar stone artefacts had been known for centuries, but their significance was not widely appreciated. Indeed, many people believed they were thunderbolts or the work of elves rather than of human origin. Unfortunately, Rigollot died in 1854, soon after the publication of his report.

Encouraged by Rigollot's findings, Boucher de Perthes published a second edition of his book in 1857, but it continued to attract little attention. His luck finally changed in 1858 when he met the Scottish palaeontologist Hugh Falconer, who in turn persuaded Prestwich and Evans to investigate the findings at Abbeville and Saint-Acheul. In April of the following year, the pair met with Boucher de Perthes and though initially sceptical, they were soon convinced by the evidence presented to them. On returning to Britain, they gave a series of presentations at the Royal Society and the Society of Antiquaries of London, in which they publicly supported Boucher de Perthes' claim. The mainstream Victorian scientific establishment finally came to accept what was termed the Antiquity of Man.

However, an ironic twist soon followed. Evans happened by chance to come upon a hand-axe on display at the headquarters of the Society of Antiquaries of London. He saw at once that it closely resembled the Acheulean hand-axes he and Prestwich had examined in France. His enquiries revealed a missed opportunity more than six decades earlier. It turned out that in 1797, Norfolk-born John Frere had written to the Society and submitted five flint artefacts found in a clay pit at Hoxne, Suffolk. The Hoxne artefacts – now known to be 400,000 years old – had been found twelve feet (3.66 m) below the ground and were associated with bones of extinct animals. Frere realised the implications of the context of the finds, and suggested that the hand-axes were *"weapons of war, fabricated and used by a people who had not the use of metals. The situation in which these weapons were found may tempt us to refer them to a very remote period indeed, even beyond that of the present world"*. Unfortunately, this radical suggestion was almost entirely ignored. Had more people taken notice of Frere, it is likely that the hand-axes would now be known as Hoxnian rather than Acheulean.

Regardless of what might have been, 'prehistory' was now firmly established as a valid concept. Science had revealed the existence of an eerie forgotten world that lay far beyond the comforting reach of the Old Testament and the texts of ancient Greek and Roman historians. In the century and a half that has followed, anthropologists, archaeologists and scientists from many other disciplines have all tried to piece together the events of this long, formative period. They have drawn together strands of evidence from many diverse sources. These include fossils, archaeological remains, indicators of ancient climate change, languages that have not been spoken for millennia, and even the atoms and molecules of which our bodies are composed. Their findings cover a span of time so vast that Ussher's six thousand year chronology is but an instant in comparison.

# 2: Our place in the Animal Kingdom

*God creates, Linnaeus arranges, Darwin explains.*

The *Scala Naturae* or Great Chain of Being was the Theory of Everything of its time, envisaging a grand hierarchy of all things divine, living and inorganic from God downwards. The concept can be traced back to Aristotle's time, although it was further developed during the Middle Ages. Beneath God came the angels, followed in order by humanity, animals, plants and finally minerals. Within these basic divisions were subhierarchies: kings and princes outranked peasants; lions ruled the animal kingdom; oak trees held sway among the plants; and gold, diamonds and marble were the top-ranking minerals. Animals were divided into three categories: those living on land, those living in water, and those living in the air. They were further categorised as those 'with' and those 'without' blood (the latter, broadly speaking, are what we would now term invertebrates). Everything had its appointed place – but there was just one problem. Where did apes and monkeys fit into the picture?

That apes and monkeys look very similar to people is inescapable. From our present-day perspective it is also unremarkable, reflecting nothing more than the close evolutionary relationship between humans and other primates. But it would have been rather unwise to try and point this out in an era when few doubted that God had created mankind in His own image. In 1616, the Italian philosopher Lucilio Vanini was burned at the stake for doing just that. Aristotle's not wholly-incorrect view was that apes and monkeys represented a category situated between humans and quadrupedal animals; but later authorities suggested that the ape was God's final effort before making Adam, and that He left this 'deformed image of man' as an example. Not for two and a half centuries would Vanini be vindicated.

While creationism remained largely unchallenged, knowledge of the natural world began to reach a point where Aristotle's system was no longer adequate. The number of species known to science increased dramatically during the Age of Discovery, as European seafarers brought back exotic specimens from all over the world.

With little or no consensus on how biological organisms should be classified, and with new animal and plant species being discovered all the time, the problem was getting steadily worse.

Enter Carl Linné, usually known by the Latinised version of his name, Carolus Linnaeus. The son of a Lutheran curate, he was born at Rashult, Sweden, in 1707. Although not the most promising of scholars, he became interested in botany (the study of plants) from an early age. In 1727, he enrolled at Lund University to study medicine, but soon transferred to Uppsala University where there were better opportunities for him to combine his medical studies with his interest in botany. His mentors included Olof Celsius, whose nephew Anders invented the Celsius ('centigrade') temperature scale. Anders' scale was originally calibrated with the freezing point of water at one hundred degrees and the boiling point at zero degrees; it was Linnaeus who later reversed the convention to produce the scale now in use.

In 1735 Linnaeus published the first edition of *Systema Naturae*, the work for he is now largely remembered. In it he adopted binomial nomenclature, whereby a species is assigned a generic name and a specific name. The generic name refers to the genus, a group of species more closely related to one another than to any other group of species. The specific name represents the species itself. For example lions (*Panthera leo*) and tigers (*Panthera tigris*) are different species, but they are similar enough to both be assigned to the Genus *Panthera*. Linnaeus did not invent this system: it had been proposed by the Swiss botanist Gaspard Bauhin over a century earlier, but it had failed to catch on. The most familiar example of this nomenclature is the term *Homo sapiens*, which Linnaeus introduced to categorise humans.

In *Systema Naturae*, Linnaeus also put forward his taxonomic scheme for the natural world. A taxonomy is a tree structure of classifications for any given set of objects. A taxon (plural taxa) is any item within such a scheme and all objects within a particular taxon will be united by one or more defining feature: 'mammal', 'primate', 'insect' and 'beetle' are all examples of taxa. Linnaeus subdivided the three Kingdoms of the Great Chain of Being (Animals, Plants and Minerals) by Class, Order, Genus and Species. Each of these taxonomic categories is nested within the next category up; thus, for example lions and tigers are two species within the Genus *Panthera*. This forms part of Order Carnivora (a group which also includes other cats, along with dogs and bears), which in turn forms part of

Class Mammalia (mammals). In 1758, in the tenth edition of *Systema Naturae*, Linnaeus classified humans as *Homo sapiens*, a species within Order Primates. Note that by convention, only Genus and Species are italicised, and the latter is not capitalised; thus our species is written *Homo sapiens* and not *Homo Sapiens*. Along with humans, Linnaeus included the Simians (apes and monkeys) and lemurs. For some reason, he also included bats, although these were soon given their own order. 'Primate' means 'of first rank', reflecting Linnaeus's view that this group ranked first in God's grand scheme of things. He saw no reason to depart from the orthodox view of creationism and – never the most modest of men – claimed that *"God creates, Linnaeus arranges"*. He was nevertheless criticised for daring to suggest any connection between humans and mere animals.

Other critics objected to the bizarre sexual imagery he used when categorising plants. For example, *"The flowers' leaves… serve as bridal beds which the Creator has so gloriously arranged, adorned with such noble bed curtains, and perfumed with so many soft scents that the bridegroom with his bride might there celebrate their nuptials with so much the greater solemnity…"*. The botanist Johann Siegesbeck denounced this 'loathsome harlotry', but Linnaeus had the last word and named an 'ugly little weed' *Siegesbeckia orientalis*; a name which it retains to this day.

Linnaeus was elevated to the nobility in 1761 and continued his work until the early 1770s, when his health began to decline. He was afflicted by strokes, memory loss and general ill-health until his death in 1778. In his publications, Linnaeus provided a concise, usable survey of all the world's then-known plants and animals, comprising about 7,700 species of plants and 4,400 species of animals. The works helped to establish and standardise consistent binomial nomenclature for these many species. Biologists now recognise at least five kingdoms (though not the long-abandoned Mineral Kingdom), but the classification system in use today is very similar to that introduced by Linnaeus.

The Linnaean system assigns humanity a place in the animal kingdom, but it has nothing to tell us about how we got there. It is based on similarities between species and higher-level taxa, not on evolutionary relationships between them. It does not tell us that humans are closely related to apes and monkeys, only that we share many features with them. Creationism holds that species are immutable and by definition does not allow the concept that one species can evolve into another. Had Linnaeus believed in evolution, he might well have devised a different system.

It was not until 1859, just months after Prestwich and Evans endorsed the work of Boucher de Perthes, that the first edition of Charles Darwin's *The Origin of Species* was published. Darwin was not the first to propose a theory of evolution: even while Linnaeus was still alive evolutionists were beginning to propose alternatives to creationist orthodoxy, most notably the French biologist Jean-Baptiste Lamarck. Indeed early editions of *The Origin of Species* avoided the word 'evolution' altogether, preferring the term 'descent with modification'.

What Darwin proposed was 'natural selection', whereby differences between individuals of the same species mean that some are better at evading predators or more successful when competing for limited resources. Accordingly, such individuals stand a better chance of reproducing and hence passing on their advantageous traits to their offspring. The classic example of natural selection is the Peppered moth, which exists in speckled light grey and all-black varieties. Before the Industrial Revolution, the light-coloured form was the most common, but the large quantities of smoke and soot produced by the factories led to many of the trees on which the moths rested becoming blackened. The previously-rare all-black moths were now better camouflaged from predators, and hence were more likely to reproduce and pass their colour scheme on to their offspring. During the mid-nineteenth century, numbers of the all-black moths began to rise, and by 1895 some 98 percent of moths in the Manchester area were dark-coloured.

Darwin developed the theory of natural selection between 1844 and 1858, but it was independently proposed by the Welsh naturalist and explorer Alfred Russel Wallace, who wrote to Darwin with a short description of the same evolutionary mechanism he was himself working on. It came at a bad time for Darwin, whose infant son had just died from scarlet fever. Unable to give the matter much thought, he was persuaded to publish a synopsis of his work, which was jointly presented with Wallace's paper to the Linnaean Society of London. That neither wished to take sole credit for their work meant that there were none of the unseemly squabbles over priority that have bedevilled so many joint discoveries down the centuries. *The Origin of Species* was published a year later, and the first edition promptly sold out.

Evolution remained unpopular in clerical circles and controversial elsewhere. Darwin was regularly portrayed as an ape by satirical media. In fact, he was not the first to propose that humans evolved from apes and *The Origin of Species* only hints that the theory may cast light on human origins. It was his friend and self-styled 'bulldog' Thomas Henry Huxley who first publicised the anatomical similarities between humans and apes, culminating in the famous 1860 debate at the Oxford University Museum. Often described as the Huxley-Wilberforce debate, it was not a formal debate but an *ad hoc* discussion that took place following a presentation by the American academic John William Draper. Huxley was opposed by Bishop Samuel Wilberforce and Darwin's former captain on the *Beagle* voyage, Admiral Robert FitzRoy, and is generally supposed to have come out on top. However, no transcript exists of the debate and there is uncertainty over exactly what was said and by whom.

Three years later, Huxley presented anatomical and other evidence for the evolution of humans and apes from a common ancestor in his 1863 work entitled *Evidence as to Man's Place in Nature*, the first book ever to be devoted to the topic of human evolution. It was not until eight years later that Darwin's 1871 work *The Descent of Man* appeared, in which he proposed that humans were most closely related to African apes. Humanity's demotion was complete: from beings created in 4004 BC in God's own image, to an ape that had evolved in Africa at some unknown time in the distant past.

# 3: Finding the Missing Link

*The idea of a 'missing link' between apes and humans goes back to the
nineteenth century, but when and where did it live?*

The phrase 'missing link' is a familiar term, widely used in the popular media in the context of human evolution, and conjuring up a
vision of an as-yet-undiscovered fossil ape that links humans to our
primate cousins. In fact, the term is something of a misnomer: there
is no single species, undiscovered or otherwise, linking us to present-
day apes. Instead, there are two diverging branches of evolution
leading back to a common ancestor, which is often referred to as the
Last Common Ancestor or LCA. *Homo sapiens* emerged from one
branch; our closest living ape relatives (now known to be chimpanzees) emerged from the other. Anything on the human side of the
split (including ourselves) is referred to as a 'hominin', although not
all hominins were our direct ancestors. The hominin family tree has
been described as more of a 'tangled bush' than a single branch, and
most hominin lineages were evolutionary cul-de-sacs that simply
died out. In the past, there were often several different hominin species living at the same time, but now only *Homo sapiens* remains. The
total number of extinct hominin species is disputed, but is probably
somewhere in the twenties or even thirties.

However, in Darwin's time there was very little in the way of fossil evidence and the existence of a single fossil species of 'man-ape'
or 'ape-man' linking *Homo sapiens* directly to apes seemed entirely
feasible. By the late nineteenth century the search was on, but academic opinion took several wrong turnings over the next few decades. Although evolution was now widely accepted, not everybody
agreed with Darwin's view that humans were most closely related to
African apes. There was consensus that human ancestors must have
lived in the tropics, where modern apes live, but some believed that
humans were more closely related to Asian orang-utans and gibbons
than they were to African apes. Indeed, by the 1920s, the prevailing
wisdom was that the Great Apes (chimpanzees, gorillas and orang-
utans) were all far more closely related to one another than any of
them were to humans.

Anthropologist Sir Arthur Keith and Henry Fairfield Osborn,

President of the American Museum of Natural History in New York both believed that divergence between apes and humans was very ancient, and had occurred in the Late Oligocene, 30 million years ago. Some argued for an even earlier split. In 1919, the British anatomist Frederic Wood Jones suggested that key features of the anatomy of apes and monkeys were completely absent from humans, and he proposed that humans were most closely related to tarsiers. The tarsiers are a group of small primates characterised by their long tarsal bones (hence the name) and very large eyes. They are only distantly related to apes and monkeys, and the 'tarsioid hypothesis' as it was known would place the split with apes in the Eocene, 50 million years ago.

Although radiometric methods used to date Earth's geologic past were less accurate then than they are now, it was clear that even the Late Oligocene was too far back in time to allow the perceived similarities between humans and African apes to reflect a common evolutionary heritage. Scholars proposed instead that they were the result of parallel evolution. Although the two lineages had long been separate, they had both followed similar evolutionary paths, with the result that certain features had appeared in both.

By the 1920s, a fossil picture was beginning to emerge. *Pithecanthropus erectus* ('erect ape-man', later renamed *Homo erectus*) had been discovered by Dutch anthropologist Eugene Dubois on the island of Java in 1891. Although it was markedly smaller brained than a modern human, it clearly was human and had lived long after the time of the 'missing link'. On the other hand, *Australopithecus africanus* ('Southern ape of Africa') discovered by Australian anthropologist Raymond Dart in South Africa in 1925, was more obviously a transitional form between apes and humans. It walked on two legs, like a human – but its brain was no larger than that of a chimpanzee.

Unfortunately, this flew in the face of another widely-held misconception about human origins: the 'brains first' view, which stated that the evolution of larger brains had preceded that of upright walking. We now know that it was the other way round. Proponents of the 'brains first' view claimed evidence in the form of *Eoanthropus Dawsoni* ('Dawson's Dawn Man'), better known as Piltdown Man, a fragmentary humanlike skull with an apelike lower jawbone that was supposedly recovered in 1912 from a gravel pit at Piltdown, Sussex. As early as 1913, some were already beginning to suspect that these now-notorious bone fragments were a hoax, but their conclusions were largely ignored. In the meantime, Dart's find was dismissed by many as an ordinary ape, not relevant to human ancestry. He was even criticised for introducing the term *Australopithecus*, which critics complained was a mishmash of Latin and Greek.

Although early post-war researchers did eventually confirm that the australopithecines were bipeds, the 'ancient split' view persisted. As late as the 1960s, the fossil ape *Ramapithecus*, discovered in the 1930s at the Siwalik Hills of India, was favoured as a likely human ancestor. *Ramapithecus* lived around 15 million years ago, and it was claimed that it was one of the earliest hominins, living soon after the split with the apes. Around that time, however, the new science of molecular biology changed the picture dramatically.

Researchers found that the genetic material of all living organisms occasionally undergoes random changes. These changes, known as mutations, typically arise from DNA copying errors during cell division, though they can also be caused by exposure to sunlight, radiation or certain chemicals. When mutations occur in reproductive cells, they are passed on to the next generation. Consequently, over many generations, mutations accumulate in genetic sequences. The resulting genetic variation within a population is known as genetic diversity. The genetic diversity of a large, well-established population tends to be higher than that of a small, recently-established population.

When populations become separated from one another, each begins to pick up its own distinct set of mutations. Thus, for example, Africans, Europeans, Asians, Aboriginal Australians and Native Americans are all genetically distinct from one another. Mutations occur at a roughly constant rate, and hence the differences between equivalent genetic sequences in two populations, or the 'genetic distance', will be related to the time since two populations last shared a common ancestor, or 'divergence time'. This principle is known as the 'molecular clock'. The same principle applies to species as well as populations, although the genetic differences are far greater between species. Again, though, the genetic distance will be related divergence time.

Early researchers lacked the gene sequencing techniques now in use, so they focussed on the immunological reactions of blood serum samples obtained from various primate species. The strength of a cross-reaction between a pair of blood serum samples is greater if the samples come from two more-distantly related species. In 1963, by applying this principle, researcher Morris Goodman demonstrated that chimpanzees, gorillas and humans were all closely related to each other – it was the Asian orang-utans who were the outliers. In other words, Darwin had been right all along: humans are closely related to African apes.

This conclusion was supported by geneticists Vincent Sarich and Allan Wilson, who worked with blood serum albumin reactions. In 1967, the pair also obtained a date for when humans had diverged from African apes. Based on the reasonably well-supported assumption that apes had diverged from Old World monkeys 30 million years ago, they calculated that the split between humans and African apes had occurred just five million years ago. These results meant that *Ramapithecus* was now firmly out of the picture.

Unsurprisingly, this challenge to the 'ancient split' orthodoxy met with considerable scepticism, but subsequent work confirmed Sarich and Wilson's findings. The findings raised the obvious question: which African ape was our closest relative – was it the chimpanzee or the gorilla? Protein studies could not provide the necessary resolution, but once gene sequencing techniques had made it possible to study DNA directly, it was found that we are slightly more closely related to chimpanzees than we are to gorillas.

Current estimates as to when we diverged from chimpanzees vary. Many are in the lower part of the range from between five to seven million years ago, little changed from Sarich and Wilson's initial estimate. However, the most recent work, relying on direct measurements of the mutation rate per generation, has suggested a slightly earlier date of seven to eight million years ago. What these results tell us is that around seven to eight million years ago there was a species of ape whose descendants include every chimpanzee and human ever to have lived. We now know when and where the 'missing link' lived – but it remains missing.

A number of early fossil hominins are now known from the period five to seven million years ago. They include *Ardipithecus*, *Sahelanthropus* and *Orrorin*, but their relationship to one another and to human ancestry remains uncertain. The fossil record remains frustratingly incomplete to this day. Whether palaeoanthropologists will ever succeed in finding their way through the 'tangled bush' of early hominin evolution and unequivocally locate the 'missing link' is doubtful. Even if its fossil remains were one day to be found, it would be very difficult to confirm their status. The missing link is likely to remain missing.

# 4: Four legs good, two legs better

*The origins of an unusual way of getting about.*

Though we don't tend to give it much thought, the way humans get about on two legs is unique. Nearly all bipeds – be they birds, kangaroos or dinosaurs – have the same basic body shape, in which the back is close to the horizontal when in motion, and the tail is used as a counterweight. Humans, by complete contrast, lack a tail and walk upright. Although other apes can also walk upright, it is not their preferred form of locomotion and they waddle rather than stride. Striding motion is a complex process requiring split-second timing. The legs alternate between a swing phase and a stance phase: assisted by the big toe, the leg in the swing phase pushes off from the ground, swings under the body while slightly flexed, and finally straightens out again prior to the foot hitting the ground heel-first. It then remains in the extended position for the stance phase, while the other leg goes through the swing phase, and so on.

The British anthropologist John Napier once remarked that human walking is a risky business, but that is only the beginning of the story. The anatomical adaptations required to get from a waddling ape to a striding human are not trivial. They include a curved lower spine; a shorter, broader pelvis; thigh bones angled inwards, allowing the legs to swing under the body; longer, more powerful lower limbs; the ability to fully straighten the legs; and an enlarged, in-line rather than opposable big toe. The foramen magnum (the hole in the base of the skull through which the spinal column enters) is repositioned from the rear to the centre of the skull. It is a radical set of transformations and for it to have evolved at all, the advantages must have been considerable.

The most obvious possibility is that bipedalism freed our hands for other purposes, such as tool-making – but, as useful as our hands have proved, this cannot be the whole picture. Freeing up our hands was a useful spinoff, but regardless of how useful they might turn out to be, spinoffs are not the primary driver of evolutionary processes. Our forelimbs weren't freed from locomotive duties to enable us to make better tools – or to build cities, drive motor cars or operate computers. The human hand was a useful spin-off from something else, but what?

Over the last fifty years, there has been no shortage of theories, many of which have focussed on feeding rather than tool-making. The 'Man the Hunter' theory of the 1960s saw bipedalism as an adaptation for hunting. Although bipeds are slower and less energy efficient than quadrupeds at top speed, at lower speeds they possess greater stamina, which has obvious advantages when tracking prey. The similar 'Man the Scavenger' theory also saw advantages in the superior biped endurance, but this time for following migrating herds and scavenging carcasses. Both seemed plausible explanations, but it subsequently became apparent that the appearance of bipedalism had considerably predated large-scale consumption of meat.

In the 1980s, anthropologists Peter Rodman and Henry McHenry proposed the 'efficient biped' model, which suggests that bipedalism evolved as a means of improving energy efficiency. During the Late Miocene from 11.6 to 5.3 million years ago, there was a trend towards a colder, dryer and more seasonal climate. These changes resulted in the breakup of continuous forests and the appearance of more open woodland and grassland savannah. Consequently, sources of food became more thinly dispersed. Although early hominins lived in the remaining wooded areas, they would regularly have had to walk long distances between patches of woodland in order to find food. Rodman and McHenry noted that humans are at least as energy-efficient as quadrupeds at walking speeds and much more so than are chimpanzees when the latter are on the ground. Even though the earliest hominins were less efficient walkers than are humans, being able to access otherwise unreachable food sources provided the evolutionary pressure for more efficient bipedalism.

Also in the 1980s, evolutionary biologist Peter Wheeler suggested that bipedalism arose from the need to reduce exposure to the sun while foraging. An upright ape will have less of their body surface exposed to the sun than one going about on all fours, and has less need to stay in the shade when the sun is high in the sky. Furthermore, being higher up off the ground, they can gain more benefit from cooling breezes. The theory dovetails neatly with the 'efficient biped' model: not only would biped apes use up less energy getting about; they would be less exposed to the effects of the sun when out in the open, crossing between wooded patches. The two theories have the added attraction of suggesting that the switch to bipedalism was simply an evolutionary response to climate change.

Another theory dating back to the 1980s is the 'Man the Provisioner' model proposed by anatomist Owen Lovejoy, but unlike the other two it was largely ignored until recently. Lovejoy followed Rodman and McHenry in proposing that bipedalism was an evolutionary response to more dispersed food sources during the Late Miocene, but suggested that it also brought an important spin-off benefit. This was the freeing-up of the forelimbs, which enabled males to bring back food and share it with females and their offspring. The advantages to females were three-fold: it ensured that they and their offspring were well-fed; it gave them more time to devote to parental care; and being well-nourished reduced the time between successive pregnancies. But what was in it for the males? They would only benefit in terms of reproductive potential if they were solely provisioning their own offspring – something they could only be reasonably confident of in a monogamous relationship.

Human reproductive biology differs from that of other primates and indeed most other mammals. In most mammal species, females are only fully sexually receptive when ovulating and hence able to conceive. At such times they advertise their condition to the males with visual, olfactory or other cues. With chimpanzees, for example, the genitals turn bright red. There are no equivalent cues in our species, but as copulation takes place throughout a woman's menstrual cycle, she has no need to advertise when she is ovulating. The typical primate cues probably disappeared from humans because there were no evolutionary pressures maintaining them, rather than because of a specific need to conceal ovulation. It is likely that on-going sexual receptivity in women evolved to reduce the appeal of infidelity and so strengthen pair-bonding.

The problem with Lovejoy's theory was that it contradicted the long-standing view that these distinctive features of human reproductive biology emerged millions of years after the first bipedal hominins. In a sexually-reproducing species, the term sexual dimorphism refers to the physical differences between the two sexes. With humans, for example, males on average are larger than females, and possess greater body strength. The most extreme example of sexual dimorphism among vertebrates is the angler fish: the small male attaches itself to the much larger female, and lives out the remainder of its life as a parasite. It becomes incapable of independent existence, serving only to fertilise the female.

Sexual dimorphism is common in primates, and typically manifests itself not just in body size but also in dental differences. In many species males have enlarged canine teeth, used for threat displays in order to gain social dominance. There is a strong correlation between mating strategy and sexual dimorphism, which in turn is related to male-on-male aggression. In monogamous species, such as gibbons, there is little difference between the size and dentition of males and females, and only limited aggression between males. By contrast, in polygamous species, male-on-male aggression is common when competing for females and sexual dimorphism is the rule. Big, burly males will be advantage over smaller weaklings, thus for example male gorillas are almost twice the size of females. Male chimpanzees are only about 35 percent larger by body weight than females, but their canine teeth are enlarged in comparison to females.

At the time Lovejoy proposed his theory, the only non-human hominins known were the australopithecines, which in terms of size display considerable sexual dimorphism. For example, Henry McHenry estimated that *Australopithecus afarensis* males measured 1.51 m (5 ft. 0 in.) tall and weighed 45 kg (99 lb.) whereas females measured just 1.05 m (3 ft. 6 in.) and weighed only 29 kg (64 lb.). These figures have been questioned, but if they are correct, then *Australopithecus afarensis* was even more sexually dimorphic than chimpanzees. However, Lovejoy challenged the importance of body size dimorphism in primate mating strategies and claimed that canine size is the determining factor. He noted that chimpanzees are far less dimorphic in body size than gorillas, despite males being no less competitive. Also, in many primate species, male body size is related to factors other than mate competition. The canine dimorphism of the australopithecines is actually fairly limited, and Lovejoy reasoned that their mating strategy was similar to that of humans.

Support for Lovejoy's views came with the discovery of *Ardipithecus*, a very early hominin genus that preceded the australopithecines and lived from 5.8 to 4.4 million years ago. It retained primitive features such as opposable big toes, useful for climbing but less so for a life on the ground, and replaced by in-line big toes in all later hominins. Its body size was minimally dimorphic, and its canine teeth were only slightly more dimorphic than those of modern humans. The male and female canines were similar in size, and the male canine was 'feminised' in shape. Rather than the pointed shape of male apes, the crown of the upper canine was a less threatening diamond shape, similar to that of the female. Overall, this suggested only limited male-on-male aggression and that *Ardipithecus* was largely monogamous, implying that the present-day human mating strategy emerged fairly early on in hominin history.

Despite the *Ardipithecus* findings, the 'Man the Provisioner' model is still not universally accepted, but further supporting evidence has come from comparative studies of the human and chimpanzee Y-chromosomes. The Y-chromosome is one of the two sex-determining chromosomes in most mammals, containing the MSY (male specific region Y) genes responsible for the development of male gonads. Given that chimpanzees and humans are so closely related, it would be expected that there is little difference between the Y chromosomes of the two species. In fact, it was found that there are considerable differences. In comparison to the human MSY, the chimpanzee MSY had lost around a third of its genes, suggesting that the human version was closer to that of the Last Common Ancestor and hence the basal hominin conditions. Other changes had led to a complete restructuring of the chimpanzee MSY.

These changes may reflect the prominent role of the Y-chromosome in sperm production, and its importance in the chimpanzee's promiscuous mating strategy. The implication is that it is the chimpanzee rather than human mating strategy that is most changed since the time of the Last Common Ancestor, and that the mating strategy of the latter had more in common with that of humans than it did with that of chimpanzees. This would be consistent with Lovejoy's suggestion that early hominins were monogamous in their mating habits.

# 5: Lucy

*She was named for a Beatles song, but was she a human ancestor?*

What is probably the best-known fossil ever found was discovered on 24 November 1974 by American anthropologists Donald Johanson and Tom Gray. They were part of a team of scientists investigating the Hadar Formation on the southern edge of the Afar region of Ethiopia. Johanson and Gray were returning to their camp in a Land Rover after a morning of mapping and surveying, when on an impulse they decided to double-check a small gully that had been previously investigated by other members of the team without success. On this occasion, however, Johanson spotted a hominin elbow bone and the pair soon found other fragmentary remains dotted around on the surface. In a state of understandable excitement, they returned to camp. Two weeks of excavation followed, resulting in the recovery of several hundred bone fragments, representing 40 percent of a single female hominin skeleton: one of the most complete ever found. Her remains were given the catalogue number AL-288-1 (denoting the first fossil to be discovered at Afar Locality 288), but she is far better known by her nickname 'Lucy'. The name comes from the 1967 Beatles song *Lucy in the Sky with Diamonds*, which was played at a party held at the base camp to mark her discovery.

The story of Lucy's discovery really began in 1968, when French geologist Maurice Taieb discovered the Hadar geological formation while he was studying the evolution of the Awash River valley, which runs through the south of the Afar region. The formation takes its name from the nearby Hadar River, a tributary of the Awash. It dates to the Late Pliocene period, and was deposited between 4.2 and 2.4 million years ago. Donald Johanson learned about the formation from a conversation with Taieb, and was intrigued by the possibility of finding early hominin remains there. Although genetic studies had recently shown that humans had diverged from African apes around five million years ago, the oldest fossil hominin known at that point was still *Australopithecus africanus*, which dated back no further than 2.8 million years ago. Johanson and Taieb collaborated with the French palaeontologist Yves Coppens to organise the International Afar Research Expedition, and a Franco-American team of scientists began working at Hadar in the autumn of 1973. In November of that year, towards the end of the first season of excavation, the team discovered a fossil knee joint that had belonged to an upright-walking hominin. Encouraged, the team returned for a second season in 1974 and it was then that Lucy was discovered.

Lucy lived 3.2 million years ago, which made her the earliest hominin yet found. The diminutive female stood just 1.1 m (3 ft. 7 in.) tall and weighed an estimated 29 kg (64 lb). Although her brain was only a little larger than that of a chimpanzee, her pelvis and leg bones were almost identical in function to those of modern humans, showing that she was a biped. Under an agreement with the government of Ethiopia, Johanson brought the skeleton back to the Cleveland Museum of Natural History in Ohio, where it was reconstructed by anthropologist Owen Lovejoy before being returned to Ethiopia.

Lucy immediately became a household name around the world, but in the meantime discoveries at Hadar continued. At a single fossil bed known as Afar Locality 333, the team found over two hundred separate fossil bone fragments representing at least thirteen more of Lucy's people. The group, which became known as the First Family, included adult males and females and four or more infants. For a long time, it was believed that they were all members of a single relatively large social group who were overwhelmed by a flash flood. However, later reconstructions of the local environment cast doubt on the hypothesis. Although the bones were deposited by the flooding of a dry channel, the event was less dramatic than had been supposed. The site was a shallow depression rather than a deep gully in which the group could have become trapped, and consideration of sediments in the channel suggest that the flow of water was fairly gentle. Just how the remains did reach the site is therefore something of a mystery, as there is no evidence that they were attacked by a predator. One possibility is that the remains do not actually represent a single group and were transported to the site one at a time by floodwater after dying from natural causes elsewhere.

Further discoveries were made in Kenya and Tanzania including a set of hominin footprints that had been preserved for 3.66 million years in volcanic ash at Laetoli in Tanzania. There was a hint of drama from the distant past – the hominins were walking through muddy ash following an eruption of a volcano 20 km (12 miles) away, and they would have been able to see the menacing sight of it smouldering on the horizon. The footprints of three individuals walking in a group were captured like a plaster casting, and the mud must then have had time to harden before further eruptions covered them in a layer of ash. They showed that these hominins had humanlike arched feet and in-line big toes, and deep heel impressions in relation to those made by the toes suggest that they were walking fully upright.

In 1978, Johanson and American palaeoanthropologist Tim White described the finds as a new australopithecine species, *Australopithecus afarensis*. Similar fossils have since been found dating from between 4.2 to 3.0 million years ago, though in 1995 the earlier examples were assigned to a separate species, *Australopithecus anamensis* ('lake' in local Turkana language) on the basis of anatomical differences in the dentition and the upper and lower jawbones. Also assigned to its own species is 'Abel', a 3.5-million-year-old fossil discovered in Chad in Central Africa and nicknamed in memory of the French geologist Abel Brillianceau, who died of malaria in 1989. 'Abel' has been described as *Australopithecus bahrelghazali*, but it might simply have been a regional variety of *Australopithecus afarensis*. Even using the strict definition of the species, the habitats occupied by *Australopithecus afarensis* varied considerably. At Hadar, Lucy and her folk apparently lived in woodland, but at Laetoli the environment was a much more open grassland savannah. If they are all the same species, then *Australopithecus afarensis* was a long-lived, geographically widespread and adaptable species – but was it a human ancestor?

The answer is that we simply don't know. Even discounting the controversial possible hominin species *Kenyanthropus platyops* (thought by some to be the badly-distorted skull of an australopithecine), *Australopithecus afarensis* was not the only hominin species in existence at that time. The recently-announced *Australopithecus deyiremeda* was found in sediment dating from 3.5 to 3.3 million years old at the site of Woranso–Mille in Ethiopia, only a short distance away from where Lucy was discovered and is said to differ from *Australopithecus afarensis* in terms of the architecture of its lower jawbone, and a number of dental differences possibly indicating a different diet. Between 2.8 and 2.6 million years ago, further australopithecine species emerged: *Australopithecus garhi* in East Africa and *Australopithecus africanus* in South Africa, along with the bigger-jawed robust australopithecines in both East Africa and South Africa. They were followed two million years ago by another South African species, *Australopithecus sediba*. It is highly likely that further australopithecine species remain to be discovered.

It was during this critical period of hominin diversification that the first humans emerged. The earliest currently-known example of *Homo* is LD-350-1, a 2.8-million-year-old partial lower jawbone also found in the Afar region, which would put *Australopithecus afarensis* in the right place at the right time to be a human ancestor. However, it is by means certain that it actually was. The relationship between *Homo* and the various australopithecine species is far from clear, and some believe that the origins of *Homo* are to be found in South Africa rather than East Africa. For all their success as a species, Lucy's people might ultimately have been just another evolutionary dead end.

# 6: The technological ape

*Experimental and archaeological evidence for tool-making by pre-human hominins.*

Until the end of 1950s, it was generally believed that the ability to make and use tools was restricted to humans. 'Man the Toolmaker' was thought to be one of the defining characteristics being human, and it was therefore assumed that the apelike australopithecines could not have been toolmakers. Then, in early 1960s, primatologist Jane Goodall discovered that chimpanzees make use of tools, often modifying objects for specific tasks. The best known example of chimpanzee tool use is for 'termite-fishing', where small sticks or plant stems are inserted into a termite mound and then slowly removed, allowing any clinging termites to be eaten. Sometimes, chimpanzees fray the ends of the sticks or stems to increase the number of termites caught. Other tools include sponges made from leaves for extracting water from deep holes, and hammerstones used to crack nuts. Chimpanzees are also capable of learning new ways of making and using tools from their companions rather than having to re-invent everything for themselves. If such behaviours are shared between chimpanzees and humans, then the implication is that tool-making is very old, predating the emergence of the very first hominins.

Any termite sticks or leaf sponges made by early hominins will have long since rotted away, but stone tools are another matter. Stone is far more durable than any organic material, and stone tools made by early hominins would almost certainly survive. The question was, could early hominins have made stone tools as opposed to termite sticks?

In 1985, archaeologist Nicholas Toth carried out a series of experiments in replicating early stone tools. At that time, the earliest-known stone tools were the Oldowan stone tools first discovered by Louis Leakey at Olduvai Gorge in the 1930s. Leakey spent more than three decades searching for the maker of these tools before discovering early human remains at the same site, which he eventually named *Homo habilis* ('Handy Man'). However, the Oldowan tools are no more than around 1.8 million years old. Toth found that although they are crude, making them does require a certain amount of skill. Could the required techniques be mastered by an ape?

Archaeologist Thomas Wynn and primatologist William McGrew concluded that the skills were no more demanding than those used to make tools from sticks or leaves and that it was entirely possible that early hominins could have made stone tools. To test the theory experimentally, Toth collaborated with primatologist Sue Savage-Rumbaugh and a male chimpanzee named Kanzi. Savage-Rumbaugh had taught Kanzi to use a large vocabulary of words displayed on a keyboard, and to understand complex sentences. Toth encouraged Kanzi to make sharp stone flakes that could then be used to obtain a food reward from a box secured with string. Kanzi was able to make flakes and obtain his reward, but only by knocking cobbles together or smashing them against another hard object. He never used any of the more sophisticated techniques used by Oldowan toolmakers, despite these being demonstrated to him. It was unclear as to whether this unimpressive performance was due to cognitive limitations, anatomical limitations, or simple lack of motivation on Kanzi's part given that the cruder flakes he produced were good enough to do the job. It was certainly possible that early hominins had done the same, but the flakes and battered rocks that resulted from Kanzi's tool-making activities can also be produced by purely natural forces. It would therefore be hard to demonstrate that such items were genuine hominin-made artefacts.

Not until the 1990s did the first tentative evidence emerge of australopithecine tool-making. Between 1992 and 1994, archaeologists recovered stone tools from sites in the Gona River study area in Ethiopia, which were found to be about 2.5 to 2.6 million years old. The tools were very basic, resembling human-produced Oldowan artefacts, and comprised sharp-edged flakes and stone cores from which the flakes were struck. In addition to serving as a source for the flakes, the cores showed evidence of pitting and bruising, suggesting that they had been used for hammering and pounding. The artefacts were unequivocally stone tools, but who were the toolmakers? No hominin remains were found with the tools and although 2.5 million years ago slightly predated the then earliest-known humans, it could not be said with any degree of certainty that the toolmakers must have been australopithecines.

However, that possibility did strengthen in 1999, when evidence of carcass butchery was found at the nearby Bouri Formation. The finds comprised 2.5-million-year-old bones of large mammals with cut-marks, apparently made by stone tools in the process of defleshing the carcasses. In addition, long bones had been broken open to extract marrow. Although no actual tools were found at this site, the animal bones were associated with hominin remains, believed to be *Australopithecus garhi*. This is one of the later species of australopithecine, but its brain was no larger than that of earlier types and there is no reason to suppose that it was any smarter. If *Australopithecus garhi* was responsible for the Gona artefacts, then it could reasonably be expected that earlier australopithecines had also made stone tools.

Taken together, the Gona and Bouri finds represented a good case for australopithecine tool making, but they did not settle matters beyond reasonable doubt. Further problematic evidence emerged in 2010 when it was claimed that animal bones from Dikika, Ethiopia, show stone tool cut-marks for flesh removal, and signs of having been struck with hammerstones to extract bone marrow. At 3.39 million years old, the remains were early enough to preclude human involvement. As with Bouri, though, no actual tools were found. In their absence there was no way to tell whether the cut-marks were produced with specially-made tools, naturally-sharp pieces of stone, or even smashed cobbles of the type used by Kanzi to obtain his food reward. Nor was everybody convinced that the bones were evidence of butchery by early hominins. Some argued that as the bones had been buried in coarse-grained, sandy deposits, it was likely that trampling by animals had produced the marks.

Without associated stone tools, or at least stone tools of about the same age, there was no way to resolve the issue, but between 2011 and 2012, these finally came to light. Well over a hundred stone artefacts were found at Lomekwi 3, a site located just west of Lake Turkana in Kenya. At 3.3 million years old, they are 700,000 years older than the Gona tools. Finds included flakes and the cores from which they had been struck. It was found that the cores had been rotated as successive flakes were struck off, confirming that the flaking was an intentional, methodical process and did not result from accidental fracturing. Researchers also managed to 'refit' one of the flakes back to the core from which it had been struck. The tools were larger and heavier than typical Oldowan artefacts, and methods by which flakes were struck from cores less effective. It was claimed that they represented a technology intermediate between the use of stone tools for pounding and hammering and the more flake-orientated Oldowan, for which the name Lomekwian was proposed.

Even though fossil evidence for early humans has now been identified from 2.8 million years ago, the Lomekwian tools predate this by half a million years. 3.3 million years ago lies firmly within the age of hominins such as *Australopithecus afarensis* ('Lucy's' people) and the poorly-understood *Kenyanthropus platyops*. Regardless of which of these species made the tools, it is now clear that stone tool technology emerged well before *Homo*. Technology has long played a role in our affairs, but humans were evidently not the first technological apes.

# 7: You are what you eat

*What the atomic composition of tooth enamel has told us about the diet and social structure of early hominins.*

About two and a half million years ago, global cooling and increasing aridity transformed the forested landscape of Africa into one of widespread savannah grasslands. For the australopithecines, this represented a crisis as their traditional foods became scarce. The australopithecines' small to moderate-sized incisors and large, thick-enamelled, flat molars were adapted for crushing and chewing nuts and other hard, brittle food items, as well as soft, sugary fruits when these were available. This dentition suited the australopithecines to habitats ranging from open savannah to the 'gallery' forests that form as corridors along rivers and wetlands, but it lacked the shearing action required for chewing meat. Without the tools for processing meat, it was assumed that the australopithecines must have been vegetarian.

One evolutionary solution to the new conditions was more powerful jaws and larger, grindstone-like back teeth. With these, the so-called robust australopithecines could handle coarse fibrous gritty plant material such as seeds, roots and tubers – foods that the dentition of earlier 'gracile' australopithecines could not readily process. The other solution was to start eating meat. The meat-eaters became tool-making humans and although the robust australopithecines survived for a long time, they eventually became extinct.

A neat theory, but as it turned out, an over-simplification. Firstly, the climatic picture was not a simple one of progressively increasing aridity. Instead, there were constant fluctuations between wet and arid conditions, with consequent shifts in the types of food that were available at any one time and place. Secondly, we now know that australopithecines were making and using stone tools at least 3.3 million years ago and the evidence from sites such as Dikika, Ethiopia suggests that these were being used to butcher carcasses. It adds up to a good case that the pre-human hominins of this era were already eating meat, but is there any further evidence?

The phrase 'you are what you eat' is literally true: an individual's diet while they are alive leaves subtle chemical signatures that can be analysed thousands or even millions of years after death, placing a very powerful tool in the hands of anthropologists and archaeologists. One widely-used technique is stable isotope analysis. Isotopes are atoms of the same chemical element but with slightly differing masses; for example nitrogen has the isotopes $^{14}N$ and $^{15}N$ which weigh 14 and 15 atomic mass units respectively. The majority of chemical elements have more than one stable (i.e. non-radioactive) isotope, and some have half-a-dozen or more. There are subtle differences between the physical and chemical properties of the isotopes of any element, and biological and geological processes will often favour one isotope over another. Consequently, in any living organism, the relative abundance of a particular isotope will be affected by factors including diet and local geology. This isotopic signature is preserved after death, thus a wealth of information can be obtained from fossil remains.

Stable isotope analysis of carbon present in the dental enamel of *Australopithecus africanus* strengthens the view that it was not a strict vegetarian. Carbon has two stable isotopes, $^{12}C$ and $^{13}C$, both of which are absorbed by plants in the form of atmospheric $CO_2$ through photosynthesis. However, plants take up proportionally less $^{13}C$ than $^{12}C$, meaning that if the two isotopes were present in equal amounts in the atmosphere, a plant would absorb more $^{12}C$ than $^{13}C$. In actuality, atmospheric $^{13}C$ is scarcer than $^{12}C$, but the proportion absorbed by plants is even less. Although all plants favour $^{12}C$, the extent to which they do so depends on the method of photosynthesis they use. There are two main photosynthetic processes known as C3 and C4. The C3 process is employed by the majority of plants, including trees, bushes and shrubs; and the much rarer C4 process occurs in plants such as grasses and sedges. C4 plants takes up slightly more atmospheric $^{13}C$ than do C3 plants. The isotopic composition of the carbon in an animal's bones, teeth and body tissues will therefore provide an indication of its diet: higher $^{13}C$ levels will indicate the presence of C4 plants in the diet.

A number of studies have been conducted on dental enamel from molar teeth of *Australopithecus africanus* fossils from the Makapansgat Valley and Sterkfontein sites in South Africa. C4 foods were found to account for 40 percent of the diet on average, although there was considerable variation between individuals suggesting that *Australopithecus africanus* was adaptable and opportunistic in its feeding habits. Their diet might have included combinations of grasses, sedges, bird's eggs, locusts, termites, rodents, lizards, and grazing mammals.

Further information about the diet of *Australopithecus africanus* has been obtained from measurements of strontium and barium levels in dental enamel. The chemical properties of these elements are very similar to those of calcium and they likewise find their way into dental enamel and bone via the food chain, though in far smaller amounts. Their abundance relative to calcium depends upon the type of diet: ratios are lower in carnivores than they are in herbivores. Researchers analysed bone and enamel samples from *Australopithecus africanus*, the robust australopithecine species *Paranthropus robustus* and early humans. It was found that the strontium/calcium and barium/calcium ratios for early humans were indicative of a meat-based diet, and those for robust australopithecines suggested that they were browsers – animals whose diet primarily comprises leaves, shoots and shrubs. Both these results were more or less as expected, but the results for *Australopithecus africanus* were less straightforward. The strontium/calcium ratios were consistent with grazers – animals who feed predominantly on grasses – whereas the barium/calcium ratios were consistent with browsers. This suggested that the diet of *Australopithecus africanus* was more varied than that of either early humans or robust australopithecines and probably involved two distinct sources. One possibility is that its diet alternated between meat and plant food at different times of the year.

The uses of such techniques are not restricted to learning about type of diet and have also provided an insight into australopithecine social structure. There are a number of stable isotopes of strontium but researchers usually focus on ratios of $^{87}Sr$ to $^{86}Sr$, which are sensitive to local geology. The bulk of dental strontium is absorbed before tooth formation is complete, so the $^{87}Sr/^{86}Sr$ ratio in dental enamel can help identify where an individual grew up. Researchers obtained dental enamel $^{87}Sr/^{86}Sr$ ratios for nineteen australopithecines whose remains were found at sites in the Sterkfontein Valley, South Africa. It was found that the isotopic ratios of the males was consistent with local geology, suggesting that they had lived and died fairly close to where their remains were found. For the females, on the other hand, isotopic ratios mostly differed from those observed locally, suggesting that they had grown up elsewhere. This pattern is seen with present-day chimpanzees, where males usually stay with their birth group for life, but females migrate to join another group. Such a social structure largely eliminates the problem of inbreeding.

While the dietary evidence isn't conclusive, it reinforces the archaeological evidence for meat-eating. It seems likely that the australopithecines responded to an unstable climate and periodic shortfalls in their favoured food items by relying increasingly on meat. Such a scenario might explain the absence of recognisable stone tools from the earlier australopithecine era. The increasingly-frequent requirement to butcher carcasses led to the gradual refinement of tool-making techniques. Early tools were probably no more sophisticated than the smashed cobbles produced by the chimpanzee Kanzi, but in time recognizable artefacts were produced, such as those found at Lomekwi 3. Lomekwian tool technology could have been mastered by earliest hominin species, but the need did not arise for millions of years. When it did, it was a case of necessity being the mother of invention.

# 8: Food for thought

*How and why did our brains become bigger?*

Why do humans have such large brains, about three times larger than those of any other primate species? Bigger, better brains might sound very appealing, but the same could be said of owning a Rolls-Royce. The problem is that they are expensive to run, and there is a pretty good case for trying to get by without. Brain tissue requires over 22 times as much energy as an equivalent amount of muscle tissue. In a modern human, the brain uses around 16 percent of the body's energy budget despite making up just two percent of the body's overall mass. While the energy costs of the smaller brains of early humans were less than those of a modern brain, they were still considerable. How might these costs have been met?

In 1995, anthropologist Leslie Aiello and biologist Peter Wheeler put forward the 'expensive tissue' hypothesis. They argued that in order for large-brained hominins to balance the books, another part of the body had to cut down its energy consumption. The brain is not the only energy-hungry organ: the heart, liver, kidneys and gut are also disproportionally-large consumers of energy. The size of the heart, liver and kidneys is more or less predetermined by the size of the animal, and only in the gut is there any scope for downsizing. In other words you can have either a big brain or a big gut, but you can't have both. Animals subsisting on a diet of low-quality hard to digest foods require large guts with complex fermenting chambers, so you will never see large-brained cows, sheep or goats. Only those with high-quality, sugar and protein-rich diets can get by with smaller simpler guts, and so make up the energy costs needed to run a large brain. Meat is ideal, being nutritious with a high protein content. As predicted by the theory, human guts are small in comparison to those of modern apes.

It is clear that significant evolutionary changes were necessary before brains could even start to increase in size, but what might have triggered these changes? The answer is almost certainly climate change. It is surely no coincidence that the first humans appeared during the Late Pliocene, at a time when global temperatures were falling and the Earth was on the brink of its first full-blown ice age for 250 million years. The transition to the Pleistocene, 2,588 million years ago, saw the full onset of glacial conditions. Cooler, arid climatic episodes alternated with warmer, wetter periods as ice sheets ebbed and flowed in higher latitudes. The expansion in brain size must have been linked to something that gave early humans a survival advantage in these new, harsher conditions.

How smart might these early humans have been? In the 1980s, anthropologist Phillip Tobias examined plaster cast of the inside of the braincase of a *Homo habilis* skull from Koobi Fora, Kenya. Tobias concluded that the brain's pattern of ridges and furrows were more humanlike than apelike. He also found that the frontal and the parietal lobes were enlarged, and that the Broca's area was expanded in comparison to the same region in australopithecines and modern apes. The frontal lobes, which control higher brain functions including planning and reasoning, are located at the front of the brain. Behind them, on the top and on each side of the brain are the parietal lobes, which carry out a wide range of functions including spatial awareness and the processing of sensory information. The Broca's area is named for nineteenth century physician Paul Broca who demonstrated a connection with speech. Damage leads to Broca's aphasia, where patients are unable to speak in a grammatically correct manner. Understandably, the suggestion proved controversial, but if Tobias is right, then *Homo habilis* might have possessed good planning skills, and employed some form of language.

Recent research shows that the Broca's area is also associated with tool-making, so one possibility is that its expansion was linked to enhanced tool-making skills as well as or even instead of the use of language. Might the evolutionary trigger for larger brains have been a need for better tool-making skills to aid survival in the challenging conditions? If so, we would expect their appearance to correspond to a jump in tool-making technology, but this is not the case. The earliest-known stone tools were made by small-brained hominins 3.3 million years ago, and comprise stone cores from which were struck sharp flakes. These crude tools predate the appearance of *Homo* by half a million years, but the tools associated with *Homo habilis* were only slightly more advanced. It was not until around 1.76 million years ago – well after the appearance of the first humans – that the more sophisticated multi-purpose Acheulean hand-axe made its appearance. A link between brain expansion and tool technologies therefore seems unlikely.

In the 1980s, British psychologists Dick Byrne and Andrew

Whiten proposed what they termed the 'Machiavellian intelligence hypothesis', although it is now known rather less dramatically as the 'social brain hypothesis'. The theory simply states that the large brains of primates enable them to use knowledge about the social behaviour of their fellows to predict their likely future behaviour, and then base their social relationships around these predictions. Sociality is a near-universal feature of primate behaviour and probably appeared very early on in primate history. Most primate species live in groups with a clear social hierarchy. Although group living is common in the animal kingdom, few species enter into the kind of complex social relationships seen in primate societies. Group living has many benefits, including food sharing and providing early warning and defence against predators, but it also has its drawbacks. Tensions can build up in non-human primate societies just as easily as they can among humans, and in response small groups form coalitions within the larger overall living group. Such alliances are built around the ability of group members to make informed choices about potential allies on the basis of characteristics such as reliability and who is likely to beat who in a fight.

The key to maintaining such alliances is grooming, a social activity in which animals remove fleas, lice, dead skin and dirt from each other's fur. Grooming is a pleasurable activity, releasing endorphins, and within primate societies, it is largely carried on within 'grooming cliques'. Members of such cliques are far more likely to back up fellow members than non-members in any fighting with third parties. Within grooming cliques and within the overall living group, individuals are constantly having to balance conflicting interests, playing one individual off against another and keeping as many happy as possible. Such primate politics are not too far removed from those characterising human affairs, and likewise the rewards of getting to the top are high. Dominant individuals enjoy greater reproductive success, and better access to food.

But does all the politicking require larger brains? British anthropologist Robin Dunbar investigated the relationship between group sizes in primate societies and relative neocortex size rather than absolute brain size. The latter is not a reliable indicator of 'braininess': large mammals such as elephants and whales have larger brains than humans, but much of the capacity is needed to coordinate body movements and perform background tasks such as breathing and maintaining the correct body temperature. There isn't enough capacity left over for humanlike cognitive behaviour. It is the neocortex or 'grey matter' that is used for higher-level brain functions, including thinking – hence the oft-heard exhortation to 'use your grey matter'. The relative size of the neocortex in mammals typically ranges from 10 to 40 percent, but in primates this rises to between 50 to 80 percent. Dunbar found that there was indeed a relationship between overall living group size and relative neocortex size, but he also found that grooming cliques were larger in cases where the overall living group was large. He suggested that it is actually grooming clique size that influences neocortex size. As overall group size increases, so larger intra-group coalitions are required – and so more 'grey matter' is required to handle the politics.

The implication of Dunbar's findings is that the first humans were living in groups larger than those of their australopithecine forebears. In the deteriorating climate of Late Pliocene, the pre-human australopithecines would have come increasingly under pressure as food and water became less readily available. One adaptive response to the crisis would have been to increase group size, to make better, more co-operative use of what resources were available. A switch to a diet of high-quality food, such as meat, might have made it possible for brains to become larger. It is ironic that climate change, such a concern today, might well have been responsible for our large brains in the first place.

# 9: Dating the Mojokerto child

*The Mojokerto Child is one of the great treasures of palaeoanthropology, but how old is it and what can it tell us about migration of early humans from Africa?*

Until the middle of the last century, many anthropologists believed that the first humans had lived in the Far East rather than Africa. Unlike Darwin, they believed that humans were more closely related to Asian orang-utans and gibbons than they were to African apes, making the Far East the key place to look for early human fossils. Although the Neanderthals were identified in mid-nineteenth century, they were clearly fairly recent and were quite possibly an archaic form of *Homo sapiens*. However, in 1891, a Dutch army doctor named Eugene Dubois discovered the first fossil remains of an extinct human species that had lived significantly before *Homo sapiens*. Excavating at Trinil on the island of Java, he recovered a partial skull and a thigh bone of what he initially described as *Anthropithecus erectus* ('erect man ape') and subsequently renamed *Pithecanthropus erectus* ('erect ape man'). The brain was rather smaller than that of a modern human, and the cranium was long and low rather than globular. Dubois claimed his fossil was a transitional form between apes and modern humans, but his conclusions were slow to gain acceptance. It was not until the 1920s that similar fossils began to turn up at Zhoukoudian, near Beijing, although Dubois rejected any connection with his own find.

A few years later, Dutch palaeontologist Ralph von Koenigswald conducted further excavations in Java. In 1936 one of his local helpers, a man named Andojo, recovered a juvenile skull near Mojokerto, in the eastern part of the island. Now known as the Mojokerto child, the infant was about a year to 18 months old at death, but we don't know their sex or the cause of death. Unfortunately, fieldwork at that time could be a little haphazard, and the find spot was not accurately documented. Nor was this the only problem faced by von Koenigswald. The following year, he made further discoveries at Sangiran, central Java, after promising to pay local people 10 cents for each find. The finds included fragments making up an almost-complete skull, but von Koenigswald's delight at this discovery was somewhat tempered when he learned that his helpers were breaking larger finds into smaller pieces to maximise their bounty. Dubois continued to reject any connections with *Pithecanthropus*, which he claimed was more apelike than any of the later finds. Despite this, the Chinese and Javanese fossils are all now considered to belong to the same species, and are included in our own genus as *Homo erectus*.

In the 1950s through to the 1970s, discoveries of hominin fossils and early stone tools shifted attention back to Africa as the focal point of human origins. *Homo erectus* was viewed as an African species that had only later migrated to Java and China. The earliest hominin fossil attributable to *Homo erectus* was thought to be KNM-ER 3733, a 1.78-million-year-old skull from Koobi Fora, Kenya – but how old were the fossils from the Far East? The prevailing view was that they were no more than one million years old.

The familiar radiocarbon dating technique cannot be used to date anything older than around 45,000 years old, so to date fossils of such great age palaeoanthropologists must rely on other methods. One of these is potassium-argon dating, which can be used for material with an age ranging from 100,000 years to several billions of years old. Potassium is an abundant element, present in many minerals and making up 2.6 percent by weight of the Earth's crust. Naturally-occurring potassium contains a small proportion of the radioactive isotope $^{40}$K, which decays to $^{40}$Ar, a stable isotope of the inert gas argon. The potassium-argon technique makes use of this decay sequence, and it is typically used for dating volcanic lava flows and tuffs (ash). Before rocks solidify from a molten state, any $^{40}$Ar present will be driven off. After they crystallise, however, all subsequent $^{40}$Ar produced by the decay process will remain trapped. The ratio of $^{40}$K to trapped $^{40}$Ar in the sample can be used to determine when the sample crystallised from the molten state. The technique was developed in the 1950s in the United States by geochronologist Garniss Curtis, physicist John Reynolds and seismologist Jack Evernden.

Potassium-argon dating is often used to estimate the age of fossil remains or stone tools by noting their position in relation to underlying and/or overlying volcanic material. The Chinese *Homo erectus* fossils were not associated with volcanic material, but the island of Java is largely volcanic in origin and possesses numerous active volcanos. In 1969, Curtis collected volcanic rock samples from the supposed find site of the Mojokerto child, which he was shown by Indonesian palaeoanthropologist Teuku Jacob, a former student of

Ralph von Koenigswald. He obtained a date of 1.9 million years, albeit with some uncertainty. But even the lower range of his estimates made the Mojokerto child far older than the one million years most believed it to be. Few anthropologists took Curtis's date seriously.

By the early 1980s, a variant of the potassium-argon technique was coming into use – the argon-argon technique. This method entails bombarding a sample with neutrons from a nuclear reactor, which converts the non-radioactive potassium isotope $^{39}$K to the argon isotope $^{39}$Ar. The ratio of $^{39}$Ar to $^{40}$Ar is then determined in a single measurement, unlike the standard potassium-argon method in which separate measurements are required for the potassium and argon. Argon-argon dating has the advantage that smaller samples are required and that a single measurement is less susceptible to errors than are two. In 1990, Curtis re-dated his 1969 samples using the new technique and obtained an age of 1.7 million years with a lower degree of uncertainty. The date was still 'too old', but there was now a feeling that it was worthy of further investigation.

Accordingly, Curtis returned to Java in 1992 with a team from the Geochronology Centre at the Institute of Human Origins, Berkeley, California, including geologist Carl Swisher. Accompanied by Jacob, they collected volcanic pumice samples from several fossil find sites before reaching Mojokerto. There, Jacob led the team to a different site from the one he had shown Curtis in 1969. He claimed that a few years after Curtis's first visit, he had met Andojo and asked to be shown the spot where he had made the discovery. It reinforced suspicions among the Berkeley team that nobody in Java really knew the exact place where the Mojokerto skull has been found.

The samples gave an age of 1.81 million years, but the team delayed publishing their results because they felt that they had a solution to the problem of the uncertainty of the skull's find spot. The skull itself was packed with volcanic pumice, and a date obtained from this material would almost certainly be correct. The only problem was trying to persuade the notoriously-protective Teuku Jacob to agree to the removal of sufficient pumice from the fossil for it to be dated. In the 2001 book *Java Man*, Carl Swisher claimed that Jacob was initially agreeable, but then changed his mind after the Berkeley team had already travelled to Java to carry out the work. They nevertheless decided to publish in the journal *Science*, and announced their results to a packed news conference. The implications of the date, if correct, were considerable. With no significantly earlier fossil material known from Africa, it could not be ruled out that the true origins of *Homo erectus* lay instead in Asia. The story made the front page of the *New York Times*, but the anthropological community remained sceptical.

Undeterred, the team made a third visit to Java in 2000. After coming across a 1937 photograph of the Mojokerto find spot in the archives of the American Museum of Natural History, they had contacted various institutions around the world and obtained six additional photographs taken between 1936 and 1938, showing the find spot from various angles. Unfortunately, extensive farming and changes in vegetation in the intervening decades made it impossible to pinpoint the exact spot shown on the photos to within more than a few tens of metres – but it was clear that it was not the spot that Jacob had shown them in 1992.

The matter was not finally cleared up until 2003, when a team led by Australian archaeologist Michael Morwood adopted a slightly different approach. Morwood's team considered the geological horizons within the Mojokerto study area, which included several containing pumice. They dated these using a method known as fission track dating. This is a relatively low-tech dating method which relies on counting tracks left in crystalline material by particles emitted when atoms undergo radioactive decay. Pumice contains minute crystals of zircon, which can be utilised for this method of dating. The team obtained a date of 1.49 million years for material from Pumice Horizon 5, which underlies the Mojokerto find spot by 13 metres (42 ft. 7 in.) and must therefore be older. The pumice was not mixed with gravels or other materials, suggesting that it had been deposited soon after it formed and that the horizon was thus the same age as its constituent pumice material. The implication was that the Mojokerto child could be no more than 1.49 million years old. It wasn't even the oldest human fossil from Java: argon-argon methods had by then been used to obtain a date of 1.51 million years old for the Sangiran fossils.

Subsequent discoveries have considerably revised our view of the early career of *Homo erectus*. Tools and fossils indicate that an early form of *Homo erectus* ('*Homo georgicus*') was present at Dmanisi, Georgia, by 1.85 million years ago, and a Chinese *Homo erectus* skull from Gongwangling, Shaanxi Province has recently been dated to 1.63 million years old. Although the earliest undisputed African example is still the 1.78-million-year-old Koobi Fora skull, a 2.33-million-year-old upper jawbone from Hadar, Ethiopia, known as AL 666-1 and long believed to be *Homo habilis*, may instead be *Homo erectus*. With the origins of *Homo* now pushed back to 2.8 million years ago in Africa, the traditional view that *Homo erectus* was an African species that later migrated to the Far East now seems to be correct, after all. The Mojokerto child, which threatened to overturn that view, has been left on the sidelines.

# 10: The Movius mystery

*Were early humans in the Far East technologically backward in comparison to their cousins in the West?*

In an age where smartphones, cameras and television sets are invariably superseded after one or two years at most, it is difficult to imagine a technology that remained in use with little change for almost one and a half million years. The distinctive teardrop-shaped Acheulean stone 'hand-axe' even outlasted the human species who invented it. First made by *Homo erectus* in East Africa around 1.76 million years ago, they persisted well into the time of the larger-brained *Homo heidelbergensis*. The Hoxne artefacts described by John Frere in 1797 are actually among the more recent examples.

The Acheulean hand-axe may be characterised as a second-generation stone tool. Unlike Oldowan artefacts, their manufacture was clearly beyond the abilities of non-human apes, and required tool makers to concern themselves with overall shape of the finished artefact and with producing a sharp cutting edge. The hand-axes were often symmetrical in two dimensions, with trimming on one edge being placed to match the opposite edge. They have been likened to Swiss army knives and would have been useful for carrying out a variety of tasks, such as butchery, and chopping or scraping wood.

It is possible that the axes also had less mundane functions. The 'sexy hand-axe' theory proposes that they were on occasion used to impress prospective mates. When a female saw a large, symmetrical axe, she might have concluded that its maker possessed the right attributes to father her children. This theory would explain why some axes are too large and unwieldy for practical use, and why axes often show little sign of ever having been used. Presumably, having served their purpose (or not), these axes were simply discarded.

Undoubtedly the biggest puzzle about the hand-axes is that while they are common in Africa, Europe and Southwest Asia, they do not occur further east. Instead, far simpler stone flake and core artefacts are found, resembling those of the earlier Oldowan stone tool tradition. This apparent discontinuity was first reported by the American archaeologist Hallam Movius in 1948, following fieldwork carried out with geologist Helmut de Terra in 1938. The boundary between the two regions was later dubbed the Movius Line by anthropologist Carleton Coon, and it has been widely accepted ever since. Movius himself took the view that there was a fundamental distinction between the progressive societies of Africa, Europe and Southwest Asia and their backward cousins in the Far East. He saw the latter as 'stagnant' and contributing nothing to the development of human culture. Could he be right? What is the explanation for the Movius Line?

The simplest explanation that the ancestors of those living east of the Movius Line left Africa before the hand-axes were invented. Until the 1990s, this scenario would not have been considered: the hand-axes were thought to have come into use around 1.5 million years ago, and *Homo erectus* was not thought to have left Africa until around one million years ago. A much earlier date of 1.81 million years ago was then obtained for the earliest *Homo erectus* in Java, making the scenario a possibility. There is still the problem that it presupposes the hand-axes were invented only once, in Africa; and that knowledge of this single invention spread freely throughout Africa and into Southwest Asia and Europe, but not to the Far East. A further issue is that since the 1990s, dates have more or less 'met in the middle': the earliest currently known hand-axe is that from Kokiselei, Kenya, dating to 1.76 million years ago. The earliest reliable dates for Java are now no earlier than 1.51 million years ago, but a date of 1.63 million years ago has been obtained for a fossil skull from Gongwangling in China. It seems likely that the Acheulean hand-axe first appeared at around the same time or possibly slightly before the first dispersals of *Homo erectus* into Eurasia.

A possibility is that not every *Homo erectus* group adopted Acheulean technology, and that the original migrants into Eurasia were among those lacking it. Subsequent migrations were responsible for the hand-axes eventually reaching Southwest Asia and Europe. Once again, though, it is necessary to assume that none of the first wave of migrants ever subsequently invented hand-axes independently. The same assumption must be made for the suggestion that population sizes at the extremities of the migration were too low to keep the skills necessary for hand-axe production alive from one generation to the next. While it is entirely feasible Acheulean technology could be lost, we have to also assume that it remained lost.

Given the extraordinary longevity of the Acheulean hand-axe, it rather stretches belief that it was only ever invented once. If so, it would make its inventor the most important human ever to have lived; one who would make Galileo, Newton and Einstein pale into insignificance. Had this one individual shared the fate of the Mojokerto child – hardly an uncommon occurrence – the hand-axe might never have been invented and the whole history of the last 1.76 million years would have been entirely different. Even now, human technology might not have got beyond crude Oldowan flakes and cobbles. It's an intriguing possibility, but it seems rather unlikely.

A more likely explanation is that human groups in the Far East began to use materials other than stone for tool-making, possibly driven by local scarcities of suitable raw material. Bamboo has been suggested as a suitable alternative, as it is can be used to make sharp knives suitable for butchery and other tasks. Such tools are far less durable than those of stone, but they are far easier to make and the raw material is far more widely available. It is possible that bamboo knives were the world's first disposable technology, but if so it would be 'archaeologically invisible'. Such implements would be unlikely to survive for over a million years, making the theory difficult to test.

However, tools made from organic materials other than wood have a better chance of being found. In 2014, archaeologists were studying a group of freshwater mussel shells that were excavated in the nineteenth century by Eugene Dubois at Trinil, Java and are now held at the Naturalis Biodiversity Centre in Leiden. Among the shells, which are around 500,000 years old, was one that had been sharpened and polished for use as a cutting tool: the earliest-known example of the use of shells for tool-making. Notably, the local availability of suitable stone for tool-making is poor.

A switch to alternative tool-making materials provides the best explanation for the Movius Line – but is it something that even needs to be explained at all? In other words, is the Movius Line an actual phenomenon or is it an artefact of our incomplete understanding of the archaeological record of Asia? Archaeologist Robin Dennell believes the latter. He notes that none of the Mainland Southeast Asian flake and core industries cited by Movius can be unambiguously demonstrated as being contemporary with the Acheulean industries to the west, and that there is no firm evidence that *Homo erectus* was even present in the region at all prior to one million years ago. In the case of China, the absence of hand-axes could be apparent rather than actual, and might reflect an incomplete archaeological record in what is after all a vast region. Rather than hand-axe users and non-hand-axe users forming two largely separate cultures, Dennell suggests that true picture is a mosaic in which Oldowan and Acheulean technologies were both in use in the same regions. To this mosaic may be added organic tool technology of the type seen at Trinil – long before we have any evidence for it elsewhere. It is now clear that the *Homo erectus* populations in Java at least were certainly not the 'backward cousins' of the hand-axe using populations in the West.

# 11: The gift of Prometheus

*When did humans first learn to use fire?*

According to Greek legend, humans gained the use of fire after the Titan Prometheus stole it from Olympus, hiding it in a fennel stalk. He was already out of favour with Zeus after an earlier misdemeanour, and this latest deed was the final straw. He was chained to a rock and his liver was gnawed by each day by an eagle, until eventually Hercules released him after killing the eagle. That fire was stolen from the gods to enable human progress is a theme that occurs in many traditions, and there is little doubt that mastering the use of fire was a vitally important breakthrough for early humans. Fire can be used for heat and lighting, for cooking, and to deter predators. In the colder regions such as Europe, fire would have been an even greater asset.

The British primatologist Richard Wrangham has argued that the ability to cook food played a crucial role in human evolution. When food is cooked, it becomes more palatable, and the amount of available nutrient is increased. Wrangham believes that once humans were able to cook food, the gut could become smaller – opening up the possibility of bigger, better brains. As we have seen, both brains and guts are 'expensive' to run in terms of the body's energy budget. A bigger brain requires savings to be made elsewhere, and Wrangham believes it was the invention of cooking that made these savings possible. If he is correct, we would expect the first evidence for use of fire to coincide with the emergence of larger-brained hominins.

Such is the importance of the early use of fire that palaeontologist Travis Pickering has insisted that *"extraordinary evidence"* is required for its acceptance, but finding this evidence is not easy. Unlike stone tool use, fire use can only be inferred from clear signs of burning having occurred. Even then, there is the problem of distinguishing controlled use of fire from natural wildfire. This is particularly a problem in Africa, where electrical storms frequently trigger outbreaks of wildfire. Archaeological evidence of hearths would certainly meet Pickering's criterion, but unfortunately it is lacking from the earliest sites where fire use has been claimed.

Localised red patches of oxidised sediment have been found at the site of Koobi Fora (FxJj20) in Kenya, and are around 1.6 million years old; and similar evidence has been reported from the slightly younger site of Chesowanja, also in Kenya. In both cases it has been claimed that they are remains from fire use by early humans, but this evidence is rather less than extraordinary.

Less tentative evidence has been found at Swartkrans Cave, near Sterkfontein, South Africa, which is about 1.0 to 1.5 million years old. Archaeologists have recovered 270 burned animal bones from the uppermost level, known as Member 3. The site was used by both *Homo erectus* and the australopithecine species *Paranthropus robustus*, and while it is generally assumed that only the former were responsible for the fires, this cannot be proved from the evidence. Unfortunately, the bones were probably moved a short distance away from where they were burned, and a natural cause cannot be ruled out. Wildfires could have ignited flammable material, including the bones, which originally lay on the floor of the cave mouth. Rainfall later washed them deeper into the gully where Member 3 formed. However, palaeontologist Bob Brain notes that while the burned bones are found throughout the 6 m (19 ft. 8 in.) thick Member 3, hardly any have been found in the earlier Members 1 and 2, despite these levels containing large quantities of vertebrate fossils. If wildfire had been responsible for the burned bones, one would expect to find them in all three levels. It's probably safe to say that on the balance of probabilities, the evidence from Swartkrans Cave demonstrates the use of fire, but it does not do so beyond reasonable doubt.

Closer to meeting the criterion of 'extraordinary' is the evidence from Wonderwerk Cave, in Northern Cape Province, South Africa. The site is about a million years old, so it dates to well after the emergence of *Homo erectus*. Archaeologists investigated a habitation layer known as Stratum 10, which was found to contain ash, minute bone fragments, and complete or fragmented bones with signs of having been burned. This material was associated with stone tools, and it occurred throughout the whole of Stratum 10. It shows that fires were occurring too frequently to be accounted for by natural causes, and in any case the habitation area was some 30 m (100 ft.) from the cave entrance (and it was even further away at the time Stratum 10 was laid down). This distance was much too far for the burnt material to been blown in or washed in from outside. The techniques used by the team were so sensitive that they were even able to rule out the possibility of spontaneous combustion of bat guano, which though rare has been known to occur in caves.

What none of this data tells is whether *Homo erectus* knew how to actually produce fire, or if they had to rely on the availability of wildfire to start their own fires. The evidence from Eurasia suggests the latter. Once early humans had left Africa, the controlled use of fire would have been a boon in the often challenging and climatically-unstable environments. One would expect widespread evidence for fire from one million years ago, by which time humans were widely dispersed across Eurasia. In fact, prior to 400,000 years ago, the evidence from Europe is non-existent and that from Asia comes from just two sites – only one of which is particularly convincing.

Locality 1 at Zhoukoudian is a much-investigated cave site near Beijing, with archaeological layers that accumulated between 500,000 and 200,000 years ago. Burnt bones and stone tools have been recovered from Layer 10, the lowest and oldest layer, and evidence of hearths has long been claimed. However, work in the late 1990s failed to find any traces of the wood ash and charcoal that would be expected at an archaeological hearth site.

There is stronger evidence from Gesher Benot Ya'aqov, a 790,000-year-old site is located on the shores of the now-drained Lake Huleh, Israel. Burned wood and small burned flint fragments found there might indicate the locations of hearths. Although it is an outdoor site, wildfire is unlikely to account for the burning: electrical storms in the region mainly occur during the wet season, making lightning-induced wildfire uncommon. Human activity is the most likely explanation, and the scarcity of wildfire suggests that the site's occupants had discovered the means to start fires for themselves. If so, they kept the knowledge to themselves.

Elsewhere there is nothing. No evidence for use of fire has been found at any European site from the Early or Middle Pleistocene. Not until 400,000 years ago do the first signs emerge at the British site of Beeches Pit and the German site of Schöningen, where charred wood, heated sediments and the possible remains of hearths have been found. From then on, however, evidence for use of fire becomes increasingly widespread throughout Europe, Asia and Africa. In Europe and western Asia, Neanderthal sites reveal clear evidence of its long-term use and management. In some cases, lignite was transported over long distances for use as fuel. Fire was used not just for heat, light and cooking but also for making pitch from birch tree bark, which they used for hafting projectile points to spears. It must be assumed that they had now developed the means to produce fire rather than having to wait for convenient lightning strikes.

That such evidence is not seen earlier suggests that until 400,000 years ago, there was little or no habitual as opposed to opportunistic use of fire, and that humans were able to occupy northern latitudes without it. Such timings make Richard Wrangham's cooking hypothesis look improbable. Notably, by this time *Homo erectus* had already given way to the larger-brained *Homo heidelbergensis*, suggesting that bigger brains led to the habitual use of fire, rather than the other way around. A little later, modern humans in Africa began to use heat treatment to improve the flaking properties of the raw materials that they used for tool-making. Given the vital role fire has played in human affairs, it is not surprising that tales of its theft from the gods are so prevalent in world mythologies.

# 12: Footprints at Happisburgh

*Who were the first Britons?*

Somewhere between one million and 780,000 million years ago, a group of adults and children walked along the foreshore of a river estuary in what is now Norfolk, leaving footprints in the soft estuarine sediment. The survival of such footprints is extremely rare, but it does sometimes happen. Hundreds of millennia passed. The coast, originally 24 kilometres (15 miles) away, was brought ever closer by the combined effects of erosion and rising sea levels. Eventually, in May 2013, the footprints briefly emerged at low tide, having being exposed by rough seas. Within a fortnight, they had vanished again, this time for ever.

At the time the footprints were made, the landmass now known as Great Britain was not an island: it was connected to mainland Europe by the Doggerland isthmus, which stretched roughly from Great Yarmouth to Eastbourne on the British side; and from Amsterdam to Boulogne on the European side. The combined peninsular landmass lay on the southern edge of the forests of northwestern Europe. The Thames flowed into the North Sea about 150 km (95 miles) north of the present estuary, close to where the coastal village of Happisburgh (pronounced 'Hazebrough') now stands. It was here that these earliest-known Britons lived, on the edges of a conifer-dominated forest.

Very few human remains from this period of European prehistory are known. The Gran Dolina ('Great Depression') cave in the Sierra de Atapuerca of northern Spain has yielded human remains from two sites, documenting a human presence there from roughly 1.2 million to 800,000 years ago. The Gran Dolina people were slightly larger brained than African *Homo erectus* and distinct from them facially, with the result that they were classified as a separate species, *Homo antecessor* ('pioneer man') by their discoverers. In all probability, though, these early Spaniards were descendants of a population of Asian *Homo erectus* that migrated westwards.

*Homo erectus* was well established in the Far East by 1.5 million years ago, but establishing a permanent presence in Europe apparently took longer. This was probably due to episodes of glaciation, which were far more severe in Europe and seem to have been responsible for the ultimate demise of the Gran Dolina people. Around a quarter of the remains from the last phase of occupation in the region show signs of damage that includes chop-marks and cut-marks, peeling where bones have been broken and bent, and marks where bones have been splintered for marrow extraction. The evidence points to butchery for food purposes, in other words cannibalism. Perhaps the plight of the Gran Dolina people became so desperate that they ended up eating each other.

Despite these difficulties, early Europeans did not remain confined to the Mediterranean region. The first evidence for an early human presence in Britain emerged in 2005, when flint tools believed to be 700,000 years old were reported from Pakefield in Suffolk. The tools were 200,000 years older than the previous earliest-known evidence for human presence in northwestern Europe. The climate at that time was significantly warmer than today, and Britain basked in Mediterranean-like conditions of hot summers and mild winters. It seemed reasonable to suppose that early humans, by now long present in southern Europe, would not be particularly out of their comfort zone in Britain at that time. The Pakefield people inhabited a mixed environment of marshland, woodland and open grassland; these habitats were home to a variety of large mammals, including hippopotamus, bison and now-extinct species of elephant and deer. An added benefit was the abundance of high-quality flint for tool-making. On the down side, humans would have faced competition from lions, hyenas and wolves. The findings supported an 'ebb and flow' model of early human settlement in Europe, where groups retreated south during times of cold climate, but expanded northwards when conditions improved.

However, it soon turned out that the Pakefield people were not the first Britons – and that their predecessors had lived in the region at a time when the climate had been far less favourable. In 2010, flint artefacts estimated to be from 780,000 to a million years old were reported from Happisburgh. This discovery was soon followed by direct evidence for the actual toolmakers. It emerged in dramatic fashion in May 2013, when a low tide exposed ancient footprints on the foreshore at Happisburgh. Erosion of the sandy beach by rough seas had revealed the footprints, but researchers now faced a race against time to record them before they were lost for good. A team led by Nick Ashton from the British Museum obtained plaster casts and 3d images of the footprints, recording a total of 152 in all. Of these, twelve yielded complete outlines suitable for analysis. It is thought that they represented five individuals ranging in height from 0.93 to 1.73 m (3 ft. 0 in. to 5 ft. 8 in.), suggesting that the group included both adults and children. The estimated foot size, foot area and stature of the Happisburgh people are consistent with estimates for *Homo antecessor*.

The date range for tools and climatic inferences were obtained by the use of a variety of techniques. The recent end of the date range was obtained by the use of palaeomagnetic dating, a technique that relies on periodic changes in polarity of the Earth's magnetic field. During intervals of 'reversed' (as opposed to 'normal') polarity, a compass needle will point south rather than north. The frequency with which reversals occur has varied considerably: at times the same polarity has been maintained for tens of millions of years; at others a change has occurred after just 50,000 years. There is no preferred polarity and the present state of affairs is only considered normal because the last switch occurred 780,000 years ago – long before the invention of the compass. Sediments associated with the tools contained traces of magnetic material with a reversed polarity, implying a date of at least 780,000 years ago. The upper end of the date range was obtained by a consideration of animal fossils found in the stratigraphic layer containing the tools: two species of deer and two species of vole that did not appear until one million years ago.

Climatologists were able to reconstruct the climate using beetle remains as indicators. Beetles are very sensitive to temperatures, and the presence and absence of particular species can be used to estimate seasonal temperatures with a reasonable degree of accuracy. The results indicated that the climate was rather cooler than that of today: summers were similar, but winters were on average at least three degrees Celsius colder. This, together with the presence of conifer-dominated woodlands, suggests that conditions were similar to those of present-day southern Scandinavia. Such conditions are known as 'late interglacial' and occurred during the latter part of the warm periods that lasted from 866,000 to 814,000 years ago and from 970,000 to 936,000 years ago, though we do not know which of these corresponds to the Happisburgh occupation.

While not particularly severe by present-day British standards, the winter cold would have worse for those used to a Mediterranean climate, and occupying the region would have presented many challenges. Edible plants were scarce during the winter months, and the daylight hours for foraging were short. The Happisburgh people were able to minimise these problems by settling in a region bordered by a variety of habitats, all of which were rich in resources. These included a large tidal river with freshwater pools and marsh on its floodplain, together with salt marsh and the nearby coast. In contrast to the nearby conifer-dominated forest, the grassy floodplain was home to a diverse range of herbivores. In addition, tubers, shellfish and seaweed were available all the year round, even in winter.

Overall, the implication of this early human presence at Happisburgh is that humans from this period were much more adaptable to challenging conditions than was previously thought. Just what form these adaptations took remains unclear. The Happisburgh people might, over many generations, have become physically adapted to the colder winter conditions. Another possibility is that they simply migrated south in winter. We lack knowledge of the technology they might have used to master the conditions, such as hunting, use of clothing, construction of shelters, and control of fire. We can be hopeful, though, that further discoveries are waiting in the sands and silts of East Anglia.

# 13: The Boxgrove people

*An archaeological site in West Sussex has provided a unique insight into use of technology by early humans in Britain 500,000 years ago.*

The small West Sussex village of Boxgrove is noted for its ruined priory and thirteenth century parish church. The population is fewer than a thousand, but the discovery of Middle Pleistocene stone tools at the nearby Eartham Quarry suggested that people have been living in the area for a very long time indeed. The finds soon attracted the interest of a team from University College London, which began excavating the quarry in 1985 and eventually had over 40 specialists and a large number of excavators on site. Despite the numbers, no human remains were found until late 1993, when a volunteer named Roger Pedersen discovered a human shin bone. This 500,000-year-old bone is more recent than the Happisburgh footprints, but it is the earliest-known human fossil from Britain. It is also one of the most massive early human leg bones known. Its size and thickness suggested that it probably belonged to a tall, powerfully-built male, who was nicknamed Roger after Roger Pedersen. He was probably about forty at the time of his death, which was a respectable age for the Middle Pleistocene.

Roger belonged to an archaic human species usually referred to as *Homo heidelbergensis* ('Heidelberg Man'), though his exact status is uncertain. *Homo heidelbergensis* was first identified from a lower jawbone found in 1907 in a sandpit at the village of Mauer, near Heidelberg in southwestern Germany, and is thought to have been the common ancestor of the Neanderthals and modern humans. The species first appeared about 600,000 years ago and is known from sites in both Europe and Africa, though some regard the African examples as a separate species, *Homo rhodesiensis* ('Rhodesian Man'). If the two are indeed separate, then European examples like Roger were actually early Neanderthals.

Regardless of such considerations, the brain size of *Homo heidelbergensis* was about 90 percent of the modern size, and was a significant increase on that of earlier humans such as *Homo erectus*. Much of the increase was in the parietal lobes, which process sensory information and are responsible for spatial awareness. How smart was

*Homo heidelbergensis*, and why should such an increase in brain power happen?

As with the initial increase in brain size when *Homo* first appeared, this further jump corresponds to a period of climate change. *Homo heidelbergensis* appears soon after the onset of the Middle Pleistocene Transition, a period characterised by ever increasing swings in the climate. Europe was hardest hit, but the effects of glacial periods were also felt in Africa. At such times, the Sahara was transformed from a rich, well-watered environment into an arid wilderness. Only in Asia did the climate remain relatively stable. In these challenging conditions, larger brains presumably conferred an advantage, but what was it? We have seen that the brains of the first humans might have been associated with larger group sizes and the larger brains of *Homo heidelbergensis* would have enabled a further increase. It is possible that as food and water became more widely dispersed, working in larger groups helped ensure continued access to these essentials. However, it is also possible that larger brains enabled *Homo heidelbergensis* to improve on the tool technology of *Homo erectus*, and so improve on their chances of survival.

Boxgrove is one of the most important Middle Pleistocene sites in Europe, and it has provided a wealth of data on the behaviour of its inhabitants. The site now lies well inland, but half a million years ago it was much closer to the shore. The region was a coastal plain of salt marshes and grasslands, on which red deer, bison, horses, elephants and rhinoceros grazed. The plain was set against a backdrop of massive chalk cliffs, 100 m (330 ft.) high, running along an indented shoreline of beaches and tidal lagoons. It was an attractive site for humans, benefiting not only from abundant game but readily-available flint from the chalk cliffs.

The site has yielded over 300 Acheulean hand-axes and the waste material left over from their production. The latter is known as debitage. These were overlain by fine silt deposits that froze them in time for half a million years. Exact places where people made hand-axes have been preserved, with struck-off stone flakes lying where they fell. The patterns of scattered flakes even highlight the arrangement of tool-makers legs while they were going about their work. In some cases, researchers have managed to 'refit' debitage to finished stone tools, painstakingly reassembling the flakes like a three-dimensional jigsaw puzzle. This has revealed the exact sequence in which flakes were detached from stone cores, and yielded valuable information about the flint knapping techniques used by *Homo heidelbergensis*.

Hand-axes were not the only stone artefacts produced at Boxgrove. At one tool-manufacturing location, set aside from other debitage was a small pile of larger flakes intended for possible use as tools in their own right. Not only was this the forerunner of later 'flaked tool' industries, it suggests that the Boxgrove tool-makers were able to concentrate on more than one goal at a time: making a hand-axe and obtaining a useful by-product.

Also informative was the short time it took the overlying silt deposits to accumulate: possibly no more than a single generation. Usually, sites from this period are separated by thousands of years, and archaeologists are only very rarely able to identify more than one location used by a particular group. By contrast, several sites at Boxgrove were used by the same group, making it possible to build up a picture of the various ways in which they were used.

At one site, located at the base of the cliff, flint nodules were tested for quality by striking off a few flakes. Suitable nodules were either knapped into hand-axes then and there, or taken away for future use. Rejected nodules were simply discarded. A short distance from the cliff, the butchered remains of a horse were found, along with ten separate piles of debitage. By refitting these, archaeologists deduced that hand-axes had been produced on the spot to assist in butchering the horse carcass. The hand-axes themselves were not found and were presumably kept for future use. The implication from this site is that the horse butchering was a one-off activity.

A different picture was seen at another site, located by edge of a water hole. Here a large number of hand-axes and smaller tools were found, together with butchered animal remains. The hand-axes were varying stages of completion, and were not only used as tools but as portable sources of stone flakes for making the smaller tools. The fact that the tools were left where they were for future use suggests that unlike the horse butchering site, this was a place of ongoing operations. The reuse of some sites but not others suggests the Boxgrove peoples stuck to habitual patterns of behaviour rather than carrying out tasks on a completely *ad hoc* basis.

Methods of tool production had become more sophisticated than those of *Homo erectus*, but the tools themselves were little changed. This suggests that *Homo heidelbergensis* carried out the same range of tasks as *Homo erectus*, although it was more efficient at doing so. *Homo heidelbergensis* was able to fine-tune the overall expertise of *Homo erectus*, but the role of technology in day to day living might not have changed significantly. *Homo heidelbergensis* still lacked the modern ability for innovation and long-range planning, but the evidence from Boxgrove suggests that the rudiments were now in place.

# 14: The Berekhat Ram pebble

*Is a 250,000 year old lump of volcanic lava the world's oldest artwork?*

In 1981, archaeologists discovered a small lump of volcanic lava at the Late Acheulean site of Berekhat Ram in the Israeli-occupied Golan Heights. The object, which is more than 250,000 years old, had been worked with a sharp-edged tool, and there are indications of head, neck, arms, shoulders and breasts. It is claimed that the pebble is the earliest-known attempt to represent the female form, though inevitably this suggestion has proved controversial. The implications are considerable – the existence of an art object implies that its maker was capable of at least some form of symbolic behaviour.

Just how close to the modern condition were the thought processes of the humans of that time? What if any language did they use? The evidence from sites such as Boxgrove suggests that while they were able to fine tune the technologies of earlier humans, *Homo heidelbergensis* and other Middle Pleistocene people lacked the modern ability to innovate. They could not, in modern parlance, think outside the box. Innovation – indeed all art, literature and science are consequences of a behavioural package anthropologists refer to as 'modern human behaviour'.

None of this would be possible without our ability to use symbols to convey information, ranging from the spoken and written word to representational art. A symbol is anything that refers to an object or an idea, and it can take the form of sound, an image or an object. Symbols may refer directly to an object or idea, for example a representational image; or they may be totally abstract, such as spoken or written words. Thus for example a drawing of a tree, the sound 'tree' or the written letters 't-r-e-e' may all be used to refer to a tree. We use symbols all the time – whenever we read a newspaper, check our email, consult satnav or admire a painting or sculpture. All of these activities involve symbolic behaviour: human society could not function without it. Modern syntactical language is a system of communication that uses symbols in the form of spoken and (in the last six thousand years) written words to enable an effectively infinite range of meanings to be conveyed.

Just when and how modern human behaviour emerged remains

hotly disputed, with two principle schools of thought. One view is that it emerged quite suddenly as a result of a genetic mutation that occurred as recently as 50,000 years ago and somehow 'rewired' the human brain. This 'smartness mutation' occurred well after the emergence of anatomically-modern *Homo sapiens*, but it conferred an enormous survival advantage on its possessors. Consequently, it rapidly spread through the human population with the result that all modern humans now possess it. The event has been described by science author Jared Diamond as the Great Leap Forward, in reference to the economic and social plan implemented in China between 1958 and 1961 by the former Communist leader Mao Zedong.

Proponents of this view claim that artefacts that are unquestionably the work of modern minds do not appear in the archaeological record prior to the transition to the Upper Palaeolithic in Europe and the Late Stone Age in Africa, around 50,000 years ago. These include spectacular polychrome cave paintings, bone and ivory carvings and enigmatic large-breasted 'Venus' figurines. It is argued the apparently sudden appearance of such artefacts reflects a fundamental shift in cognition and the emergence of modern syntactical language. But others claim that evidence of behavioural modernity – albeit less clear-cut – is to be found much earlier. On this second view, there was no Great Leap Forward, and the elements of modern human behaviour emerged only very gradually over tens and possibly hundreds of millennia.

If this second view is correct, then it is likely that *Homo heidelbergensis* was capable of at least a limited form of symbolic behaviour and that it possessed a form of language. An endocast of the inside of the Kabwe skull from Zambia has shown that the Broca's area was enlarged relative to the corresponding area in the right hemisphere. As we have seen, this area of the brain is associated with speech, suggesting a degree of linguistic competence, but we cannot tell how complex any language was in comparison to that of modern humans. It has been suggested that tool-making techniques were now too complex to be learned by simply watching tool-makers at work, and a complex grammatical language was necessary to provide training. On the other hand, it could have been that teachers only required a combination of pointing gestures and simple, non-grammatical instructions to instruct their students.

More direct evidence of symbolic behaviour comes from Twin Rivers, a complex of caves in southern Zambia. The site was first studied in the 1950s, but in 1999 a team led by British archaeologist

Larry Barham recovered over 300 pieces of coloured minerals known as ochres from levels dating from between 266,000 to 400,000 years old. They included the minerals haematite, limonite and specularite, which can be used to produce a range of colours including red, yellow, brown and purple. The pieces show signs of grinding and rubbing to obtain powder. Further evidence for processing was provided by a quartzite cobble, recovered in 1954, that was found to be stained with traces of specularite. It seems very likely that the pieces found at the site were used as pigments as they do not occur naturally in the environs of the site and must have been brought in from elsewhere.

Although it is possible that the powdered ochres were simply used for medicinal purposes or hide processing, the range of colours and the effort required to obtain and process the different materials suggests otherwise. Barham believes that the ochres were used primarily for ritual body painting and possibly for cave painting as well, although no evidence of the latter has been found or is likely to have survived after so long. He also believes that the existence of rituals implies language as it is difficult to see how else the meaning and significance of such group activities could be communicated.

The most tantalising evidence that *Homo heidelbergensis* was capable of some form of symbolic behaviour is the Berekhat Ram pebble. Its age is not open to any doubt: it was found in an archaeological layer that was sealed between two volcanic basalt flows and accurate dating of these bracketed the age of the artefact to between 250,000 and 280,000 years old. Sceptics point out that it takes a degree of imagination to see the pebble as depicting a woman, and it certainly bears very little resemblance to the finely-crafted 'Venus' figurines from the European Upper Palaeolithic. It is nevertheless beyond dispute that the pebble has been worked with a tool, and it has no obvious utilitarian function.

If the Berekhat Ram pebble is indeed an attempt to portray a woman it would be the oldest-known example of representational art anywhere in the world. Crude as it is, it could represent the first glimmerings of a sculptural tradition that would one day lead to the works of Michelangelo, Donatello and Rodin.

# 15: New Man's Valley

*The discovery and rediscovery of the first Neanderthal fossil.*

Of all the early extinct human species, none have captured the public imagination to anything like the extent of the Neanderthals. The idea that tens of thousands of years ago, people very much like ourselves shared the planet with another human species is understandably intriguing, almost the stuff of science fiction. The term 'Neanderthal' comes from Neander Thal (Neander Valley), a limestone valley near Düsseldorf through which flows the River Düssel. The Neander Valley is named for Joachim Neander, a local seventeenth century Calvinist theologian who is best known for composing the popular hymn *Praise to the Lord, the Almighty*. The name 'Neander' is a Greek transliteration of his original family name Neumann (the equivalent English surname is Newman), which had been adopted by his grandfather as was a fashion at the time. Thus the literal meaning of Neanderthal, ironically, is New Man's Valley.

It was at this otherwise undistinguished location that the first recognised specimen, Neanderthal 1, was discovered in August 1856. By the middle of the nineteenth century, the Industrial Revolution had transformed Dusseldorf into a boom town. Limestone was much in demand for both the steel and construction industries, and two years earlier extensive quarrying had commenced in the Neander Valley. The discovery was made by quarry workers at Feldhofer Cave, a small cave on the south wall of the valley that was named for a local farm. The workers recovered a skullcap, two thigh bones, three bones from the right arm, two from the left arm, part of the pelvis, fragments of a shoulder blade, and ribs. At first, it was thought that the bones had belonged to a cave bear, but they were then examined by a local schoolteacher and amateur naturalist, Johann Carl Fuhlrott, who pronounced them to be human. He also noted that the remains were unlike those of modern humans. The cranial vault of the skull was long and low, quite different to globular cranium of present-day people. In addition, the browridges were massive in comparison to those of a modern human. The simple fact that the bones were fossilised implied that they were very old.

Fuhlrott suspected that the quarry workers, unaware of the importance of the find, had saved only the larger bones.

Believing that they were of scientific interest, Fuhlrott showed the remains to Hermann Schaaffhausen, Professor of Anatomy at the University of Bonn, and the pair jointly announced the discovery in Bonn in 1857. Schaaffhausen believed that the Neanderthals were an ancient northern European race that predated the early Germanic and Celtic peoples, but his colleagues were rather more sceptical. Pathologist Rudolf Virchow also believed that the remains were of a modern human, whose deformities were due to rickets in childhood and osteoarthritis later in life. The unusual skull shape was the result of powerful blows to the head. Anatomist F. Mayer claimed that the Feldhofer remains belonged a Mongolian Cossack who had deserted on the way to the 1814 Battle of Paris, taken refuge in the cave, and died there. According to Mayer, the massive browridges were the result of many years of wincing in pain from his deformities.

It was not until 1863 that the Irish anatomist William King suggested that the Feldhofer remains might represent an entirely new human species, for which he proposed the name *Homo neanderthalensis*. King formally described the species under that name the following year. In doing so, he ensured that Joachim Neander gained a second claim to fame, but it was actually a close-run thing. It turned out that the Feldhofer Cave discovery had not been the first Neanderthal to be found. A juvenile skull had previously been recovered in Engis Cave, Belgium between 1829 and 1830 and an adult female skull was found at Forbes Quarry, Gibraltar in 1848. In neither case was their significance recognised at the time, but by 1864 the Gibraltar skull had attracted the attention of the British palaeontologists Hugh Falconer and George Busk. The pair described it under the name *Homo calpicus* (after Mons Calpius, the Roman name for Gibraltar), by which time King had already published and secured priority for the name *Homo neanderthalensis*. This formal name remained unchanged even after the spelling of Neander Thal was changed to Neander Tal in 1901, although the informal term Neanderthal is often spelled 'Neandertal'.

Recognition was still slow to come. In 1864, Darwin was shown the Gibraltar skull, but it evidently did not make a lasting impression and he referred to Neanderthals only briefly in his 1871 work *The Descent of Man*. Darwin's associate Thomas Henry Huxley was also sceptical as to whether the remains were anything but slightly abnormal *Homo sapiens*. As late as the 1890s, Eugene Dubois dismissed the Feldhofer remains as having nothing to do with human ancestry. By this time, however, more Neanderthal finds were coming to light, including well-preserved skeletons of one male and one female from Spy Cave, Belgium. In this case, stone tools were recovered in association with the remains. The tools were of a type now known as Mousterian, an industry largely associated with the Neanderthals. It takes its name from the site of Le Moustier in southern France, where similar tools were found in 1863.

The Mousterian is an example of what is known as a prepared-core industry. Prepared-core techniques entail shaping a stone core to a pre-planned form, from which flakes of a desired size and shape are then struck. Depending on the shape of the core, the resulting flakes may be oval or triangular. Such techniques maximise the use of raw materials, because many flakes may be struck from the same core. Instead being confined to making multi-purpose hand-axes, Neanderthals were able to make a variety of tools for specific purposes. Prepared-core industries replaced Acheulean hand-axes between 300,000 and 250,000 years ago, although their origins probably can be traced back to sites like Boxgrove where it was realised that flakes produced as a by-product of hand-axe manufacture could often be useful as tools in their own right. Gradually, the emphasis shifted to the flakes themselves becoming the main product. Prepared-core methods include the Levallois technique, named for the Parisian suburb of Levallois-Perret where examples of pre-shaped cores were discovered in the nineteenth century.

What of the Feldhofer Cave, where the first recognised Neanderthal remains were found? The limestone excavations completely destroyed the cave without a thorough survey being carried out. By the end of the nineteenth century, its exact location had been forgotten. In the 1920s the area was turned into a park and Feldhofer Cave would have been lost to science forever but for the efforts of two archaeologists from the Rhineland Archaeological Service. In 1997, Ralf Schmitz and Jürgen Thissen set about relocating the site, using old plans of the quarry and nineteenth century sketches and paintings of the valley as it had been before the quarrying operations had started. From these they identified a rock that still stands in the park, so they dug exploratory trenches nearby. The odds were seemingly stacked against success, but on sifting through rocks and quarrying debris they found the teeth of bats and pieces of stalactites: items which are only found in caves. Realising they had located the site of Feldhofer Cave, Schmitz and Thissen continued their investigations. Eventually, they unearthed 62 human skeletal fragments. A number of cranial pieces were found to either fit or represent elements missing from the skull of the original nineteenth century find. Another small piece of bone exactly fitted its left knee joint. It was established that the finds represent three individuals – the 1856 find, a second adult and an adolescent. In addition, they recovered a large number of stone tools and animal remains showing evidence of butchery. Radiocarbon dating of the remains indicates that the Feldhofer Cave Neanderthals lived 42,000 years ago. The operation was a spectacular success for investigative archaeology. The recovery of missing pieces from a fossil as historically-important as Neanderthal 1 has been likened by palaeoanthropologist Chris Stringer to finding one of the lost arms of the Venus de Milo.

# 16: Were they really dimwits?

*Just how smart or otherwise were Neanderthals?*

With the possible exception of the dinosaurs, no species has been the butt of as many unwarranted slurs as the Neanderthals. Politicians and other public figures whose views are seen as outdated are regularly described as 'Neanderthals', as are football hooligans, and the term has long been used as a synonym for blundering stupidity and general dim-wittedness. When you consider the harsh conditions in which they managed to survive, it is obvious that such comparisons are inappropriate, but were the Neanderthals behaviourally modern? It's a classic case of 'it depends on who you ask'. The cognitive abilities of the Neanderthals is one of the most contentious areas of palaeoanthropology: there is a reasonable amount of evidence, but interpretations of it are still hotly disputed.

Some believe that the archaeological record shows that Neanderthals were behaviourally less advanced than modern humans. One suggestion is that because Neanderthals lived at high latitudes, they experienced lower light levels than people living in the tropics, and required larger eyes to compensate. This in turn required a larger visual cortex, leaving less brainpower available for other functions including the ability to manage complex long-distance social networks, and to develop and pass on innovations.

But does this argument hold water? A recent survey of the archaeological record suggests that it does not: the Neanderthal diet was every bit as diverse as that of modern humans; no evidence was found to suggest that the social networks of the latter were larger, or that their hunting techniques and capacity for innovation were necessarily superior. Sophisticated Neanderthal technologies included manufacturing pitch for hafting spear points and making specialised bone tools for working animal hides. The latter were made from deer rib fragments, which were ground and polished to a predetermined size and shape. They are thought to have been a type of tool known as a *lissoir* (French 'to make smooth') for preparing animal hides, used by present-day leather-workers to make them softer, tougher and more waterproof. Dating to 51,500 years ago, they are the earliest-known specialised bone tools in Europe. Although the lissoir is a purely functional artefact, the ability to grind and polish bone in such a manner is thought to be indicative of behaviourally modern minds.

However, the major battleground between proponents and sceptics of behavioural modernity in Neanderthals has long centred on the evidence for symbolic behaviour. Burial of their dead has long been thought to the make one of the best cases for Neanderthal rituals and symbolic behaviour – but were Neanderthal burials funerals as we understand them? The Neanderthals were not the first hominins to intentionally bury their dead: the site of Sima de los Huesos in northern Spain was used as a burial pit by *Homo heidelbergensis* (or possibly proto-Neanderthals) around 50,000 years before the Neanderthals emerged. The remains of over thirty individuals have been found at this site, but it is thought that corpses were simply dumped there in order to dispose of them. By contrast, Neanderthals are usually interred singly or in small groups, and in association with residential sites, suggesting something other than simple hygienic disposal.

One of the best-known Neanderthal burial sites is Shanidar Cave in the Zagros Mountains of Iraq. In lower levels of the site, dating from around 80,000 to 70,000 years ago, intentional burials were found. The burial of one individual, a 30 to 45-year-old male known as Shanidar 4, yielded what was at first interpreted as evidence that flowers had been placed in the grave. Soil samples gathered from around the body were later analysed for pollen, in an attempt to reconstruct the climatic and vegetation history of the site. In addition to the usual pollen found throughout the site, some samples yielded whole clumps of pollen and it was suggested that this had come from flowers deposited during the burial – but if so, why were other human remains in the cave not accorded similar ritual treatment? A later re-evaluation of the grave suggested a purely natural origin for the pollen: it had probably been introduced into the grave by a gerbil-like rodent known as the Persian jird, which stores large numbers of seeds and flowers in its burrow.

A similar picture is seen at other Neanderthal sites where evidence of grave goods has been claimed. Artefacts and once-meaty bones have been found in burial infill, and it has been suggested that the latter were intended to provide sustenance for the deceased on their journey to the next world. However, it is just as likely that such items were accidentally introduced when the grave was filled in after the bodies were interred. Overall, there is no conclusive evidence for ritual or symbolic behaviour at any Neanderthal burial site. Nevertheless, the burials must have been a more than a way of simply disposing of dead bodies. As was the case at Sima de los Huesos, there are far simpler ways of achieving this. There must have been a perceived need to preserve the remains of kin. Regardless of their capacity for symbolic behaviour, it suggests that Neanderthals felt the loss of friends and family just as keenly as do modern people.

Another long-running source of controversy has centred on sites in northern Spain and western and central France associated with the Châtelperronian culture, which was confirmed as a Neanderthal culture after remains found at one of the sites were identified as a Neanderthal rather than a modern human. Châtelperronian sites include La Grotte des Fées, at Châtelperron in central France, for which the culture is named. Other Châtelperronian sites include the Grotte du Renne at Arcy-sur-Cure in north-central France and Saint Césaire in southwestern France. Artefacts found at these sites combine typical Neanderthal Mousterian stone tools with articles more characteristic of modern humans such as end scrapers (long flakes or blades with a sharp edge at one end) for working animal hide and burins (chisels) for working wood, bone and antler. Other seemingly-modern items include projectile points, awls, pins and burnishing tools made from bone, and beads and pendants made from animal teeth, ivory, bone and shell. Living spaces at Châtelperronian sites include features usually associated only with modern humans, including floors paved with limestone plaques. The Châtelperronian people showed evidence of modern human behaviour – but was it of independent Neanderthal origin?

The Châtelperronian is dated very closely to the time of the transition from the Middle to Upper Palaeolithic, which is when modern humans finally reached Europe. The Aurignacian, a modern human culture named for Aurignac in southwestern France, spread rapidly across Europe in the period from 46,000 to 41,000 years ago, and Aurignacian people would certainly have come into contact with the Neanderthal population. Many think that it is too much of a coincidence that all these trappings of modernity appeared just as modern humans showed up, and believe that the Neanderthals simply borrowed this technology and culture from their new neighbours.

Archaeologist Sir Paul Mellars attributed the Châtelperronian to what he terms a 'bow wave effect', i.e. technological and cultural diffusion from the modern human populations in North Africa and Asia, some way in advance of the actual dispersal of modern humans into Europe. He noted that such connections have been widely documented among recent hunter-gatherers, who have spread technological ideas and items such as highly-prized shells and raw materials over long distances.

The issue really turned on whether the Châtelperronian could be shown to pre-date any possible Aurignacian influence. Much controversy focussed on the reliability of the stratigraphy at the classic Châtelperronian sites of La Grotte des Fées and Grotte du Renne – but then later work rendered these arguments moot. New radiocarbon dates for the Châtelperronian showed that it did not begin until soon after modern humans reached Europe; even Mellars' 'bow wave effect' was not necessary to invoke the possibility of modern human influence.

By now though, evidence for Neanderthal symbolic behaviour was emerging from sites elsewhere in Europe. From two Neanderthal sites in Spain came shells that had been coloured with pigment and perforated for use as beads, along with evidence that minerals had been mixed in a shell 'powder compact' for possible use as cosmetic. Bird bones damaged by the removal of flight feathers were found at a cave site near Verona in northern Italy. As none of the species involved had any value as food and the feathers were too long for use as fletching elements in spears, the implication was that they had been removed for ornamental purposes – possibly to make a headdress. The sites ranged from 45,000 to 50,000 years old and predated the arrival of modern humans in the region – but they were not early enough to entirely preclude the 'bow wave' effect.

Even more compelling was a 39,000-year-old rock engraving found at Gorham's Cave, a much-studied Neanderthal site on the eastern side of Gibraltar. The deeply-etched cross-hatched pattern is carved into the dolomite bedrock of the cave, and was wholly covered by an undisturbed archaeological level containing Mousterian artefacts. As these are of purely Neanderthal origin, the association of the engraving with Neanderthals is secure. Researchers carried out a number of tests to demonstrate that the engraving was intentional. They used a variety of tools and cutting actions on blocks of dolomite rock similar to the rock face at Gorham's cave and found that results best matching the engraving were achieved by using a pointed tool to create and enlarge a groove. Considerable care and physical effort was required to produce similar markings. The researchers also used the sharp tools to cut pork skin on a dolomite slab to rule out the possibility that the pattern had been produced accidentally while cutting meat or working animal hides. Again, though the rock engraving predated the arrival of modern humans in the area, it did not predate the earliest modern human cave paintings in Europe. The sceptics still had room to manoeuvre.

Proponents of Neanderthal symbolic behaviour continued to argue their case. Their view was that even if an Aurignacian influence was accepted in all of these cases, Neanderthals must have been behaviourally modern in order to understand and implement the newcomers' tool technology and make use of Aurignacian cultural elements. Against this view, Sir Paul Mellars argued that any technology exchanged between Neanderthals and modern humans would not necessarily have had the same social and cognitive meanings for the two species.

The decisive breakthrough came in March 2015 when evidence was announced of Neanderthal jewellery from 130,000 years ago, predating any possible influence from modern humans by at least 80,000 years. The evidence emerged from a study of eight white-tailed eagle talons that were found at the Neanderthal site of Krapina, Croatia over a century ago. Researchers found 21 cut marks on the talons, and there were areas of high polish consistent with 'use wear' as the talons rubbed against each other. The implication is that they were mounted in a necklace or bracelet – clear evidence of symbolic behaviour. Furthermore, it was concluded that the talons come from at least three different eagles, suggesting that they represented live captures rather than recovery from dead birds. The white-tailed eagle is fairly rare, and carcasses uncommon. However, it is also an aggressive apex predator, far from easy to catch or trap, and it was clear that considerable effort had gone into obtaining the talons.

The study left little doubt that Neanderthals possessed a symbolic culture long before modern humans reached Europe. The achievements of the Neanderthals were considerable and they certainly were not the dimwits of popular imagination. A change in public perception is long overdue, as is an end to the use of the word 'Neanderthal' as a pejorative.

# 17: The Neanderthal in us

*Possible interbreeding between Neanderthals and modern humans was the subject of much speculation before geneticists finally confirmed that it had indeed happened.*

The confirmation that modern humans had interbred with Neanderthals was one of the biggest news stories of 2010. The topic had long been of interest to scholars and laypeople alike, and there was no reason to suppose that it could not have happened. Closely-related species can often interbreed, and in some cases such inter-specific unions can lead to fertile offspring – for example grey wolves and coyotes. While Neanderthals would certainly have appeared strange to modern humans and vice versa, they would not necessarily have seemed unattractive to each other. For a present-day modern human, sexual relations with a Neanderthal might be somewhat hazardous, given the considerably superior physical strength of the latter – but modern humans living 50,000 years ago were rather more powerfully-built their present-day counterparts, so this was probably less of an issue.

It all sounded feasible, but strong evidence was lacking. No convincing fossil evidence of a Neanderthal/modern hybrid has ever come to light. It was claimed that the 24,500-year-old skeleton of a 4-year-old child found at Abrigo do Lagar Velho, Portugal in 1998 is such a hybrid, but most were sceptical and felt it was more likely that the individual was simply an unusually stocky modern juvenile. Had the child been buried at a Neanderthal site, the case might have been stronger, but the burial was typical of the Gravettian, an Upper Palaeolithic culture that is firmly associated with modern humans.

More recently, it has been suggested that a 34,500 year old Neanderthal lower jawbone from Riparo Mezzena, northern Italy, belonged to a hybrid. There are signs of a chin, a feature normally seen only in modern humans. This might have arisen from interbreeding with the modern humans known to have been living only a short distance away at Grotta di Fumane. Again, though, the evidence isn't conclusive. Modern people can have a weak or receding chin, and there is no reason to suppose that a Neanderthal could not sometimes have an unusually prominent chin.

Researchers turned to genetics, but at first failed to obtain definitive answers. Comparisons of Neanderthal mitochondrial DNA with that of modern humans failed to demonstrate that interbreeding had taken place. In the meantime, however, a project had been underway for some years at the Max Planck Institute for Evolutionary Anthropology to sequence the Neanderthal genome, using genetic material recovered from the remains of three Neanderthal individuals found at Vindija Cave in Croatia. The Vindija remains are more than 35,000 years old, and obtaining usable genetic material from them posed a major challenge. Only around five percent of the DNA extracted was actually of Neanderthal origin: the rest was from fungi and bacteria that had accumulated and grown among the remains after death.

In May 2010, the researchers were finally in a position to publish a first draft of their findings, along with the dramatic news that between one and four percent of the genome of modern non-Africans was derived from Neanderthals. In other words, the answer to the answer to the million dollar question was 'yes they did, but not in Africa'. The researchers compared the Neanderthal genome with those of five present-day individuals: an indigenous South African San, a Yoruba from West Africa, one from Papua New Guinea, one from China and one from France. The results showed that Neanderthals were more closely related to non-Africans than to Africans. This is not particularly surprising, as Neanderthals are not known to have lived in Africa. Any interbreeding has generally been supposed to have occurred within the known range of the Neanderthals, in Europe and western Asia. What was unexpected was that no difference was found between Papua New Guinean, Chinese and French individuals in terms of their degree of relatedness to Neanderthals.

The Neanderthal range is now known to have extended from Europe to the Altai Mountains, but no Neanderthal fossils have ever been found in Papua New Guinea or China. The result contradicted the expectation that the highest levels of Neanderthal ancestry would be found in Europeans. The implication was that interbreeding must have happened at a time before the ancestors of the present-day East Asian, Australasian and European populations diverged from one another – presumably soon after modern humans first left Africa, and long before they reached Europe. If the population that left Africa was small, only limited interbreeding would be necessary to leave the Neanderthal contribution fixed in the modern non-African genome for all time, as numbers increased during the subsequent peopling of the world. Conversely, later encounters in Europe, would leave little genetic trace. Modern populations were by that time large in comparison to Neanderthal groups.

However, follow-up research indicated a more complex picture. It was found that non-Africans were not, after all, equally related to Neanderthals – but the highest levels of Neanderthal ancestry were found in East Asians rather than in Europeans. Curiouser and curiouser. Could the Neanderthal range have extended all the way into the Far East, and could the ancestors of today's East Asians have encountered and interbred with a second Neanderthal population? It cannot be ruled out, but it seems unlikely.

It is more likely that the differences between the present-day European and East Asian populations are due to the differing effects of natural selection in the two regions. Researchers found that the distribution of Neanderthal genes was not random, and that many useful Neanderthal genes have been incorporated into the modern genome; for example those involved with the production of keratin, a protein that is used in skin, hair and nails. In East Asian populations, many genes involved with protection from the sun's UV rays are of Neanderthal origin. It is likely that this transfer of Neanderthal genes helped modern humans to adapt to conditions away from Africa that the Neanderthals had long been accustomed to.

Conversely, adverse genes were selected against. Neanderthal DNA was found to be largely absent from the X chromosome and genes associated with modern testes. The implication is that the presence of Neanderthal DNA in these regions of the modern genome led to reduced male fertility, or even sterility and that Neanderthals and modern humans were at the limits of biological compatibility. Oddly enough, some deleterious genes do have a Neanderthal connection, including those implicated in type 2 diabetes, Crohn's disease, depression, an increased tendency to blood clotting, and a range of skin conditions. Possibly, some these genes were once advantageous, and it was only the later dietary and social changes of Neolithic and later times that triggered adverse effects.

The possibility of increased male sterility is a complication if we are talking about the Neanderthal component of the modern genome originating largely from just one or two episodes of interbreeding involving small populations. Some believe that instead of one-off 'pulses', interbreeding occurred throughout the Neanderthal range – but only very occasionally. Mathematical studies suggest that the Neanderthal component of the modern genome could be accounted for even if interbreeding only occurred once every 70 to 80 generations. Such a low rate could be due either to social factors or to only a limited reproductive compatibility between the two species.

However, ancient DNA recovered from an early modern European suggests that interbreeding occurred rather more often. The material was obtained from Oase 1, a 40,000-year-old lower jawbone found at the cave site of Peştera cu Oase ('Cave with Bones') in Romania. Researchers found that from five to eleven percent of the Oase 1 individual's genome was of Neanderthal origin and that long stretches of Neanderthal DNA remained uninterrupted by later admixture with modern humans. From this, it was estimated that Oase 1 had had a Neanderthal ancestor no further than four to six generations back.

Our knowledge is far from complete, but we can be confident that techniques for recovering DNA from ancient human remains will continue to be refined, that further discoveries will be made, and that our understanding of this critical period of the human story will continue to improve. The latest work suggests that around 20 percent of the Neanderthal genome survives in the present-day population, although no one individual possesses more than a small fraction of this amount. With a current world population of seven billion, there is now more Neanderthal DNA in existence than ever before. The Neanderthals are not entirely extinct.

# 18: The fate of the Neanderthals

*Were modern humans responsible for the demise of the Neanderthals?*

The demise of the Neanderthals has long gripped the imagination of general public. Having survived for hundreds of millennia in the unstable and periodically glacial conditions of western Eurasia, they disappeared soon after modern humans arrived on the scene. Invariably, *Homo sapiens* is the prime suspect – but was it genocide or competition? Did the first modern humans in Europe hunt down and exterminate the Neanderthals, or did they simply outcompete them? It is all too easy to invoke the horrors of our recent past and suggest that the Neanderthals were victims of genocide. We do not have a particularly good record, even with members of our own species. Is there any reason, though, to suppose that relations between a group of modern humans and Neanderthals would be any more or any less friendly than those between two groups of modern humans?

We don't know, because there are only a few documented cases of violence between either individuals or groups prior to the Neolithic. The world's earliest-known homicide victim goes by the name of Cranium 17, a largely complete 430,000-year-old cranium recovered in 52 pieces from the Sima de los Huesos burial pit in northern Spain. Although most of the breakages occurred long after death, researchers identified two unhealed depressed fractures consistent with blunt force trauma from the same weapon, resulting in penetration of the bone-brain barrier. Either of the injuries would probably have been sufficient to kill, and two suggests deliberate intent. That both injuries were caused by impact with the same object more or less rules out the damage having been caused by the body landing on a hard object when it was dropped into the pit. Cranium 17 represent the earliest reasonably clear-cut case of interpersonal violence between humans leading to death. It demonstrates that this rather depressing aspect of human behaviour has an ancient origin.

Cranium 17's attacker was presumably a member of the same species, but what of inter-species violence? The earliest evidence of possible violence between modern humans and Neanderthals comes from Shanidar Cave in Iraq. The alleged victim is a Neanderthal male, Shanidar 3, who was probably in his early forties and suffered a sharp force trauma to his ninth left rib. The injury, inflicted with a knife or spear-point, was not immediately fatal, although Shanidar 3 died a few weeks later before healing was completed. His death could even have been due to an unrelated cause, because prior to the injury he was suffering from an arthritic disease of the right foot that would have slowed him down. In the harsh world of the Neanderthals, such a disability could often prove fatal.

In an attempt to learn more about the circumstances of Shanidar 3's injury, researchers used a crossbow to fire replica stone spear points at the ribcages of pig carcasses. A variety of different draw weights were used to replicate the impact forces associated with both thrusting spears and long-range projectiles. The results suggested that the likeliest cause of the injury was an impact from a long-range projectile weapon. At the time of the study, it was not thought that Neanderthals had possessed projectile weapons, and it was therefore assumed that Shanidar 3 had been attacked by a modern human. Shortly afterwards, however, 280,000-year-old obsidian projectile points were discovered in Ethiopia. The points predate the emergence of modern human by 80,000 years, and although they were not actually made by Neanderthals they demonstrate that archaic humans were capable of making long-range projectile weapons.

There might also be an alibi for *Homo sapiens*. The radiocarbon dates placing modern humans at the scene of crime were obtained in the 1960s, and suggest that Shanidar 3 was attacked 50,000 years ago. These early radiocarbon dates are now not considered wholly-reliable, and the actual date might be nearer 60,000 years ago – a time when there were no modern humans in the region. Combined with the 'new evidence' from Ethiopia, it would not be possible for a jury to find *Homo sapiens* guilty of carrying out the attack.

The only other example of violence involving Neanderthals is St. Césaire 1, a young adult male whose remains were found at La Roche à Pierrot, a rock shelter near the village of St. Césaire in southwestern France. St. Césaire 1 lived around 36,000 years ago. Using tomography and computer reconstruction techniques, researchers created a virtual model of St. Césaire 1's skull and found a healed fracture at the apex of the cranial vault. The injury was consistent with a deliberate blow from sharp object. An accidental injury, such as falling onto a sharp edge, a rock-fall, or a hunting accident, was thought to be less likely as these injuries typically affect the side rather than the apex of the cranial vault. The injury was not fatal, and St Césaire 1 survived for at least several months after the attack.

Who was the assailant? Unlike the much earlier Shanidar Cave incident, there is no doubt that modern humans were in France at the time St Césaire 1 was attacked. Possibly food shortages led to conflict with another group, though not necessarily one of modern humans. It is equally likely that St Césaire 1 was attacked by a member of his own group, although we can only speculate about the circumstances. The attack could have been a premeditated assault, or it could have happened during an argument. The disagreement might have arisen over a female, or a struggle for dominance within the group.

These two incidents fall rather short of evidence for genocide. Science author Jared Diamond has suggested that the Neanderthals suffered the same fate that befell the Native Americans, Aboriginal Australians and other indigenous people after the arrival of European colonists, and that they were wiped out by a combination of disease, killing and displacement from their land. This view recalls another less-than-meritorious aspect of the European colonial era: as is well known, the diseases the Europeans brought with them proved even more destructive than their desire for conquest and gold. The problem with this analogy is that diseases such as smallpox, flu, tuberculosis, measles and cholera all originally affected animals and only crossed the species barrier when farmers began keeping livestock and poultry. The first modern humans to reach Europe were hunter-gatherers, who would have had little or no exposure to such diseases. They also lived in relatively small, individual groups and could in no sense be likened to the Spanish Conquistadors.

If incoming modern humans were indeed responsible for the demise of the Neanderthals – and the evidence is only circumstantial – then it seems more likely that the newcomers simply outcompeted Neanderthals for the same resources than a scenario involving genocide and conquest. The question, then, is what gave modern humans the edge? Were they simply smarter than the Neanderthals? As we have already seen, there is a growing body of evidence that the Neanderthals were a lot smarter and their technology more sophisticated than was believed only a few years ago.

The real explanation might be related to simple demographics. A number of studies using genetic material obtained from Neanderthal remains have indicated that population sizes were very low. The genetic diversity of mitochondrial DNA obtained from Neanderthals living from 70,000 to 38,000 years ago was found to be just a third of that of present-day populations. Genetic diversity is related to population size, and researchers estimated that the population included fewer than 3,500 females of child-bearing age. Genetic material from Neanderthal remains found in the Altai Mountains showed that inbreeding was common. There is also evidence for a population collapse in the more northerly parts of Europe around 48,000 years ago, corresponding to several brief but severe climatic episodes. Genetic diversity of populations there were low, even by Neanderthal standards.

A Spanish cave site, El Sidrón, in the Asturias region of the country has provided disturbing insights into Neanderthal family life – and death. The remains of twelve individuals have been recovered from the site, together with 400 stone tools. The group comprised three adult males, three adult females, three adolescent males, two juveniles and one infant. The finds were made deep within the limestone cave complex and were probably brought down from the surface when a violent storm caused an upper gallery to collapse. The whole assemblage is around 49,000 years old.

It was found that the genetic diversity of the group was lower than would be expected for unrelated Neanderthals, suggesting that they were related to one another. All three of the adult males carried the same mitochondrial lineage, whereas the three adult females all carried different lineages. As mitochondrial DNA is inherited solely from the maternal line, the males must all have shared the same maternal lineages.

The females, on the other hand, all carried different maternal lineages, and must not have originally been members of the group. This suggests that in Neanderthal groups, mature males remained within their family birth group, but females came from outside. Such a social system is known as patrilocal, where men remain in the family home and women move to the home of their new husband upon marriage.

But there was a more sinister aspect to the discoveries. All the El Sidrón individuals had suffered from stunted growth, presumably arising from malnutrition. This was indicated by numerous dental hypoplasias, or deficiencies in dental enamel formation occurring as a result of arrested growth. Five group members had experienced two episodes of growth arrest, and one adult had experienced four. It is clear that life was very difficult for this extended Neanderthal family, but their ultimate fate was even worse. Many of the bones had been cut with stone tools or smashed open for their marrow. While we shall never know exactly what happened, it seems likely that the El Sidrón Neanderthals were killed and eaten by members of a neighbouring group who were themselves on the brink of starvation.

The overall picture that emerges from these studies is that the position of the Neanderthals was precarious even before the arrival of modern humans in Europe. Archaeological evidence based on site numbers suggests that modern humans soon outnumbered Neanderthals by as much as 10:1. Sheer weight of numbers might have enabled the modern humans to expand their overall territory at the expense of the Neanderthals.

Computer simulations have been used to analyse the relationship between climate data for specific periods and the geographical distribution of archaeological sites associated with Neanderthal and modern human populations. The simulations used a computer program which was capable of 'learning' by refining its predictions of regions occupied the two populations at any one time until they matched known archaeological data. The program was then used to predict what regions the two populations would have occupied during the various climatic phases of the Upper Palaeolithic. It was found that in each case the geographical range of the Neanderthals contracted, and that of the incoming modern humans expanded – and eventually the Neanderthals were left with nowhere to go.

Estimates as to just how long the Neanderthals survived after the arrival modern humans in Europe have varied over the years, ranging from as 10,000 years to no more than a few centuries. The most recent radiocarbon dating of Neanderthal sites suggest that they went extinct in the period between 41,000 and 39,000 years ago, about 5,000 years after the first modern humans arrived. At the peripheries of Europe, they might have hung on for much longer: possibly until as late as 28,000 years ago at Gorham's Cave, Gibraltar.

A sharp climatic downturn 40,000 years ago might have delayed the expansion of modern humans into the Iberian Peninsula. Computer simulations show that the region became a semi-desert, forming an arid buffer zone between the two populations. With the advance of modern humans temporarily halted, the south of the peninsula would have become a refugium for late-surviving Neanderthals. But once they were gone from this safe haven, the long story of the Neanderthals was at an end.

Or was it?

# 19: An unexpected journey

*Who were the diminutive 'hobbit people' who survived on the island of Flores until just 12,000 years ago?*

The Indonesian island of Flores is part of the Lesser Sunda, an archipelago in maritime Southeast Asia. The name comes from the Portuguese word for 'flowers' and is a legacy of Portugal's lengthy colonial presence in the region. It is thought that the first settlers of Australia passed through Flores as they 'island hopped' through the Indonesian archipelago, and in 2003 a joint Australian and Indonesian team led by anthropologists Peter Brown and Michael Morwood investigated Liang Bua, a limestone cave in western part of the island. They were hoping to find evidence of the original migration to Australia, but instead they made a discovery that made international headline news.

The finds included a partial human skeleton lacking only its arms, and a complete human lower jawbone. The remains, which were formally designated LB1 and LB2 respectively, were 18,000 years old. The bones were not fossilised and were described as having the consistency of blotting paper. What was remarkable was their size, or lack thereof. The team claimed that LB1, which almost immediately gained the nickname 'Flo', had been a 30-year-old woman who had stood no more than 1.06 m (3 ft. 6 in.) tall, weighed no more than 16 to 36 kg (35 to 79 lb.), with a brain size of just 380 cc – comparable to that of an australopithecine. Yet she lacked the large back teeth of an australopithecine, her facial proportions were humanlike rather than apelike, and she was apparently a fully-committed biped. Accordingly, Brown and Morwood classed her as belonging to a new human species, *Homo floresiensis*. Later finds included the remains of at least nine individuals, Oldowan-type stone tools, and animal remains. The finds ranged from 95,000 to 12,000 years old, but stone tools from other Flores sites show technological continuity with the Liang Bua artefacts and are up to a million years old.

*Homo floresiensis* was almost immediately nicknamed the Flores Hobbit. The team attributed its small size to a phenomenon known as insular dwarfism, which occurs when animals are living on an island where predators are few but food scarce. Over the course of many generations the animals 'downsize', as smaller offspring require less food and will have a better chance of survival in situations where predators pose no threat. There is relatively little animal life on Flores and the only predator is the Komodo dragon. The only other large species on Flores was an extinct elephant known as *Stegodon sondaari*, which had undergone insular dwarfism of the kind proposed for *Homo floresiensis*. These animals were still fairly large and were comparable in size to a water buffalo. If early humans such as *Homo erectus* had reached Flores, then it was suggested that the same fate could have befallen them. The team claimed that despite its tiny brain, *Homo floresiensis* was as smart as any early human species, capable of complex behaviour and cognition.

Not everybody accepted that *Homo floresiensis* was genuinely a new human species. The Indonesian anthropologist Teuku Jacob claimed that Flo was a modern human suffering from microcephaly, a developmental disorder leading to a smaller brain. Jacob believed that she was a modern human of Australomelanesian extraction. He found little support for his views, but a few years after his death in 2007, his former colleagues revived the theory, this time claiming that Flo had suffered from Down syndrome.

Assuming that *Homo floresiensis* is indeed a new human species, then from what did it evolve? The most obvious possibility is Asian *Homo erectus* because it was present in mainland Asia and is generally thought to have been the first hominin to leave Africa. However, some studies have suggested that while the skull was consistent with *Homo erectus*, the limb proportions of *Homo floresiensis* had more in common with an australopithecine and the feet were a mosaic of apelike and humanlike features. This suggests that *Homo floresiensis* evolved from something more primitive than *Homo erectus*.

A similar conclusion was drawn by researchers who considered how insular dwarfism may affect brain size. They concluded that a smaller-brained hominin than Asian *Homo erectus* is a more plausible ancestor. Even with an upward-revised estimate of 420 cc for the brain size of *Homo floresiensis*, not all of the brain reduction from Asian *Homo erectus* can be explained in terms of a simple downsizing model. Although no fossil evidence has been found, it is possible that pre-*erectus* humans or even tool-making australopithecines could have left Africa long before *Homo erectus*.

Against this, it has been suggested that the most primitive aspects of the dentition of *Homo floresiensis* were comparable to *Homo erectus*, which would rule out a pre-*erectus* ancestor. It is possible that *Homo erectus* was unusually variable in terms of both body and brain size, and that in its earliest guise, it was less modern than is generally supposed. The hominins from Dmanisi, Georgia, have been cited as examples of early *Homo erectus*, with brain sizes at the lower end of the *erectus* range.

Despite these suggestions, there is evidence that the cognitive abilities of *Homo floresiensis* were fairly advanced. The prefrontal cortex and the temporal lobes corresponding to a region of the brain known as the Brodmann area 10 are large in comparison to those of early hominins. The prefrontal cortex is the frontmost part of the frontal lobes and the temporal lobes are located on both of the lower sides of the brain, below the parietal lobes. The function of the Brodmann area 10 is not well understood, but it may be involved in processes such as taking initiatives and planning future activities. If so, it implies that *Homo floresiensis* was able to plan ahead, respond to unexpected situations, draw upon memories, and communicate effectively with fellow group members.

Another major issue is how did *Homo floresiensis* reach Flores in the first place? Unlike Java and many other islands in the Indonesian archipelago, Flores has never been connected to the mainland, even during ice ages when sea levels dropped. Consequently, it has been widely assumed that Flo's forebears must have had the ability to build boats. Against this, there is no direct evidence to suggest that humans built boats until very late in the prehistoric era. We know that modern humans must have used boats to cross the sea from the Southeast Asian archipelago to Australia, but could archaic humans have made sea crossings by boat?

There have been suggestions that African *Homo erectus* could have reached Eurasia by boat, but the construction of a suitable watercraft and the navigational skills required to make a voyage across the open sea are generally accepted to have been beyond the abilities of early humans. Accordingly, the consensus is that early humans dispersed from Africa exclusively by overland routes, but in the case of Flores, no overland route has ever existed. Does this mean that Flo's ancestors must have reached Flores using some form of primitive watercraft – possibly logs lashed together – or are there other possibilities? The answer is 'yes': they could have been swept out to sea and stranded on Flores by a natural occurrence such as a flash-flood or a tsunami, possibly surviving on a raft of matted vegetation until they made landfall. This is believed to have been how the ancestors of the New World monkeys reached South America from Africa, and we can safely assume that these early monkeys did not build boats. Such an unexpected journey seems to be the likeliest explanation for the early human presence on Flores.

Undoubtedly the most speculative idea is that *Homo floresiensis* survived into modern times and that it is the origin of tales about the Ebu Gogo. These small, humanlike folk are said to have been living on Flores when the Portuguese first arrived 400 years ago, and it has been claimed that they were still being seen as recently as 100 years ago. It was also suggested that similar folk are the basis of legends such as the Orang Pendek from Sumatra, and even leprechauns in Ireland. As intriguing as this idea is, it is unlikely in the extreme. So-called 'little people' are very prevalent in world folk traditions and if all were due to actual dwarf humans, concrete evidence would surely have emerged by now. However, if endemic dwarf humans can arise on Flores, there is certainly no reason to suppose similar species could not arise elsewhere. It is quite possible that evidence from similarly isolated locations may come to light in the future.

Notably, the most recent artefacts of *Homo floresiensis* are 12,000 years old, which coincides with the disappearance from the fossil record of the dwarf elephants. These animals might have been an important source of food, and their extinction probably in turn brought about the demise of *Homo floresiensis*. It therefore seems unlikely that the Ebu Gogo were *Homo floresiensis*. It remains an open question whether or not these diminutive folk ever came into contact with modern or indeed any other humans during their million year sojourn on Flores.

# 20: The Denisovans

*In 2010, geneticists discovered a new and previously unsuspected archaic human species that had encountered and interbred with modern humans.*

Denisova Cave is remote cave located by a small river in the Altai Mountains of southern Siberia. It takes its name from a hermit called Dionisij (Denis) who reputedly lived there in eighteenth century, but if this is true he was only the latest in a long line of inhabitants. Previous occupants include nomadic herders going back to Neolithic times, and archaeologists believe that the cave was first used by humans as long as 125,000 years ago.

The discovery of a phalanx bone from a human little finger was not at first a cause for any great excitement. The small bone had apparently belonged to a child aged between five and seven years old. It was found in a small side chamber at the back of the cave, in deposits thought to be 30,000 to 48,000 years old. The cool, dry Siberian climate preserved some of the bone's genetic material, and researchers were able to isolate mitochondrial DNA fragments and sequence the entire mitochondrial genome. As we inherit our mitochondrial DNA solely from our mothers, this led to the find being dubbed X Woman, despite being a juvenile of unknown gender.

At the time in question, Neanderthals, identified as such by their mitochondrial DNA, were known to have been living less than 100 km (60 miles) away at Okladnikov Cave (and were later identified at Denisova Cave itself). There is also archaeological evidence to suggest that modern humans reached the Altai no later than 43,000 years ago. The expectation, therefore, was that the mitochondrial DNA from the bone would match that of either Neanderthals or modern humans, but it matched neither. Instead, it was found that X Woman had last shared a common ancestor with Neanderthals and modern humans about a million years ago - long before either species appeared. On the other hand, the divergence was too recent for X Woman to be a late-surviving descendant of Asian *Homo erectus*. She (if indeed X Woman was a 'she') was a member of a hitherto-unknown human species.

The next step was to sequence X Woman's nuclear genome, and this was completed a few months after the mitochondrial genome had been sequenced. It turned out that X-Woman lacked the male sex-determining Y-chromosome and was indeed female. In the meantime, an upper molar tooth from a young adult had been discovered at the cave site, and mitochondrial DNA obtained from it confirmed that it had belonged to a different individual to the owner of the finger bone. With two individuals now known, the term 'X-Woman' was dropped in favour of 'Denisovan'.

The Middle Pleistocene fossil record of Southeast and East Asia is very sparse and the Denisovan tooth, probably a third or possibly second left upper molar, fails to support a connection with any of the few remains that have been found. The tooth is fairly large, lying within the size range of *Homo erectus* and *Homo habilis*. It is above the size range typical for Neanderthals, early modern humans, and the very few third upper molars that have been recovered from other late archaic hominins in the region. The tooth shares no recent features with Neanderthals or modern humans, hinting at the distinctiveness of the Denisovans. A second, even larger third upper molar tooth was discovered in 2010. Only two upper third molars from Late Pleistocene modern human fossils are known to be larger than the Denisovan molars. Based on genetic considerations, the 2010 discovery is 60,000 years older than the other tooth and the finger bone.

The data from the nuclear genome enabled better estimates to be made of the relationship between Denisovans, Neanderthals and modern humans. It was found that the Denisovans had diverged from Neanderthals 640,000 years ago, and from present-day Africans 804,000 years ago, meaning that they were more closely related to Neanderthals than to modern humans. Denisovans and Neanderthals are both Eurasian species whereas modern humans are an African species, so this result was not unexpected.

What was a major surprise was the discovery that 4.8 percent of the nuclear genome of present-day New Guineans is of Denisovan origin, which is a considerably greater contribution than that from Neanderthals. Evidently our ancestors were quite happy to interbreed with any archaic humans they came into contact with. No less remarkable was the implication that the Denisovan range had once extended from southern Siberia to the tropics. In terms of both geography and ecology, this is a larger range than that of any human species with the exception of modern humans.

Follow-up studies soon confirmed the presence of Denisovan genetic material in some other modern populations of the Wallacea group of islands lying to the east of Borneo, and also in Aboriginal Australians, Fijians and Polynesians. Significantly, though, it was largely absent from mainland populations. The small Denisovan component found there is likely to have been introduced by recent migrations of modern humans from the island region.

During the colder periods of the last Ice Age, sea levels were far lower than today, and more westerly islands of Southeast Asia formed part of an extended mainland known as the Sunda peninsula. At the same time, Australia, New Guinea and Tasmania were conjoined into a single continental landmass known as Sahul. Between the two is an archipelago of deep-water islands that never become a part of either landmass. They are known collectively as Wallacea after naturalist Alfred Russel Wallace, and include Sulawesi, Lombok, Sumbawa, Komodo, Flores, Sumba and Timor.

The most obvious explanation for the findings is that the interbreeding occurred in Wallacea as the first modern human settlers 'island hopped' their way to Sahul. Consistent with this view is the recent discovery of stone tools from Sulawesi which are at least 118,000 years old and are unlikely to be the work of modern humans. As with the Flores 'hobbits', it is likely that these archaic humans were accidentally stranded on Sulawesi.

Another possibility is that modern humans and Denisovans did interbreed on the mainland (regardless of whether they also did in Wallacea), but that the present-day population of the Asian mainland are largely descended from a second group of migrants that arrived after the Denisovans had become locally extinct. A genetic study carried out in 2011 suggests that this was indeed the case: following the initial dispersal of modern humans from Africa, there were two eastward migrations. The first of these led to the peopling of New Guinea and Australia, but East Asia was largely peopled by the second wave of migrants.

As with when modern humans interbred with Neanderthals, advantageous genes were apparently 'imported' from Denisovans. The human leucocyte antigen (HLA) system helps the immune system to recognise and combat pathogens, and it is believed that a number of genes associated with this system are of Denisovan origin. These could have provided immunity to pathogens to which the incoming modern population had not been previously exposed, and conferred a survival advantage upon those acquiring them from the Denisovans.

It was found that the Denisovans had interbred with other human species as well as our own. They interbred with Neanderthals in the Altai region, but they also interbred with another, unidentified archaic human species as well. Given that the Denisovans and Neanderthals diverged from one another after they had diverged from modern humans, one would expect the two to be equally closely related to ourselves – but this is not the case. Scattered genetic fragments totalling around one percent of the Denisovan genome are much older than the rest of it, meaning that they are less closely related to us than are Neanderthals. This suggests that the Denisovans interbred with archaic humans whose ancestors split from the common ancestor of the Neanderthals, Denisovans and modern humans before the three diverged from one another. A date of at least 1.1 million years ago was suggested for the split. We don't know which particular species was involved, but the timing suggests that it was Asian *Homo erectus*.

An unexpected twist came in 2014 with the successful extraction of mitochondrial DNA from the 400,000-year-old thigh bone of an archaic human from the Spanish site of Sima de los Huesos. This site has yielded a very large number of fossils representing over thirty individuals, which exhibit a mixture of *Homo heidelbergensis* and Neanderthal characteristics. As such, they are thought to be proto-Neanderthals, and it was expected that the material would show an affinity to genetic sequences obtained from later Neanderthal remains. Instead, it more closely resembled those of the Denisovans. Matters were partially cleared up a year later when the nuclear genome was sequenced, and it was found that the Sima de los Huesos people were indeed more closely related to Neanderthals than they were to Denisovans and modern humans. How, then, to explain the mitochondrial results? One suggestion is that the Denisovan material arose from interbreeding. A more likely interpretation is that mitochondrial lineages originally present in the Denisovan/Neanderthal common ancestor subsequently disappeared from the Neanderthal line, but persisted in the Denisovans. It and other genetic lineages could have been lost in a population bottleneck of the type known to have affected Neanderthal populations. As to what the Denisovans themselves looked like, we know very little other than they had large molar teeth. Comparisons between pigment genes in modern humans and Denisovans suggest that the latter were dark-skinned, with brown eyes and hair.

At some stage, fossil evidence will emerge that can be identified as Denisovan by successful extraction of DNA and we will have a clearer idea of what this extinct branch of humanity looked like. While we are probably now stuck for good with an informal term that sounds compellingly like a humanoid race from *Star Trek*, paleoanthropologists will be able to describe the species and assign it a formal name such as *Homo denisovaiensis* or *Homo altaiensis*.

The confirmation that modern humans interbreed with at least two species of archaic humans shows that the conventional view of *Homo sapiens* entirely replacing archaic populations is not entirely accurate. It is clear that much remains to be learned about even this comparatively late stage in the story of human evolution.

# 21: Claustrophobics need not apply

*The discovery of a hitherto-unknown early human species deep inside the Rising Star Cave in South Africa.*

On 7 October 2013, Professor Lee Burger posted a rather unusual appeal on the Facebook page of the American Association of Physical Anthropologists. He was seeking a small group of individuals with the requisite top-notch professional and team skills for a short-term excavation project, but there was a catch: applicants had to be 'skinny and preferably small', and claustrophobia was not an option. US-born Berger, a palaeoanthropologist at the University of the Witwatersrand, Johannesburg, already had one major discovery under his belt. In 2010, he had announced the discovery of *Australopithecus sediba*, the first new hominin species to be discovered in South Africa for decades. The find was made two years earlier when Matthew, Lee's nine-year-old son, discovered a hominin collar bone embedded in a rock at Malapa, part of a now-eroded cave system located in the Cradle of Humankind World Heritage Site about 15 km (9.3 miles) northeast of the hominid-bearing sites of Sterkfontein and Swartkrans, and about 45 km (28 miles) from Johannesburg.

Berger felt that other cave systems in South Africa had the potential to yield hominin fossils, so in 2013 he recruited a team of cavers to search the Rising Star cave system, 50 km (30 miles) northwest of Johannesburg. The cave had been well explored over the years, but the team came across a narrow 18 cm (7 in.)-wide shaft that dropped vertically for 12 m (39 ft.) into an unexplored chamber. Caver Steve Tucker made the descent into the chamber, where he found and photographed a fossil skull and jawbone lying on the floor of the cave. Berger could see that the remains were too primitive to be those of a modern human. Convinced that Tucker had found hominin fossils, he wasted no time in obtaining funding for an expedition from the *National Geographic*.

But funding was the least of the problems. Before they could even face the narrow drop into what became known as Dinaledi Chamber ('chamber of stars'), researchers would have to pass through another tiny shaft known as Superman's Crawl and then climb a steep section known as Dragon's Back. Berger placed his advertisement for 'small, skinny' scientists believing at best there might be three or four people in the world who would fit the criteria. In the event, within days 57 suitable candidates had applied from which he chose six, all women. By 7 November, just a month after the Facebook appeal, the Rising Star Expedition had set up camp at the cave system, and three days later Berger's 'underground astronauts' (as he termed them) entered the cave. Working in six-hour shifts, they soon recovered more fossil material than had been found in the whole of South Africa in the previous 90 years. Meanwhile, back on the surface, a large team began preparing and cataloguing the fossils, making extensive use of social media to report progress. The number of fossils climbed steadily, reaching 500 on 21 November and 1,000 on 25 November. In total, the expedition recovered 1,550 fossils comprising 15 individuals, including males, females and infants. Yet they had barely scratched the surface; work at the Rising Star cave system will continue for years to come.

In an unusual move, Berger then invited thirty young postdoctoral researchers from fifteen countries to help him evaluate the massive fossil haul at a workshop in Johannesburg. They were accompanied by twenty of Berger's more senior colleagues, who had worked with him on the *Australopithecus sediba* discovery. This exercise in 'paleodemocracy' did not please everybody. Some questioned the wisdom of handing over such important fossils to inexperienced researchers, but for the latter it was the opportunity of a lifetime.

In September 2015, Berger and his colleagues announced their findings. The remains represented a new human species, *Homo naledi*, taking its name from the word 'star' in the local Sotho language. With multiple examples of almost every bone in the skeleton, it was possible to describe the new species in great detail. *Homo naledi* was comparable in height and weight to a small-bodied modern human or a large australopithecine, with an estimated stature of around 1.5 m (5 ft.) and weighing 40 to 55 kg (88 to 121 lb.). The brain was tiny, ranging from 465 to 560 cc, overlapping entirely with the range of values known for australopithecines. Within *Homo*, only the Flores 'hobbits' are smaller-brained. The reconstructed skeleton exhibits both humanlike and apelike features, but in a combination that has not been seen with other hominins. The feet and lower limbs are humanlike, but the upper thighbone, pelvis and shoulders are apelike. The hands and wrists are humanlike, though the fingers are curved suggesting *Homo naledi* spent time in the trees as well as on the ground. Overall, *Homo naledi* is the most primitive, small-brained hominin ever to have been included in *Homo*, but the shape of cranium and lower jawbone and the dentition is more consistent with *Homo* than *Australopithecus*.

The first and most obvious question is where does *Homo naledi* belong in the human family tree? Sceptics have claimed that it isn't a new species at all and is simply an early, primitive form of *Homo erectus*. It has been suggested that skull characteristics supposedly distinguishing *Homo naledi* from *Homo erectus* are in fact also present in the latter. Until more independent studies are published, it is probably too soon to jump to any conclusions.

Frustratingly, no dates are yet available for the fossils. It may be assumed that they lie well beyond the range of radiocarbon dating, but there is no readily-datable material in the chamber. Calcium carbonate flowstones have been found to have been contaminated with materials from associated muds, making them unsuitable for uranium series dating (see Chapter 27). At some stage these difficulties will undoubtedly be overcome and a date published, but for now all we have to go on is the primitive characteristics such as the small brains. These suggest that the species emerged close to the base of the human family tree 2.5 to 2.8 million years ago, although the Dinaledi remains themselves could be more recent.

*Homo naledi* might not necessarily have been an ancestor of any later humans; instead it could have been one of a number of early hominins possessing various combinations of apelike and humanlike traits. 'Apelike' and 'humanlike' are merely labels we have attached to these traits, which in reality were adaptations to differing environments. We might learn more when comparisons are made with the LD-350-1 early human lower jawbone from Ethiopia, claimed to represent the earliest dated *Homo* remains.

No less problematic is the question of how the fossils reached Dinaledi Chamber in the first place. There is a near-absence of non-hominin fossils in Dinaledi Chamber – yet these are abundant in the adjacent Dragon's Back. This completely rules out the remains having being swept into Dinaledi Chamber by a flash flood, as it would have left a mixture of hominin and non-hominin remains in both chambers. Carnivores could also be ruled out: even if there had been a carnivore that preyed exclusively on *Homo naledi*, why would it drag its prey into such an inaccessible location? In any case, none of the bones showed any evidence of having been gnawed by carnivores.

The remains of the two *Australopithecus sediba* were also been found in a deep cave, but it is believed that they accidentally fell into a 'death trap' – a deep shaft leading down into the cave. However, there was no evidence that any such shaft had ever connected Dinaledi Chamber to the surface. The fossils accumulated over time, so it could also be ruled out that a single group had for some reason entered the chamber and become trapped there.

The only explanation that avoids all of these issues is that the remains were deliberately placed in the chamber as part of a post-mortem ritual. As an explanation, it seems improbable in the extreme. We have no evidence for mass deposition of corpses prior to Sima de los Huesos, 430,000 years ago. Even then, it is believed that this represented nothing more than a hygienic disposal of the corpses rather than any form of ritual. Also, in complete contrast to *Homo naledi*, the brain size of the Sima people was only slightly below that of modern people. In this case, even hygienic disposal can be ruled out, as there is no evidence that the Rising Star cave system was ever inhabited, and there would surely be no need to use such an inaccessible chamber.

Should we fall back on Sherlock Holmes' rule that when you have eliminated the impossible, whatever remains, however improbable, must be the truth? Should accept that early humans were far more behaviourally complex than has long been believed? Again, it is too soon to jump to conclusions. For now, all that can be said is that we don't yet know just how the fossils reached the cavern.

# 22: Enter *Homo sapiens*

*Fossil evidence for the earliest examples of 'our' type of human.*

Although it has been said that a Neanderthal would attract very little attention on the New York subway, there are significant differences between modern and archaic people. The most immediately obvious difference is that in comparison to people living today they were more powerfully built. However, the same could be said of *Homo sapiens* from that period. It was not until much later that the comparatively puny form typical of present-day people appeared. From an anatomical point of view, the most important differences between archaic and modern humans are in the shape of the skull. While they appear completely normal to us, the face and cranium of a modern human are actually quite unlike those of Neanderthals or other early humans. Rather than being long, low and oval-shaped, the cranium is globular; and the face and eyes are tucked under the braincase. The browridges are less massive; the forehead is steep rather than flat and receding, and there is a bony protuberance from the lower jawbone – the chin. The appearance of these distinctive features in the fossil record confirms the emergence of 'our' type of human.

Since the 1990s, the date when it is believed that *Homo sapiens* first took the stage has been pushed steadily backwards. In 1967, a team led by Richard Leakey recovered two sets of human fossils in the basin of the Omo River in southwestern Ethiopia. Although the remains were found on opposite sides of the river, they were both located in the same geological stratum of a 100 m (330 ft.) thick layer of sediment known as the Kibish Formation, and hence were roughly the same age. Known as Omo I and Omo II, they comprise respectively a fragmentary skull together with a partial skeleton, and an almost-intact skull. Dating of mollusc shells found in the sediment suggested that the fossils were around 130,000 years old.

When reconstructed, the skulls were both found to be basically modern in appearance, albeit Omo II is less so than Omo I. Omo I has a globular braincase and steep forehead, a prominent chin, small browridges, a rounded occipital region (the back of skull), and the shape and size of the teeth are similar to those of modern people.

Although it is more robust (big boned) than a present day skull, Omo I is unmistakably *Homo sapiens*. The cranial capacity of the more complete Omo II skull is a hefty 1435 cc (larger than the present day average of 1350 cc), but unlike Omo I, it retains some primitive features, notably a more receding forehead, a less rounded occipital region, and a prominent occipital torus. The latter feature is a horizontal ridge at the back of the head for the attachment of the rear neck muscles. There was also a slight ridge along the midline of the braincase known as sagittal keeling, which occurs in archaic humans but is not found in modern humans. Although Omo I and Omo II were almost certainly not exact contemporaries, it is unlikely that they lived far enough apart in time for significant evolutionary change to have occurred. Instead, it is probable that the more primitive Omo II was a late-surviving member of a more archaic lineage. Perhaps the two belonged to different populations, which lived in the region at different times.

The dating of the remains was a source of controversy for more than three decades, with many arguing for a more recent date – possibly as recent as 40,000 years old. Some believed that the more modern Omo I remains were simply a recent intrusion into the older sediment layer. Not until 2005 did a team lead by geologist Ian McDougall from the Australian National University, Canberra, revisit Omo Kibish with the intention of obtaining more secure dates for the fossils.

In the meantime, three skulls reliably much older than 130,000 years had come to light at another Ethiopian site, Herto. Argon-argon dating of volcanic material from above and below the remains established that they were between 154,000 and 160,000 years old. Two of the skulls belonged to adult males; the third to a six-year-old child. The cranial capacity of the better-preserved adult skull was found to be 1,450 cc and again, this is pretty respectable, lying at the high end of the modern human range. Although the finds were close enough to present-day humans to be considered the same species, they were very robust and still possessed some primitive features. It was suggested that the Herto people were not entirely modern, and that they represented an intermediate between *Homo rhodesiensis* (African *Homo heidelbergensis*) and fully-modern *Homo sapiens*. But results from the reappraisal of Omo were to put paid to the idea that the Herto people were the earliest representatives of our species.

McDougal's team used original documentation from the 1967 expedition to pinpoint the exact locations of the two fossil finds, and they recovered bone fragments that had been missed in the original excavation of the Omo I site. These were found to fit the Omo I skull, thus confirming that the investigators were at the right spot. Subsequent work confirmed that both sets of remains were indeed from the Member I geological stratum. Crucially, they found that Member 1 was sandwiched between two layers of volcanic ash from nearby eruptions, and the both fossils had lain just above the lower layer. Argon-argon dating was used to date the lower ash layer, and it was found that the Omo remains were actually 195,000 years old, making them at least 35,000 years older than the Herto remains and by far the oldest-known fossil remains that are recognised as *Homo sapiens*. As we shall see in the next section, genetic evidence suggests that *Homo sapiens* emerged around 200,000 years ago, although not necessarily in East Africa.

The changes that led to our distinctive skull shape might not have been that dramatic and probably arose from nothing more than a reduction in the length of the sphenoid bone – a butterfly-shaped structure located at the base of the skull in front of the temporal bones and the base of the occipital bones. But why did this change happen at all? During infancy, cranial bones are thin, and bone tissue formation is not yet complete. The shaping of the frontal and parietal bones, which form the front, and the roof and sides of the skull, are largely driven by the increase in brain volume. Thus the development of the brain case reflects that of the brain itself.

At birth, modern humans have a long, low braincase, similar to those of Neanderthals and other archaic humans. Only later, between the age of one and two years old, does the braincase of a modern infant take on its characteristic globular shape. Virtual reconstructions of Neanderthal remains of various ages have shown that this 'globularization' phase did not occur with Neanderthal infants, and hence they retained the long, low-shaped brain case into adulthood. The globular braincase of *Homo sapiens* reflects a change in the actual proportions of the brain from the archaic condition, with enlargement of the parietal lobes. These are located at the top and on each side of the brain, and carry out functions including the processing of speech-related sounds (or written words). Their expansion might have played a crucial role in the development of language.

The anatomical and behavioural features now associated with modern humans might have appeared at different times and places across much of Africa. Isolated human populations, each possessing some modern characteristics, periodically encountered one another and interbred. Over time, more and more of these characteristics began accumulate in single populations, until eventually a population that was recognisably *Homo sapiens* emerged. This population, possibly numbering between 2,000 and 10,000 individuals, would have had a competitive edge over other human populations, and from it the world's current population is largely descended. It is possible that Omo I was a member of this founding population, though the presence of the more primitive Omo II suggests that Omo I's people migrated into the region from elsewhere. Regardless of where it finally came together, the full *Homo sapiens* 'package' would enable the earliest modern humans to spread across Africa and, eventually, the rest of the world.

# 23: Mitochondrial Eve

*She lived 200,000 years ago, and the entire world's population is related to her on their mother's side.*

She lived in Africa about 200,000 years ago. We don't know for certain in just what part of this vast continent she lived, but it was probably either East Africa or South Africa. In comparison to a present-day woman, she was likely to have been of sturdy build, though less so than her Neanderthal contemporaries living in Eurasia. Her people were few in numbers. Other than these sparse details, we know just one thing about the woman now popularly known as Mitochondrial Eve: every single living person today can trace their lineage on their mother's side back to this one woman, who lived at the very dawn of *Homo sapiens*.

Although the earliest humans are now known to have existed as long ago as 2.8 million years ago, our 'kind' of humans - *Homo sapiens* or modern humans – are a far more recent phenomenon. Our species emerged in Africa around 200,000 years ago and later spread to Eurasia, Australia and eventually to the New World. In the process, they replaced archaic populations then living in Eurasia. This view, commonly referred to as the Out of Africa or replacement hypothesis, was first proposed in the 1960s. At that time, the prevailing view was that archaic humans such as *Homo erectus* and Neanderthals were actually early forms of *Homo sapiens*, and that modern humans emerged gradually from these regional populations. There was sufficient interbreeding between them for them to all be classed as a single lineage, which evolved over time until what we see today emerged. This rival theory is known as the multiregional continuity hypotheses.

Today we know that the Out of Africa model is largely correct, although the multiregional view is not wholly wrong. The archaic populations did not entirely disappear as modern humans interbred with Neanderthals and at least one other archaic species, the Denisovans. Until the 1980s, however, there was no real consensus as to which model was correct. A key prediction of the Out of Africa theory is that modern humans should appear in the African fossil record before they show up elsewhere. However, much of the fossil evidence now favouring a recent African origin for *Homo sapiens* has only come to light or been accurately dated in the last twenty years or so.

Unable to resolve matters with the fossil evidence then available, researchers turned to genetics for a solution. Although techniques had advanced since Vincent Sarich and Allan Wilson's blood serum studies of the 1960s, they were still fairly primitive by today's standards. Most of the studies involved ordinary nuclear DNA, which resides in the nuclei of cells in 23 pairs of chromosomes. However, the breakthrough came when Wilson decided to focus on mitochondrial DNA.

Mitochondria are small, membrane-enclosed bodies which reside in the cells of living organisms. They carry out a number of functions, but their principle role is to generate a substance known as ATP, which is used to store chemical energy. For this reason, mitochondria are often described as the cell's 'batteries'. It is thought that they were originally free-living bacteria that took up residence inside the cells of more complex organisms about two billion years ago, and established a symbiotic relationship with them. Although they have long since ceased to be capable of an independent existence, mitochondria have retained a small amount of their own DNA, known as mitochondrial DNA (mtDNA) to distinguish it from nuclear DNA. All mammals, including humans, inherit mitochondrial DNA solely from their mothers, because the mitochondria in a sperm cell are located in the whiplash tail. This is discarded after fertilisation, and so it never becomes part of the fertilized ovum.

For researchers studying human populations, mitochondrial DNA offers two major advantages over nuclear DNA. Firstly, it is inherited exclusively from the maternal line and does not recombine with paternal DNA, making it far easier to track mitochondrial lineages over many generations. Secondly, it accumulates mutations ten times faster than ordinary nuclear DNA. This means that over a comparatively short period of time, distinct genetic lineages known as haplogroups will emerge and can be traced. The longer a population has been established, the more haplogroups it will contain.

Working with two of his PhD students at the University of California, Berkeley, Rebecca Cann and Mark Stoneking, Wilson studied patterns of mitochondrial DNA variation in 147 people, drawn from five geographic populations around the world: Africa, Asia, Australia, Europe and New Guinea, and in January 1987 the team published their results in the journal *Nature*. They had discovered that the entire human population of the world could be arranged into a single family tree with 133 different maternal lineages. The tree showed a distinct split between the African and non-African populations, with the former showing the greater number of lineages.

This result implied that the African population was the longest established, as would be expected if modern humans originated there. The team were also able to estimate the extent to which the various genetic lineages had diverged from one another since the time of their common ancestor, taken to be one woman. By applying the 'molecular clock' principle, they were able to show that this had been about 200,000 years ago. In other words, everybody living in the world today can trace their mitochondrial DNA to one African woman who lived about 200,000 years ago. This date was about ten times more recent than would be expected if the multiregional theory was correct.

The story appeared on the front cover of *Newsweek*, under the headline *"The Search for Adam and Eve"*. Inevitably, this one woman soon became known as 'Mitochondrial Eve', but the term is misleading as she was not the only woman alive at the time. Her significance is that she is the only woman of her time whose mitochondrial lineage has survived to the present day. Those of all her contemporaries ended at some point with women who failed to have any daughters – an example of a phenomenon known as genetic drift.

Genetic drift refers to random changes in the frequencies in which genes occurs in a population. In small populations, over a number of generations, the effect can result in some genes predominating and others disappearing altogether, even if the former confer no particular advantage on their possessors. An analogy for genetic drift is seen in small isolated villages where all the villagers end up with the same surname. If for example Mr and Mrs Smith are the only Smiths in the village and they have only daughters, then the surname Smith will disappear from the next generation. Over enough generations, the villagers will 'drift' to just one surname. The phenomenon would be unlikely to happen in a large population, and the fact that only Mitochondrial Eve's mitochondrial lineage remains indicates that the population to which she belonged was small – possibly numbering between 2,000 and 10,000 individuals.

The Berkeley group's statistical techniques were later challenged, and it was also noted that they had examined only a small portion of the mitochondrial DNA genome. However, subsequent studies have confirmed the original result. Some of these simply considered more extensive regions of the mitochondrial DNA genome, but later work included the male Y-chromosome and ordinary recombining DNA. In all cases, a recent African origin was indicated for *Homo sapiens*.

As we have seen, the earliest currently-known examples of our species are the 195,000-year-old Omo I and Omo II skulls from the Omo River in southern Ethiopia. Their age is a good fit to the estimated date for Mitochondrial Eve, and is much earlier than those any non-African remains. With most palaeoanthropologists now accepting an African origin for our species, the next task was to try and pinpoint in which part of Africa Mitochondrial Eve had lived. Unfortunately, mitochondrial studies cannot provide a fine enough geographical resolution to settle matters, and can only tell us that she was part of a fairly small population that lived in either East Africa or South Africa. However, a recent study of nuclear genome diversity supports a South African origin. If this conclusion is correct, then modern human fossils even older than the Omo remains may await discovery in South Africa.

# 24: Fluctuation

*The archaeological record of early modern humans in Africa suggests a puzzling mixture of innovation and conservatism, but do we have the entire picture?*

The archaeological record of early modern humans during the African Middle Stone Age suggests a strange mixture of innovation and conservatism. The technologies in use, for the most part, do not appear to be a significant advance on those of earlier humans, but there are sporadic exceptions: bursts of innovation followed by reversion to more conservative technologies. Hi-tech solutions were seemingly abandoned, not to reappear for tens of thousands of years. Or were they? Was the Middle Stone Age really a period of technological fluctuation, and if so, why?

The first example of a technology clearly in advance of anything previously seen appeared 165,000 years ago at Pinnacle Point, a series of caves on the coast in Western Cape Province, South Africa. The caves were discovered in 2000 during preparatory work for the construction of a golf course. The Pinnacle Point people manufactured and used stone tools known as microliths, almost 100,000 years before they were previously thought to have come into use.

Microliths are small blades with a width of less than 10 mm (0.375 in.), which can be hafted or set into bone or wooden handles of tools, or to the shafts or tips of spears. This means that instead of having to repair or discard an entire tool when worn or damaged, only the affected microlith needs to be repaired or replaced. Despite the obvious advantages of what archaeologist Steven Mithen has described as Stone Age 'plug-in pull-out' technology, microliths were then seemingly abandoned and there was a reversion to far simpler prepared-core industries no more advanced than those of contemporary Neanderthals in Europe.

Another site where advanced technologies were in use is at Katanda on the Upper Semliki River in the Democratic Republic of the Congo. Evidence has been found of a sophisticated fishing industry at three locations there 90,000 years ago, utilising barbed and unbarbed bone points thought to have been used for river fishing – the world's first-known fishing tackle. The pieces were carefully manufactured, and a stone grinder was used for finishing. Bone and antler tools represent high-performance technologies, although the polishing and grinding they require means that their initial production is labour intensive.

Extensive remains of large adult catfish have been found at the Katanda sites, but those of younger fish are absent. This implies that fishing was only carried out at the beginning of the rainy season, when the catfish spawn near the shore. They were evidently caught as part of an overall seasonal strategy, rather than on an *ad hoc* basis. There is a scarcity of fish vertebrae, suggesting that the catch was processed at the site, and edible parts were taken away and eaten or stored elsewhere. The Katanda people were evidently competent hunters and fishers who planned their lives around the seasonal availability of game and fish – yet after this, bone tools did not become widespread and were not seen again for another 10,000 years. Was this precocious technology no more than a flash in the pan?

Probably the best known examples of technological hiatus are those which followed the Stillbay and Howieson's Poort periods in South Africa. The Stillbay tool industry is named for the village of Stillbaai on the southern coast of South Africa. It is noted for its finely-worked elliptical and leaf-shaped spear points, which were made from high-quality materials such as chert, quartzite and silcrete (a concrete-like material formed from silica and soil grains). Advanced tool types included end scrapers and chisel-like burins, similar to those seen during much later European Upper Palaeolithic. End scrapers were used for scraping animal skins and burins for working bone and antler materials. Implements made from bone included awls and projectile points.

Two further examples of advanced Stillbay technology are the use of compound adhesives and pressure flaking. A compound adhesive is one in which two or more components are mixed before use, such as Araldite. Traces of a mixture comprising red ochre and plant gum have been found on spear points. Experiments have shown that this mixture forms a tough bond, preventing the spear tip from breaking away from its haft when used. The Stillbay people would have had to experiment at length to find ingredients that gave satisfactory results, as well as learning to use fire to harden the adhesive after application.

Pressure flaking is a technique used for finishing a stone artefact by exerting pressure with a sharp tool to unfinished edges of the piece. Before this can be done, heat treatment must be applied to the unfinished stone artefact to improve its flaking properties. It was once thought that the technique came into use no earlier than the European Solutrean period, about 20,000 years ago, but experimentation and microscopic studies has shown that it was used during the final shaping of Stillbay points made from heat-treated silcrete.

The Stillbay industry was widespread but short-lived, lasting for less than a thousand years from 71,900 to 71,000 years ago. It was succeeded not by comparable industries but by an apparent return to typical Middle Stone Age prepared-core industries that lasted for around 6,000 years. At the end of this hiatus period, another innovative culture arose, known as Howieson's Poort. This was characterised by small crescent-shaped and trapezoidal microliths that were presumably hafted into wood or bone handles. It was current from around 64,800 to 59,500 years ago before it too disappeared, and once again there was an apparent return to more typical Middle Stone Age technologies.

Like the Stillbay, the Howieson's Poort was widespread, and variants of it have been identified over large areas of central and southern Africa. It is notable that the start and end dates of both the Stillbay and Howieson's Poort industries were more or less simultaneous at archaeological sites spread across a wide area, suggesting that both were associated with long-range social networks.

Why would technologically-sophisticated people with extensive social networks abandon these industries in favour of less advanced tool technologies? Were advanced tools and techniques repeatedly invented, only for the technology to be lost on each occasion? Could their appearance and subsequent disappearance reflect expansions and contractions in populations? If populations fell to a level where the social networks could no longer be sustained, innovative technologies could no longer be transmitted and would rapidly disappear.

In the case of Howieson's Poort at least there is no evidence for a social collapse at its end, and sites do not seem to have been abandoned at any stage. In some cases, Howieson's Poort tools have been found associated with post-Howieson's Poort tools. The change to less sophisticated technologies occurs very gradually and in parallel at many widely separated sites. The picture is of an evolutionary development of a different style of weapons and domestic tools rather than of a social collapse and breakdown of cultural transmission.

The answer may be that the loss of technology is apparent rather than real. Recent work at Pinnacle Point has identified a microlithic industry originating approximately 71,000 years ago, at about the time Stillbay came to an end, and predating Howieson's Poort by six millennia. Given the much earlier presence of microliths at the same location, the discovery suggests that this technology was an early and enduring development. The apparent appearance and disappearance of complex technologies may be nothing more than an artefact of the limited number of sites that have been excavated in Africa.

It may also be naïve to assume that the Stillbay and Howieson's Poort technologies were necessarily 'better' than those that followed. It is possible that changes in technology were adaptations to changing conditions and it is only from our perspective that some technologies seem more advanced than others. Animal remains from the site of Sibudu Cave in KwaZulu-Natal suggest a gradual change from species favouring closed woodland such as pigs, duiker and bushbuck to buffalo and wildebeest, which prefer open environments. Shifts in tool types could simply reflect environmental change and the types of animals available as prey. Perhaps the less complex technologies were simply better suited to the job – if indeed they really were less complex.

Again, though, this may be an illusion. Archaeologists also identified a new tool tradition at Sibudu Cave, which they have named the Sibudan. It emerged around 58,000 years ago, just after the Howieson's Poort era came to an end. Though it was similar in many ways to typical African Middle Stone Age industries, the Sibudan is distinct from them. Artefacts from six different archaeological layers were found to be linked by common features, which identify them as belonging to a distinct tool tradition. Many of these features are considered to be hallmarks of a sophisticated stone tool-making technology, including standardisation of tool types and production methods. Overall, the Sibudan suggests that post-Howieson's Poort tool technologies were anything but rudimentary or unsophisticated.

The picture that is emerging of the African Middle Stone Age is one of technological and cultural sophistication that emerged very soon after the first appearance of modern humans and persisted thereafter. The technological hiatus periods probably represent nothing more than an incomplete archaeological record and the lack of a full understanding of the actual technologies in use at any one time. As is so often the case, absence of evidence should never be taken to be evidence of absence.

# 25: Middle Stone Age graphic art

*Do engraved ochres and eggshells demonstrate the existence of graphic art traditions in Middle Stone Age South Africa?*

At first glance, they don't look like much. Two small rectangular pieces of reddish-brown ochre, scraped and ground flat on two sides and then engraved with a sharp tool upon the newly-ground facets to produce a cross-hatched geometrical design. As pieces of modern art, they would undoubtedly divide opinion – but they were actually carved 73,000 years ago.

The carved ochres were found at Blombos Cave in 2002, and although it is likely that they were both the work of the same individual we cannot be certain. The cave is located on the southern coast of South Africa in a limestone cliff 35 m (115 ft.) above sea level and 100 m (330 ft.) from the coast, though when occupied the coastline was further away. Originally discovered by archaeologist Christopher Henshilwood, it is one of the most extensively researched sites from the African Middle Stone Age.

Henshilwood has been familiar with the site since his childhood, since it is located on land owned by his grandfather. As a boy, he had found a number of comparatively recent prehistoric artefacts. In 1991, he returned there as a PhD student, hoping to discover similar artefacts. Instead, he found bone tools and stone points that dated from a far earlier period, over 70,000 years ago. After completing his PhD at the University of Cambridge, Henshilwood obtained funding to commence excavations at Blombos Cave, and he continues to lead work at the site to this day.

Three Middle Stone Age phases of occupation have been identified. These are known as M1 (73,000 years ago), M2 (subdivided between an upper phase 77,000 years ago and a lower phase 80,000 years ago) and M3 (125,000 years ago). Each phase contains a number of occupation layers, but they are quite shallow indicating that the cave was only occupied sporadically and for relatively short periods of time. The ochres were presumably left behind when their maker's group decided to move camp, abandoning any non-essential possessions they had acquired during their stay.

The later occupations of the cave are associated with the Stillbay tool industry, which as we have seen was one of the cutting-edge industries of the African Middle Stone Age, noted for its finely-worked leaf-shaped stone spear points, and the use of bone to make awls and projectile points. However, the most important discovery at Blombos Cave has been the engraved ochres. Several thousand pieces of ochre have been found at the site, and in 2002, Henshilwood reported the two engraved ochres from the 73,000-year-old M1 phase, which were catalogued as AA 8937 and AA 8938. Both had been engraved with cross-hatched patterns, using a sharp stone tool to make wide grooves upon surfaces previously prepared by grinding. On AA 8938, in addition to cross-hatching, the pattern is bounded top and bottom by parallel lines, with a third parallel line running through the middle. The fact that the two pieces are so similar suggests a deliberate intent, rather somebody absent-mindedly scratching away at the pieces with a sharp object. Later excavations recovered engraved ochres from all three Middle Stone Age phases of the site, although they were less spectacular than AA 8937 and AA 8938.

Henshilwood rejects the possibility that the patterns are a by-product of testing for the quality of powder from the ochres, as this would require only a few lines, not a carefully-constructed pattern. He also rules out absent-minded doodling, because great care and attention were required to engrave the patterns and ensure that all the various incisions matched up. He believes that not only were the patterns made with deliberate intent, but recurring motifs on ochres found in all three of the Middle Stone Age phases are indicative of a tradition of engraving geometric patterns that persisted for tens of thousands of years.

The engraved ochres from Blombos Cave are not the only early example of an enduring graphic tradition. At Diepkloof Rock Shelter, another South African site, located in Western Cape Province, there is evidence of a tradition that changed stylistically over time. In common with Blombos Cave and many other South African sites, Diepkloof Rock Shelter was repeatedly occupied over the course of tens of millennia.

People lived there from before 130,000 years ago up until around 45,000 years ago, a period that spanned the pre-Stillbay, Stillbay, Howieson's Poort, and post-Howieson's Poort periods. Archaeologists recovered 270 engraved fragments of ostrich eggshell, representing at least 25 complete eggshells and dating to around 60,000 years ago. A 12 mm (½ in.) diameter hole had been punched in an apex fragment, suggesting that the eggshells might have been used as water flasks. To this day, ostrich eggshells are used for this purpose by indigenous Kalahari people. Their size and durability makes them ideal: they are by necessity sturdy, as they have to be able to withstand being sat on by a 100 kg (220 lb.) female ostrich.

The Diepkloof eggshells feature two principle designs. The first is a hatched band motif consisting of two long parallel lines, intersected at roughly right angles by shorter, regularly spaced lines. Within this style, craftspeople exercised a certain amount of variation of both the width of the bands and the spacing of the hatching. This design later changed to one featuring parallel or slightly diverging lines, suggesting that the dominant style varied over time. Although there was some scope for individual expression, the engravings were standardised and consisted of repetitive patterns made in accordance with a set of rules.

The most obvious question is what was the significance of the geometric patterns seen at Blombos and Diepkloof? They may well have meant something quite specific to the people who made them, though just what that might be we simply do not know. Henshilwood points out that the Christian cross would appear equally mysterious to somebody unfamiliar with the religious iconography of the last two millennia. Another possibility is that the designs represent traditions analogous to twentieth century abstract art movements such as the De Stijl school of the Netherlands.

Another question is if humans were able to produce abstract art over 100,000 years ago, why does figurative art not appear until much later? The earliest unequivocal examples of figurative art do not appear until around 40,000 years ago. One possibility is that humans were still not yet entirely behaviourally modern and were unable to make figurative images, though Henshilwood rejects this possibility. He notes that there are many cultures that do not make figurative art, and many others do so using perishable materials that would not survive for tens of thousands of years. The recent discovery that rock art from the island of Sulawesi is almost as old as European cave art implies the existence of a much older tradition of figurative art.

Henshilwood believes the fact that the ochre engravings were intentionally created and depict distinctive geometrical patterns is enough to demonstrate that they are the product of a society of behaviourally-modern humans. Given the weight of evidence for technological sophistication during the Stillbay and Howieson's Poort periods, and indeed much earlier, we should not find this unduly surprising.

# 26: Going global

*How, why, when and where did modern humans first leave Africa?*

Although the first humans are now thought to have lived around 2.8 million years ago, fossil and genetic evidence has shown that *Homo sapiens* is a far more recent phenomenon, originating in Africa just 200,000 years ago. The next question is just when and under what circumstances did our ancestors leave Africa and go on to populate the rest of the world? To leave Africa there are theoretically four routes into Eurasia: from Morocco across the Straits of Gibraltar; from Tunisia to Sicily and thence to Italy; from Egypt across the Sinai desert into the Levant; and across the Bab el-Mandeb Strait between the Red Sea and the Gulf of Aden. In practice, perhaps surprisingly, there is no evidence that early modern humans crossed into Europe from North Africa, which leaves just the last two routes.

The Sahara and Sinai can only be crossed during the warm, wet periods between ice ages, known as interglacials. At such times, these normally inhospitable regions green and the Levant becomes a northeasterly extension of Africa. Plant leaf waxes indicate that trees grew in the Sahara, and satellite radar images have revealed networks of now-buried river channels that provided an uninterrupted freshwater corridor across what is now arid desert. By travelling along this humid, life-sustaining corridor, it was possible to leave Africa. Three such favourable periods have been identified in the last 200,000 years: the first during the warm Eemian period from 120,000 to 110,000 years ago; the second from 50,000 to 45,000 years ago; and the third during the early part of the current Holocene epoch.

Paradoxically, the remaining route is only available during cold, arid periods. The Bab el-Mandeb Strait – meaning 'The Gate of Tears' – is a narrow waterway at the southern end of the Red Sea, separating Djibouti from Yemen. At the present time, it is 18 km (11 miles) across at its narrowest point, about half the width of the Strait of Dover. On a clear day, Yemen is clearly visible from the shores of Djibouti. The crossing is nevertheless treacherous, with swift currents that flow southwards into the Gulf of Aden between November and June. These currents have earned the Strait its name, and could have swept primitive watercraft out into the Indian Ocean. However, at times when glacial conditions affect higher latitudes, sea levels drop worldwide and the strait narrows to just 11 km (6.8 miles). To make the crossing at such times was probably well within the abilities of African Middle Stone Age seafarers.

On the face of it, the northern route is the most obvious, as it does not involve any form of water crossing at all. Fossil evidence from the Levant does indeed point to modern humans having left by this route, probably around 115,000 years ago. In the 1930s, the British archaeologist British archaeologist Dorothy Garrod and palaeontologist Dorothea Bate recovered the remains of big-boned, but unmistakably modern people at the site of Mugharet es-Skhul, near Haifa in Israel. Similar remains were found a few years later at the site of Jebel Qafzeh, south of Nazareth. The similarity of the remains to those of early modern people from Jebel Irhoud in Morocco suggests that these Levantine people originated from North Africa.

At the time, it seemed reasonable to suppose that the Levantine people had gone on to settle the rest of the world, moving westwards towards Europe and eastwards towards India – but later discoveries showed that by 75,000 years ago, modern humans had left the region and it had been re-occupied by Neanderthals. The obvious conclusion is that the Neanderthals drove the modern humans out of the Levant, but timing coincides with a sharp and prolonged drop in global temperatures. Rather than a Neanderthal conquest, it is more likely that the modern population either died out or retreated back to Africa as a result of the climate change.

Perhaps 'failed migration' is too strong a word to use for an excursion that probably lasted for tens of millennia. But mitochondrial DNA studies following on from 'Mitochondrial Eve' suggested that it petered out without contributing to the genetic makeup of the world's present-day non-African population. Instead, researchers learned that the non-African world had been populated by members of a single branch of Mitochondrial Eve's descendants. This branch, or mitochondrial haplogroup, was designated L3, and it emerged in East Africa around 85,000 years ago. Members of L3's non-African daughter haplogroups, of which there are three, went on to populate the rest of the world. Known as M, N and R (the latter actually a very early branch of N), these emerged between 65,000 and 60,000 years ago. Overall, the results suggested a migration via the southern route 65,000 to 60,000 years ago, which corresponded to a glacial period and lowered sea levels.

According to the 'Out of Africa' model that soon became orthodoxy, there was just one migration from Africa. The three founder haplogroups M, N and R all are roughly the same age, suggesting that all were associated with the same migration. Had they been associated with separate migrations at different times, it would be expected that their ages would reflect the dates of these migrations. The mitochondrial data has also been used to estimate that this founding group included no more than 500 to 2,000 reproductively-active women, though the total number of men, women and children taking part in the migration would of course have been greater. A total of around 3,000 individuals has been suggested.

In what has become known as the 'coastal express train scenario', it is proposed that descendants of the original migrants adopted a 'beachcomber' lifestyle, harvesting readily-available seafood as they dispersed rapidly eastwards along the rim of the Indian Ocean. In all probability, the dispersal was aided by the use of watercraft, which could transport colonists together with sufficient food, water, and other supplies needed to traverse long stretches of inhospitable coast. Settlements were likely established in river estuaries, where food, potable water and timber were readily available. As populations grew, overcrowding would have stimulated the search for new estuarine habitats further along the coast. Eventually, the migrants reached Indonesia, and aided by the low sea levels they crossed to the then conjoined landmass of New Guinea and Australia. The latter was reached at least 50,000 years ago, but Europe was not settled by modern humans until migrants arrived there from South Asia about 46,000 years ago. Meanwhile, other groups moved into Central and East Asia; finally, around 15,000 years ago, migrants from Siberia crossed the then-existing land-bridge into the New World.

Scattered along the route of the projected initial coastal migration are isolated populations long thought to have been aboriginal because their culture and appearance marks them out from surrounding people. They closely resemble Khoisan Africans, being short in stature with tightly curled hair and an epicanthic fold. They include the inhabitants of the Andaman Islands in the Bay of Bengal, the Semang from the Malay Peninsula, the Mani people of Thailand and a number of indigenous groups in the Philippines. Along with New

Guineans and Aboriginal Australians all possess localised but very ancient branches of the three founder mitochondrial haplogroups M, N and R. The implication is that these groups settled along the rim of the Indian Ocean a long time ago, and that they have remained in more or less the same place ever since. Researchers applied a statistical technique known as founder analysis to the genetic data, with the aim of identifying and dating migrations into new territory. The results suggest that the settlement took place at least 60,000 years ago, and that these peoples are indeed the relict populations left over from the original migration out of Africa.

The first hint that matters might be more complicated than this model suggests came in 2007, when evidence emerged that modern humans had been in India at the time of the Toba eruption, 73,000 years ago. The eruption of the supervolcano beneath Lake Toba in northern Sumatra is the largest volcanic event of the last two million years, ejecting at least 2,500 cubic km (600 cubic miles) of magma. Blown by southerly winds, this blanketed much of the Indian subcontinent in a layer of ash 10 to 15 cm (4 to 6 in.) deep and drifted in places to up to 6 m (19 ft. 8 in.). While the effects of the eruption on global climate are disputed, the Indian subcontinent would certainly not have been the healthiest of places to be. Nevertheless, there is reason to suppose that modern humans were there at the time, and that they lived to tell the tale.

Stone artefacts were recovered from both above and below a 2.55 m (8 ft. 0 in.) thick ash deposit near Jwalapuram, an archaeological study area in the Jurreru River valley of Andhra Pradesh, southern India, and the two sets of artefacts have enough in common to suggest that they were made by people who lived through the catastrophe. Though no actual human remains were recovered, the tools and tool-making technology bore a closer resemblance to African tool industries associated with modern humans than they did to the industries typical of archaic humans in Eurasia. There is no doubt that the date of Toba eruption is correct, and it is at least 8,000 years before the genetic estimates for the exodus from Africa. The date of the exodus itself would of course have to have been even earlier. A problem for those trying to stretch the genetic dates to accommodate an earlier exit is that recent work suggests that the dates for M, N and R have been overestimated rather than underestimated.

An even more significant challenge to the standard Out of Africa model emerged in 2011 with evidence suggesting that modern humans were living on the Arabian Peninsula as much as 127,000 years ago. Though largely arid desert today, this vast subcontinent has not always been inhospitable, and on occasions warm and wet climate phases have transformed it into a fertile, habitable ecosystem. At such times, it might have acted as a 'pump', drawing in populations from the Levant, India and East Africa. Although dry, cold periods would have seen these populations largely die out, some regions would have remained habitable and might have served as refugia for human populations. These regions included the Red Sea basin and Yemeni highlands, and the southeast Arabian coastal zone. In addition, large portions of the Persian Gulf were exposed by the reduced sea levels. The appearance of freshwater springs in the exposed basin might have transformed the Gulf into a coastal oasis comparable in size to Great Britain.

Although many archaeological sites are known in the region, there are few reliable estimates of their age and very little is known about the makers of the tools found at these sites. However, in 2011, secure dates were obtained for stone tools from Jebel Faya, a mountain in the United Arab Emirates lying due south of the Straits of Hormuz, and from the Dhofar region of southwest Oman. The Jebel Faya finds were made in a rock shelter known as FAY-NE1, located 180 m (600 ft.) above sea level at the northeast end of the mountain. The site contained archaeological layers dating from comparatively recent times all the way back to the Middle Palaeolithic. Stone tools from the latter period were found in three layers: those in the oldest of these ranged in age from 127,000 to 95,000 years old. This timespan overlapped with the modern human occupation of the Levant, but the tools were completely unrelated to those of the Skhul and Jebel Qafzeh people. Instead, it was suggested that the manufacturing techniques had more in common with those known in East and northeast Africa.

It was proposed that modern humans had crossed the Bab el-Mandeb Strait just before the onset of the Eemian warm period, while sea levels were still low enough for it still to be readily crossed. From southern coast of Yemen, the subsequent favourable conditions enabled groups to spread both inland and along the coast all the way to Jebel Faya. During the cooler, arid periods that followed, the Jebel Faya people became cut off from groups living further south, but they were able to survive. Critics argued that the Jebel Faya artefacts could not be identified with any particular East African tool industry, and that the tools were not necessarily African or even made by modern humans.

However, no such objections could be made for Dhofar findings, which were announced in November 2011. These are firmly associated with the Nubian Complex, a Middle Stone Age industry from the Middle and Lower Nile Valley. Divided into Early and Late phases, the Nubian was first reported from northern Sudan in the 1960s. Nubian artefacts have been found from Sinai to the Horn of Africa, with dates ranging from roughly 120,000 to 100,000 years old. In 2010, an archaeological project was mounted to investigate tentative reports of Nubian artefacts in Yemen. During two seasons of fieldwork, a large number of Late Nubian Complex artefacts were recovered. An age of 106,000 was obtained for the open-air site of Aybut Al Auwal, which is entirely consistent with Nubian dates from Africa. It is even possible that the Late Nubian phase originated in Arabia and later spread back to East Africa. The Dhofar findings provided unequivocal evidence of cultural exchanges across the Red Sea by modern humans some 40,000 years before genetic estimates for the migration date.

Up to this point, no unequivocal fossil evidence had been found for an early migration from Africa barring that from the two Levantine sites, although controversial evidence had been claimed from two sites in southern China. An age of up to 140,000 years old was reported for the Liujiang Skull, discovered in 1958, but the exact geological position of the find was not documented and the skull could be as little as 30,000 years old. A lower jawbone from Zhirendong ('*Homo sapiens* cave') in Guizhou Province was securely dated to 106,000 years old, but it is possible that it belonged to an archaic rather than modern human.

Definite evidence finally emerged from southern China in 2015, when 47 teeth were discovered at the newly-excavated site of Fuyan Cave in Daoxian, Hunan Province. The teeth were found to be at least 80,000 years old and possibly as much as 120,000 years old. The teeth were compared with those of Late Pleistocene humans from Europe, Asia and Africa and were found to fall consistently within the *Homo sapiens* size range. They are generally smaller than other Late Pleistocene samples from Asia and Africa, and are closer to European Late Pleistocene samples and the teeth of present-day people. They resemble the latter far more closely than they do the teeth of Neanderthals or *Homo erectus*.

The question now was how to reconcile this evidence with the genetically-derived Out of Africa model. The simplest possibility is that all these early migrants eventually died out and did not contribute to the present-day gene pool. A more interesting possibility is that Out of Africa is not so much wrong as incomplete. There are two major elements of the theory that are not invalidated by the new data. The first of these is the coastal express train scenario. Regardless of its exact point of departure or whether it was the first dispersal, it provides a simple explanation for the presence of modern humans in Australia before they reached Europe.

The second element is the expansion and branching of mitochondrial haplogroup L3. There is no reason to suppose that the data placing the origin of this haplogroup in East Africa 85,000 years ago should be wrong. The subsequent expansion followed the easing of a severe drought that had affected tropical Africa for many millennia. It is uncertain why East African populations carrying other haplogroups did not also expand; possibly a group in which haplogroup L3 was dominant possessed a technology that put them at an advantage over other groups.

The technology might have been tailored clothing, the invention of which is thought to coincide roughly in time with the initial global dispersal of modern humans from Africa. Researchers started with the assumption that body lice diverged from head lice at about the time tailored clothing came into use, as they took advantage of the new niche that had opened up. Data from mitochondrial and nuclear DNA showed that the body louse originated in Africa 72,000 years ago give or take a few millennia.

With all of this in mind, there is every reason to suppose that modern humans were present in Arabia from the Eemian onwards, and that mitochondrial lineages could have been shared between Arabian and East African populations. These included haplogroup L3, and while the climate was favourable, early L3 lineages spread across the Arabian Peninsula as well as East Africa. It is probable that mitochondrial lineages other than L3 were also present in smaller amounts in Arabia, as they were in East Africa. When the climate deteriorated 74,000 years ago, groups retreated to refugia, including the Red Sea basin, the southeast Arabian coastal zone and the expanded coastal oasis of the Persian Gulf. There, they came to rely increasingly on seafood rather than game animals.

Eventually, one group began to expand along the coastline of Iran, Pakistan, India, and eastwards. This group – from which the world's current non-African population is largely descended – was initially small enough for genetic drift to eliminate all mitochondrial lineages except for two emerging branches of the dominant L3 haplogroup. These eventually became M, N, and subsequently R. Other early branches of L3 probably continued to exist in all three Arabian refugia, but they were erased by later population bottlenecks and/or more recent population movements.

The expansion did not begin until after 74,000 years ago and is therefore unconnected with the Daoxian people and, in all probability the Jurreru people. Where did these people come from, and what happened to them? They could have originated from the Levant before the cold set in, or from Arabia, or from both. If modern humans were established in these places prior to 100,000 years ago, then it is actually quite hard to believe that nobody at all ventured further afield for another 30,000 years or more. The Jurreru people survived Toba and were likely still present when the later migrants reached India. Other groups may well have been scattered across southern Asia, and interbreeding with the migrants presumably occurred. But if these groups were all small in numbers compared to the newcomers, their mitochondrial lineages would soon have disappeared due to the effects of genetic drift. On the other hand, it is entirely possible that portions of their nuclear genomes survive; being inherited from both parents, these would have been less susceptible to the effects of genetic drift than the mitochondrial lineages. Whether or not this is actually the case we don't yet know, but it is to be hoped that future genetic studies will clarify the fate of these early pioneers beyond Africa and Southwest Asia.

# 27: The first Australians

*Controversy over when humans first reached Australia.*

Given its considerably greater distance from Africa, it is perhaps surprising that Australia was settled by modern humans before Europe. After what might have been a lengthy sojourn in Arabia, early modern human migrants from Africa pushed eastwards along the rim of the Indian Ocean until they reached the Sunda peninsula. From there, it is likely that they took advantage of the lower sea levels and 'island-hopped' across the Wallacea archipelago to Sahul (the then-conjoined landmass of New Guinea and Australia), establishing a chain of colonies stretching all the way back to the Asian mainland. There are two main island-hopping routes from the Sunda peninsula: an eastern route via Maluku to New Guinea, and a southern route via Timor to Arnhem Land in Australia's Northern Territory. Either route requires between eight to seventeen separate crossings, with one leg of at least 70 km (44 miles) and three or more of at least 30 km (18 miles). At the mid-point of such a voyage, even on a clear day, the land in both directions is out of sight – a daunting prospect even if you know that there is land where you are going. Much later, Polynesian seafarers would learn to recognise characteristic cloud formations that reveal the presence of land, and possibly this is how the colonists located islands that lay over the horizon.

Just when the first settlers reached Sahul has been the subject of a long-running debate. Some argue for a 'long chronology' of 60,000 years or more; others for a 'short chronology' of around 40,000 years. The earliest-known human remains in Australia were found between 1969 and 1974 at Lake Mungo, one of a series of 19 dried up lakes making up the Willandra Lakes system in the southwest of New South Wales. These once-extensive bodies of water would have been attractive to early settlers, although they have been completely dry for the last 14,000 years. The cremated remains of two individuals, now known as Mungo 1 and Mungo 2, were discovered in 1969 by archaeologist Jim Bowler.

The finds were reconstructed by anthropologist Alan Thorne, and comprise about 25 percent of a lightly built female skeleton, along with a few fragments of a second individual. The female was informally dubbed 'Mungo Lady'. In 1974, Bowler discovered a full skeleton, Mungo 3, only 450 m (1,500 ft.) from the cremation site and lying in the same geological stratum. He and Thorne excavated the remains, which had been covered in ochre as part of a burial ritual – the earliest-known example of this practice. Mungo 3 was also lightly built, but male, and inevitably became known as Mungo Man. Shells associated with the cremation were radiocarbon dated to about 30,000 years ago, but in 1999, Thorne attempted to date the remains of Mungo Man with a relatively new technique that had been devised in the 1980s – luminescence dating.

Buried objects containing crystalline materials gradually accumulate a radiation 'dose' from the weak, naturally-occurring radioactivity of surrounding materials. The dose takes the form of electrons trapped by defects in the material's crystalline lattice. The rate at which the electrons accumulate depends upon background radiation levels and by measuring these along with the number of trapped electrons in a sample, the time it has taken for the 'dose' to accumulate can be estimated. There are three methods that can be used to measure the number of trapped electrons, and the choice of method depends on the type of material to be dated. Thermoluminescence (TL) involves heating the sample to expel the trapped electrons. As they escape, they emit light, which provides a measure of their numbers. Optically Stimulated Luminescence (OSL) works on the same principle except the electrons are expelled by an intense light source. Electron Spin Resonance (ESR) involves making a direct measurement of the magnetic 'signal' of the trapped electrons. TL is used mainly for materials such as ceramics and bricks, where any initially trapped electrons were driven off during the process of firing, and thus setting the 'clock' running. OSL is used for quartz and sand grains, where exposure to sunlight drives off trapped electrons and the 'clock' is started when the material is buried or otherwise ceases to be exposed to sunlight. ESR is mainly used for dental enamel, which is deposited while an individual is alive and accumulates very few trapped electrons during that period.

Thorne applied ESR to Mungo Man's dental enamel and OSL to sandy sediments underlying the geological layer from which the remains had been recovered. In addition, he applied a more established radiometric technique, uranium series (U-series) dating, to date calcium carbonate deposit that formed on Mungo Man's skeletal material. This technique relies on the decay of the uranium isotope $^{234}U$ to the thorium isotope $^{230}Th$. It is used to date calcium carbonate materials such as speleothem (stalagmites and stalactites), which precipitate from natural water. Uranium is slightly soluble in water, and such materials contain uranium in small amounts; but thorium is insoluble, and will not be present in freshly-precipitated speleothem. The amount of thorium present in a sample will, therefore, serve as a measure of how much time has passed since it was precipitated.

A date of 62,000 years old was obtained, suggesting that the Mungo remains were twice as old as had been previously believed and making them older than any modern human remains found outside of Africa. Understandably, many were sceptical and Jim Bowler noted that the sand grains used for the OSL dating had been collected from sediments 300 m (1,000 ft.) from the actual burial site. Using sediment samples from a more secure context, Bowler and his colleagues obtained an age of 42,000 years for both Mungo Man and Mungo Lady. They also obtained ages of 46,000 and 50,000 years old for stone tools that were found below the burial layers, and are the earliest evidence for a human presence at the Lake Mungo. In 1992, Mungo Lady was returned into the keeping of local Aboriginal groups, though in practice this means that her remains are kept under lock and key at the Mungo National Park museum.

The controversy of the age of the Mungo remains has been echoed at other key sites in Australia and New Guinea, where the 'long chronologists' and 'short chronologists' continue to battle it out. At the Nauwalabila I and Malakunaja II rock shelters in Arnhem Land, long chronologists have obtained ages of 50,000 to 60,000 years old for stone tools, based on OSL dating of surrounding sand. These results are disputed by the short chronologists, who claim that termite activity could have affected the results by bringing sand grains upwards and shifting the artefacts downwards. This would have led to an artificially early date being obtained for the latter. The short chronologists believe that the sites are no more than 42,000 to 45,000 years old, and that there is no convincing evidence that humans reached Australia much before then.

It should be appreciated that the original colonists in all probability inhabited coastal sites that were later submerged as sea levels rose, and that inland sites could be reasonably expected to show more recent dates. Even if the short chronologists are right about the age of currently-known sites, there are no grounds for ruling out an earlier arrival in Australia. We know practically nothing about when and where the first colonists reached the now submerged Sahul coast, nor do we know how long it took for them to subsequently spread from their presumed landing points in the north to sites like Lake Mungo in the southeast. If, however, we accept that the latter was settled at least 46,000 years ago, then even a conservative estimate would suggest that modern humans reached Australia at least 50,000 years ago.

# 28: Deus ex Speluncam

*What was the purpose of the magnificent cave art of Ice Age Europe?*

The cave art tradition of Ice Age Europe lasted for more than twenty thousand years, during which time artists produced work best summed up by Pablo Picasso who, on visiting the Lascaux Caves in the Dordogne region of France, supposedly remarked that modern artists "...*have invented nothing*". Archaeologist and Catholic priest Abbé Henri Breuil described the caves as 'The Sistine Chapel of Prehistory'. At around 18,000 years old, the cave paintings of Lascaux are among of the more recent examples of cave art, but the much earlier cave art at Altamira and Chauvet is regarded as being of equal merit.

The cave paintings at these and other sites are perhaps the most spectacular examples of the artwork that heralded the arrival of modern humans in Europe 46,000 years ago. There is a sharp discontinuity in the archaeological record between the largely-utilitarian objects of the Middle Palaeolithic and art objects that are unquestionably the work of behaviourally-modern humans, including not just cave art but sculptures, carvings and enigmatic figurines of large-breasted women with exaggerated sexual characteristics. Though the latter bear little resemblance to the Roman goddess, they are usually referred to as Venus figurines. They are commonly believed to be fertility symbols, though their true purpose is unknown.

Cave art is known from around 320 sites, of which around 90 percent are located in the Franco-Cantabrian region of northern Spain and southwest France. The artwork predominantly comprises animals hunted for food, such as reindeer, horses, bison, aurochs (wild cattle), ibex and mammoths. Other animals depicted include birds, rhinos, felines, bears and wolves. Humans were portrayed only very rarely, and fewer than twenty examples are known. Some are therianthropic ('beast-man', i.e. part human, part animal), such as the highly-stylised, bird-headed, male figure in the Shaft of the Dead Man at Lascaux. However, stencilled outlines and positive prints of human hands are fairly common, as are representations of female genitalia. Purely abstract symbols also occur, including meandering rows of dots or circles, macaroni-like engravings, and triangular and rectangular tectiform (roof-shaped) designs. Images were made by either engraving the rock surface or applying pigment to it by a variety of techniques. These included painting with fingers, brushes, or pieces of animal hide, spray-painting through a tube, or spitting the pigment onto the rock surface from the mouth. The pigments used included ochre for a range of colours from yellow to deep maroon, black manganese dioxide, and mixtures of the two. As they generally worked far from natural daylight, artists relied on artificial illumination from pine torches or animal fat lamps.

What we do not know with any certainty is what motivated artists to produce this artwork over such an immense period of time. When the first cave art was discovered in the middle of the nineteenth century, it was seen as *art pour l'art*, or art for the sake of art. The caves were seen as Upper Palaeolithic art galleries, created and appreciated by people with time on their hand for activities beyond the daily round of hunting, gathering, and tool-making. The problem is that much of the artwork is located deep inside the caves, or in narrow passages, far from where it could easily be appreciated. At Lascaux, for example, the Shaft of the Dead Man is, as the name implies, a shaft some 6 m (17 ft.) deep. Present-day critics often complain that modern art is inaccessible, but for Upper Palaeolithic cave art this was literally true.

During the first half of the twentieth century, explanations based on totemism and hunting magic were in vogue. Totemism is a belief system in which human groups identify themselves with a particular species of animal or plant, for example 'Black Oak People' or 'Cave Bear Clan'. The word 'totem' originates from the North American Indian Ojibwe *odoodem*, meaning a clan or kinship group. It was suggested that the cave images were the equivalent of a totem pole, but the problem is that a totemic culture would portray only their emblem species in caves rather than the multiple species usually found. Hunting magic is the belief that making an image of an animal or person can influence the subject portrayed. Proponents argued that if people were making images in places where there work could not readily be appreciated, it must have been for magical purposes. The key lay in making rather than viewing the image, and the purpose was to ensure successful hunting. Artists depicting predators hoped to gain for themselves the strength and hunting skill of these animals, and abstract images represented traps or weapons.

Later explanations focussed on structuralism, a philosophical movement that originated early in the twentieth century with the work the Swiss linguist Ferdinand de Saussure. In the 1940s, the French anthropologist Claude Levi-Strauss applied it to anthropology and proposed that the language, kinship systems, and mythology of any human culture can be explained in terms of 'binary opposites' (for example up/down, life/death and male/female), and the relationships between them. Two of his compatriots, archaeologists Andre Leroi-Gourhan and Annette Laming-Emperaire, then applied the model to cave art, interpreting animals and abstract designs as male or female symbols. They viewed horses and stags as male symbolisations, and bison and aurochs as female. Similarly, line or arrow-like figures were seen as male genitalia, and broader triangular designs female.

Some have noted that not only is the cave art concentrated geographically in the Franco-Cantabrian region, it also focussed in time and was at a peak from 22,000 to 18,000 years ago. This period corresponds to the Last Glacial Maximum, the coldest part of the last Ice Age, when northern and central Europe was uninhabitable. The Franco-Cantabrian region lies at what was the most southerly part of the open tundra and steppe environment of Ice Age Europe, and supported large numbers of herd animals, whose migration trails followed river valleys flowing westwards from the Massif Central and northwards from the Cantabrian Mountains. It was an ideal location for hunter-gatherers to target migrating herds, but as the climate deteriorated in the build-up to the Last Glacial Maximum, increasing numbers of refugees were forced southwards into the region as their homelands became frozen wastelands.

It has been suggested that cave art was a response to the resultant population crowding, which created a need for ritual and ceremonial activities to maintain social cohesion and mark out distinct territories. The need had existed in the past, but the problem was exacerbated by the Last Glacial Maximum. Cave art might have been a social and cultural adaptation to the extreme conditions and an integral part of Ice Age hunter-gatherer ideologies. The major sites such as Lascaux and Altamira might have served as ritual centres for annual congregations of regional groups. It is also possible that the production of the art was controlled by religious leaders who used it to reinforce their position within these societies. During the subsequent climatic upturn, populations spread out once more and repopulated northern and central Europe. The 'crowd stress' eased and with it the need for distinct territories. After more than twenty millennia, the era of cave art was at an end.

This view is widely accepted, although models that posit religion and ritual as a means of creating social cohesion have been criticised. Religion and ritual do indeed create social cohesion – but this, critics argue, is more a description rather than an explanation. It doesn't tell us why religion and rituals exist, unless one supposes that people consciously invented them for that purpose. It is very difficult to argue that the tribal elders of Franco-Cantabrian settlements sat down to discuss introducing rituals to deal with the problems of crowd stress.

An alternative explanation has been put forward by South African archaeologist David Lewis-Williams. Drawing on ethnographic studies of present-day South African and North American rock art and traditions, he suggests that Upper Palaeolithic cave art was created as part of a shamanistic belief system. Present-day shamanistic religions are based on the belief that shamans can leave their bodies and travel to other realms of existence, where they communicate directly with powerful spirits and act as mediators between the living and the spirit worlds. Lewis-Williams believes that many aspects of religion can be explained in terms of the neurological architecture of the human brain. He notes that religions are often based on the belief in a multi-tiered cosmos, with other realms of existence located 'above' and 'below' that of our every-day experience. The Western concepts of Heaven and Hell are only one example of such a cosmology. Lewis-Williams suggests that widespread belief in the existence of other realms arises from visions and hallucinations experienced in what are known as altered states of consciousness.

Human consciousness may be thought of as a spectrum, along which the brain's state of consciousness is constantly shifting. At one end of the spectrum is the outward-directed consciousness that we use to interact with our environment. Beyond this is a more introverted states where we solve problems by inward-directed thought. Further on, we reach a state of day-dreaming, and beyond this the brain normally reaches the boundary between wakefulness and sleep (known as the hypnagogic state) before entering a state of dreaming. However, there is a second, very different trajectory which may be induced by psychotropic substances, intense concentration, chanting, clapping, drumming, prolonged rhythmic movement and hyperventilation. Sensory deprivation, of the type that may be experienced in the depths of cave networks, may also induce this second, intensified trajectory.

Those who have experienced it report that it leads through three stages. In the first stage, an individual experiences phenomena including grids, sets of parallel lines, bright dots, thin, meandering lines, and 'fortification' patterns. The latter, familiar to sufferers of migraine with aura, comprise arcs of shimmering zigzag lines, often resembling the battlements of a castle. During the second stage, the brain interprets these phenomena as objects with personal significance, for example religious manifestations. As individuals pass from the second to third stage, they pass through a vortex or tunnel, at the end of which is bright light. On the surface of the vortex there sometimes appear images of people, animals and monsters. As the third stage is reached, individuals experience not only visual hallucinations but may hear voices or experience sensations such changing into animals.

Lewis-Williams believes that the phenomena experienced on intensified trajectory are what give rise to perceptions of an alternate reality. All human brains are wired up the same way and hence experience broadly the same phenomena, though how these are interpreted varies from culture to culture. Shamanistic practices are based on the belief that people with the requisite powers are able to access the other realms, though in reality they are experiencing illusions resulting from the behaviour of their nervous systems in altered states of consciousness. These hallucinations may be what is depicted in the cave art of the European Upper Palaeolithic, and they could lie at the root of all belief systems from that era through to the present day. If Lewis-Williams is right, then Upper Palaeolithic shamans saw images of animals and geometrical patterns seemingly 'projected' onto the walls of the caves and the paintings represented the 'fixing' of these images. It is notable that the cave paintings lack any naturalistic setting: there are no trees, rivers or grassy plains, suggesting that they are mental images, completely unconstrained by the natural world. The people of these times saw the subterranean passages and chambers that made up the caves as the entrails of the spirit world. By entering them, they were physically entering a nether realm where they could see 'fixed' visions of spirit-animals.

However, Lewis-Williams goes further and suggests that the origins of social stratification may also be found in such belief systems. Those who could master the techniques necessary to enter the altered states of consciousness and thus access the spirit world were accorded higher status than those who could not. The cramped nature of the caves themselves suggests such a structure. At Lascaux, only the Hall of the Bulls at Lascaux is large enough to accommodate communal ritual activity. The carefully-composed images there must have been the result of a coordinated effort involving highly-skilled people and use of scaffolding. Notably, this hall is the nearest part of the complex to the surface, and it might have served as an antechamber into deeper parts of subterranean realm.

In lower levels at Lascaux, individual images do not appear to form parts of larger compositions, and are often superimposed upon each other. Lewis-Williams believes that they were the result of uncoordinated participation by different isolated individuals over a long period of time. It is in these regions of cave complexes that hallucinogenic images were 'fixed'. In moving through the narrow passages, people might have felt that they were passing through the vortex experienced by those in altered states of consciousness.

The most inaccessible part of the Lascaux complex is the Shaft of the Dead Man, which can only be reached with ropes and ladders. Floor space is limited, and only a few people could have occupied it at a time. At the base of the shaft is a portrayal of a highly stylised man with the head of a bird, four-fingered birdlike hands, and a prominent erection. He is apparently confronting a partially-eviscerated bison. Below him, a bird is perched atop a post. With its back to this scene and its tail raised is a rhinoceros, and on the opposite side is a black horse. In shamanistic terms, the death of the bison parallels the metaphorical 'death' of a shaman as he enters the spirit world and his fusion with his spirit-helper, a bird. It is notable that high levels of naturally-occurring $CO_2$, are found in the shaft, which might have induced altered states of consciousness if people stayed down there long enough.

Lewis-Williams believes that the use of cramped, inaccessible galleries and shafts, only capable of accommodating a few people at a time, was a deliberate choice. It suggests that only a few select individuals were permitted to enter the lower regions of Lascaux and other caves. Even areas where communal rituals took place, such as the Hall of the Bulls, might have been off limits to the majority of the population. Art and religion might thus have been born in a process of social stratification.

# 29: Who was Kennewick Man?

*Why does an 8,500 year old fossil skull look so unlike a present-day Native American?*

Kennewick Man was discovered in 1996 in the Columbia River, Kennewick, Washington State. The 8,500-year-old remains comprised a human skull and skeletal parts including the pelvis, in which a stone spear tip was embedded. They belonged to a man who had died aged between 40 and 55 years old, but he did not resemble a broad-headed, broad-faced Native American. He looked more like a European, with a long and narrow skull, a narrow face, and a jutting chin. A reconstruction of his face by forensic anthropologist James Chatters is said to bear a striking resemblance to the actor Sir Patrick Stewart, widely known for his role as Captain Jean-Luc Picard in *Star Trek: the Next Generation*. As many *Star Trek* episodes involved time-travel, there has inevitably been speculation that Kennewick Man actually *was* Picard, who had failed to return from one of his missions.

In fact, Kennewick Man's teeth suggest an Asian rather than European origin, and his skull features are similar to those of the Ainu people of Japan and indigenous people of the South Pacific. He seems to have led a tough life: aside from the spear injury, he had suffered many other injuries and bone fractures. On the other hand, he had eaten well: carbon and nitrogen isotope analysis of collagen extracted from his bones indicated a diet that had included seafood and salmon. Kennewick Man was not alone in his distinctive appearance: skulls of ancient Americans differ from those of present-day Native Americans up until around 5,000 years ago. These people are known as the Paleoindians, but who were they and why were they so unlike present-day Native Americans?

The most obvious possibility is that there were two successive migrations into the New World, with the Paleoindians arriving first and later being replaced by ancestors of modern Native Americans. The New World was the last habitable part of the globe to be settled by humans, but the number of migrations involved has been the subject of lengthy debate. Today, Alaska is separated from eastern Siberia by the Bering Strait, which is 55 km (18 miles) wide, but this has not always been the case. From 25,000 years ago until as recently as 10,000 years ago, sea levels were so low that the strait and parts of the adjoining Chukchi and Bering Seas became dry land. The result was a landmass stretching from the Verkhoyansk Range in eastern Siberia to the Mackenzie River in northwest Canada. Known as Beringia, this so-called 'land bridge' was 1,600 km (1,000 miles) from north to south and linked Asia to North America. The region was cold but free of ice, and was probably an open landscape covered with grasses and herbaceous tundra and steppe vegetation.

It is via the Beringia land bridge that humans are thought to have first reached the New World, although the process was not a simple migration from East Asia. Instead, a number of genetic studies have shown that the first Americans were descended from a population that lived in Central Asia. These include sequencing the genome of MA-1, a young boy whose remains were found at the 24,000-year-old site of Mal'ta in southern central Siberia. Results indicated that 14 to 38 percent of present-day Native American ancestry may be traced back to the ancient population to which he belonged. Notably, the Mal'ta boy showed no close affinity to present-day East Asians.

Modern humans learned to master the extreme conditions of the Russian Arctic as early as 45,000 years ago. Mammoth remains bearing injuries consistent with having been hunted were recovered near the Sopochnaya Karga (SK) meteorological station, at a latitude of fractionally below 72°N; and 30,000-year-old tools made from rhinoceros and mammoth ivory have been found at the Yana Rhinoceros Horn site at 71°N. The Yana River lies some 1,200 km (750 miles) west of the Bering Strait, although there is no unequivocal archaeological evidence for a human presence further east until much later.

Genetic studies suggest that a population subsequently became isolated in Beringia for between 7,000 to 15,000 years before they entered North America. During the Last Glacial Maximum the way onwards into North America was blocked by ice sheets, and arid wastelands barred the way back into Asia. Beringia itself remained habitable, although the population probably contracted slightly when the cold was at its worst. Eventually, as the last Ice Age neared its end, conditions improved and migrants were able to reach North America. The earliest archaeological evidence from Alaska is the 14,000-year-old site of Swan Point, but Monte Verde in southern Chile was inhabited at least 14,500 and possibly as long ago as 18,500 years ago. Consequently, the date of the first entry to North America must have been well before 14,000 years ago.

For a long time, it was believed that the first Americans belonged to the Clovis culture, which is named for Clovis, New Mexico, where distinctive leaf-shaped stone projectile points were first identified in the 1930s. The Clovis phenomenon was widespread, and sites are known across much of the United States, Mexico and Central America. However, recent work suggests that the earliest Clovis sites are no more than 13,250 years old, which is well after the arrival of the first migrants from Beringia. Despite being so widespread, the Clovis phenomenon was fairly short-lived and ended around 12,900 years ago. At this point, it broke up into a number of localized successor cultures, for example the Folsom Culture of New Mexico.

The 'Clovis First' viewpoint persisted for many decades, but since the 1970s, evidence of a pre-Clovis human presence in the New World has continued to accumulate. The sites of Buttermilk Creek (Texas), Manis (Washington State), and Paisley Cave (Oregon) predate Clovis by several centuries, as does Swan Point, and Monte Verde predates it by well over a millennium. The Clovis phenomenon corresponds to a period of favourable climatic conditions, and it probably represents an expansion of the descendants of the first migrants. It falls well within the Paleoindian period, before any supposed second migration.

In the 1980s, the American linguist Joseph Greenberg suggested that there had been three migrations into the New World, corresponding to each of the three language 'families' spoken by Native Americans: Amerind, Na-Dene and Aleut-Eskimo. The great majority of languages spoken by Native Americans are Amerind. The second group, Na-Dene, comprises languages spoken mainly in northwest Canada, Alaska and along the Pacific Coast; and Aleut-Eskimo is restricted to the Aleutian Islands and the Arctic. As Amerind is the most diverse family, Greenberg suggested that it corresponded to the earliest migration. It was followed by the Na-Dene, and finally the Aleut-Eskimo migrations.

Greenberg's conclusions were regarded as no more than tentative, but a 2012 genetic study suggested that they may be correct. It was found that most Native American populations are descended from a single ancestral population. However, Aleut-Eskimo speakers inherit almost half their ancestry from a second migratory group. Meanwhile, the Na-Dene-speaking Chipewyan from Canada inherit roughly one-tenth of their ancestry from a third migration. However, later work has produced contradictory results, with one study suggesting that the Amerind and Na-Dene were both part of the same initial migration.

What these studies do not show is any evidence for a population replacement around 5,000 years ago, and indeed they suggest that the bulk of Native Americans are descended from the original pioneers who entered the New World during the latter part of the last Ice Age. This conclusion has been reinforced by ancient DNA recovered from the remains of a young boy interred at a Clovis burial site in Montana and from those of an adolescent female found at a 13,000-year-old cave site in the Yucatan Peninsula, Mexico. Genome sequencing showed that the boy belonged to a population directly ancestral to many present-day Native Americans, and it was found that the female belonged to a mitochondrial haplogroup found only among present-day Native Americans. That her skull was typical of the Paleoindian form was a further indication of continuity between Paleoindians and present-day Native Americans.

If this is the case, then why does Kennewick Man look so unlike a Native American? One possibility is that the present Native American skull shape evolved from that of the Paleoindians as a result of changes in diet during the transition from hunter-gathering to farming between 8,000 and 2,000 years ago. The other possibility is that the skull data has simply been misinterpreted. For example, what is to be made of the Wizards Beach skull from Nevada? Although 9,200 years old, it falls comfortably in the range of present-day Native Americans. In order to address the problem, researchers applied statistical methods to a large number of skulls dating from the Late Pleistocene and Early Holocene, and present-day human skulls from Africa, Eurasia and the New World. The results suggested that when variations in shape were considered over a wide geographical range (such as from Australia to South America), or over a lengthy period of time (from the Late Pleistocene to the present day), the skulls formed a continuous spectrum of variation and could not be grouped into discrete categories. The same pattern of continuous variation was also seen when New World skulls were considered on their own. The supposed Paleoindian and Native American forms were shown to be no more than extremes at opposite ends of a continuum, and most of the New World examples fell well between the two extremes.

As for Kennewick Man himself, ownership of his remains has

generated almost as much controversy as his origins. The remains were found on land under the jurisdiction of the United States Army Corps of Engineers, and under US federal law, they may be claimed by any Native American tribe that can establish cultural affiliation. The Umatilla tribe have attempted to exercise this right in order to bury the remains according to tribal tradition. The US Army were happy to hand over the remains, but scientists hoping to study them were rather less enthusiastic. The remains were placed in the care of the Burke Museum, Seattle, while legal action dragged on. Eventually, in 2004, an appeal court ruled that the law protecting Native American human relics does not apply to anything as old as Kennewick Man. But the scientists' case was based on the perceived differences between Kennewick Man's skull and those of present-day Native Americans. Recently, however, ancient DNA was obtained from Kennewick Man and his genome sequenced. The results confirmed that he was indeed an ancestor of today's Native Americans, and the row has re-ignited.

# 30: No place like home

*The tendency of people to live in one place predates the first farming communities by ten thousand years.*

About 23,000 years ago, a group of six brushwood huts on the shores of the Sea of Galilee caught fire and were burned to the ground. We don't know whether the fire was an accident, or whether the huts were deliberately burned possibly to eliminate pests. The huts were subsequently rebuilt twice, but the settlement's days were numbered. Water levels in the lake were rising, and presently the site was submerged and sealed under a layer of silt and clay. The remains of the settlement were preserved below the waters until 2009, when a period of drought caused lake levels to fall, so revealing the site now known as Ohalo II.

During the Last Glacial Maximum, the Fertile Crescent, in common with other parts of the world, experienced a cold, dry climate. While much of the region became inhospitable, woodland and forest-steppe persisted in the Mediterranean coastal regions and in the northern Zagros, and it was in these parts that hunter-gatherers were able to live a reasonably comfortable life. The landscape was one of grasses, shrubs and flowers, and thinly-scattered trees. Plant foods were abundant, as was game including sheep, goat, aurochs, wild boar, gazelle and deer. The hunter-gatherer populations of the Levant during this period were termed Kebaran by British archaeologist Dorothy Garrod, following her 1931 excavations at Kebara Cave in Mount Carmel.

A number of Kebaran sites have since been excavated, but the most important is Ohalo II. This site, from which much of our understating of the period has come, was discovered by archaeologist Dani Nadel in 1989 when water levels temporarily dropped by several metres. The site was occupied around 23,000 years ago, at which time the Sea of Galilee formed the northern part of the much larger Lake Lisan ('tongue' in Arabic). Ohalo II covered an area of 2,000 sq. m. (21,500 sq. ft.), around 500 sq. m. (5,380 sq. ft.) of which has been excavated, and excavations revealed the six burnt huts. The Kebaran saw a shift in emphasis from big game to smaller animals, and the Ohalo II people hunted gazelle and deer, trapped hare and birds, and caught fish from the lake. From the preserved remains, no fewer than 142 different plant species have been identified, including emmer wheat, barley, brome and other small-grained grasses, acorns, almonds, pistachios, olives, legumes, raspberries, figs and grapes. These were collected from a range of habitats, including the nearby Mount Tabor.

Much information has been obtained from the remains of Brush Hut 1, a kidney-shaped structure arranged in a north-south direction with a floor space of 12 sq. m (130 sq. ft.). Brush Hut 1 was the largest and best preserved of the six huts. It was built with thick branches of tamarisk, willow and oak, which were then covered with brushwood, leaves and grass. Three successive floors of occupation have been identified, although the uppermost Floor I was only partially intact. Floor II exactly overlaid Floor III, suggesting that the hut had been rebuilt soon after the fire destroyed its predecessor.

Archaeologists examined the distribution and type of almost 60,000 seeds and fruits, and around 8,000 stone tools, chips and fragments from Floor II. From this, they were able to deduce that the use of domestic space inside the hut was consciously planned rather than haphazard, and that the activities of food preparation, tool-making and sleeping took place in different parts of the hut. In this respect, this humble brushwood dwelling was no different to a modern home.

In the northern part of the hut, a 40 cm (1 ft. 7 in.) long slab of basalt was embedded in the floor for use as a grinding stone and work surface. It was surrounded by scattered plant remains, suggesting that somebody had squatted by it while using it for food processing. The plants processed included cereal grains and plants with known medicinal properties, although there is no way of knowing if the latter were actually been used for this purpose. Other seed and fruit remains found on the hut floor probably came from building and roofing materials.

Near the entrance to the hut, flint-knapping debris was scattered in a pattern suggesting that two or three individuals sat facing the light from the door while they knapped stone tools. Just outside the entrance were found the remains of flowers which – barring the disputed Neanderthal floral tributes at Shanidar Cave – is the earliest-known use of flowers.

The use of space in the Floor III hut differed from that of its successor. Unlike Floor II, there was a hearth, located at the centre and surrounded by the seeds of grasses that had probably been used for bedding and for seating. The floor III space held almost 55,000 seeds and fruits, which were organised into four groups indicating separate food preparation locations around the central hearth. The groups included cereals, medicinal plants, and brome and other small-grained grasses used as staples.

Outside the huts were six open-air hearths and a group of burned stones covered with ash. The latter is thought to have been a crude oven and given the evidence for processing cereals with the grinding stone, it suggests that the Ohalo II people baked dough made from grain flour. The site also contains a single shallow grave holding the remains of a man aged between 35 to 40 years old. He was buried in a supine position, with hands crossed over his chest, legs flexed and heels touching the pelvis. Three stones were set under his head to support it, and a small gazelle bone was also placed near it. He had been suffering from severe physical disabilities including a chronic bone infection of his lower ribcage, and an atrophied upper arm resulting from a shoulder injury. He would have been unable to hunt or perform hard labour, suggesting that there was a social commitment to caring for sick and disabled members of the community.

There are three lines of evidence that suggest that Ohalo II was occupied for much of the year. Firstly, the differing ripening seasons of the grains and fruits harvested at the site suggests that it was occupied at least during spring and autumn. The second line of evidence is the patterns of growth of the teeth of gazelle remains found at the site, which were determined by examining acellular cementum. This is the bone-like tissue that anchoring tooth roots to the surrounding socket. It is formed in successive bands, with thicker bands forming during the wet season, and thinner bands during the dry season. Analysis of the outermost band can reveal the time of the year death occurred to within two months, and from this it was shown that the animals were hunted in winter and spring. Finally, based on their present-day migratory patterns, birds whose remains were found at the site were caught between September and November, and between February and April. From this data, it may be inferred that Ohalo II was not a temporary seasonal camp, and was used as a year-round base.

Ohalo II was still far too small to be described as a village, but it marks the beginning of an ever-increasing shift towards a sedentary lifestyle that would continue over the next ten millennia. The Kebaran culture and its successor, the Geometric Kebaran, persisted for around ten thousand years before the emergence of one of the most successful and widespread cultures of the late Ice Age – the Natufian. The Kebaran people were hunter-gatherers, not farmers. However, the establishment of sites that were in use throughout the year like Ohalo II was a critical step on the road to the world's first 'agricultural revolution' and a radically new way of life.

# 31: Prime suspect

*Were humans responsible for the Late Quaternary mass extinction?*

Between 50,000 and 10,000 years ago, the Earth experienced a mass extinction event which devastated the megafauna of the Pleistocene world. Australia and the New World were hardest hit, but no habitable continent remained unscathed. In all, around 180 large mammal species and many giant flightless birds went extinct, including mammoths, mastodons and giant deer with antlers spanning 3 m (10 ft.). The Late Quaternary extinction event was one of the largest extinction events since the demise of the dinosaurs, and significantly it was the first to occur since the appearance of *Homo sapiens*. Its timing coincides suspiciously with the dispersal of our species around the world.

The extinction was first recognised by early geologists towards the end of the eighteenth century and by the early nineteenth century, two possible causes were being proposed as possible causes for the extinctions – climate change and human activity. The latter became popular after 1860, and humanity has been prime suspect ever since. The 'overkill' hypothesis put forward by geoscientist Paul Martin proposes that humans rapidly hunted the megafauna into extinction, killing them faster than they could breed. Other theories that implicate human activity emphasise habitat destruction as a result of land clearance, and the introduction of invasive predatory species.

There is no doubt that human activity since the last century has led to a dangerous loss of biodiversity. Theories that implicate humans in the Late Quaternary extinction event are understandably popular with environmental campaigners, who see it as a harbinger of worse to come if humanity does not mend its ways. Against this, it is argued that we cannot extrapolate such losses back to the Late Pleistocene without further evidence, or without considering alternatives such as the constant climate change that characterised the Pleistocene. Nineteenth century climate change theories were based around either sudden catastrophic deep freeze or drought, but modern hypotheses are based around break-up or disappearance of habitats, reduction in local plant diversity upon which large herbivorous mammals rely, and disruptions to the delicate equilibrium between plant and animal species in complex habitats.

A third possibility, which has gained traction in recent years, is that 12,900 years ago, the Earth suffered multiple impacts and airbursts from an asteroid or comet that had previously broken up in space. Though far less severe than the impact thought to have brought about the extinction of the dinosaurs, it was still sufficient to trigger an 'impact winter' that brought about the extinctions. The time of supposed impact corresponds to a period of cooling known as the Younger Dryas, but sceptics point out that this was probably caused by meltwater from the icecaps cutting off the Gulf Stream as temperatures rose in the latter part of the last Ice Age.

Despite innumerable studies worldwide, there is to this day very little consensus on the cause of the extinctions, or indeed if there was a single cause. Studies have tended to focus on obtaining extinction dates for various species of megafauna by determining just when they disappear from the fossil record. Such studies have ranged in scope from tracking the extinction of single species in single regions to global chronologies of multi-species extinction dates versus arrival dates of modern humans. The main problem with these studies, even when backed up with advanced statistical methods, is the need to assume that absence of evidence equates to evidence of absence. Just because we have found no evidence that Species X existed past Date Y doesn't necessarily mean that it was extinct by then.

With this in mind, researchers have also followed other lines of enquiry, looking for 'proxies' or secondary indicators that can demonstrate the presence or absence of megafauna in a particular place at a particular time. Once such proxy that has been used in a number of studies is *Sporormiella*, a fungus which grows on the dung of large herbivores. It requires digestion by herbivores to complete its life cycle, and produces spores on their dung. The spores have been found in the dung of mammoths and other extinct megafauna. Consequently, their presence can be used to track ancient herbivore populations.

In one such study, carried out in the United States, researchers led by Jacquelyn Gill from the University of Wisconsin, Madison investigated *Sporormiella* spore levels in an 11.5 m (38 ft.) sediment core extracted from Appleman Lake in Indiana. At any time, rainfall will wash spores on dung excreted within the lake's watershed into the lake itself, so their levels in lake sediments will be an indicator of the local herbivore population at that time. It was found that *Sporormiella* spore levels were initially high, but began to decline 14,800 years ago, and fell to levels indicating the extinction of megafauna 13,700 years ago. This data suggests a decline culminating in local extinction of the megafauna, occurring over the course of 1,100 years. Last occurrence dates of fossil megafauna suggest that some species persisted in North America until at least as late as 11,400 years ago. Taking the two results together, the overall picture is one of a gradual decline over the course of 3,400 years rather than a sudden extinction event caused by an extraterrestrial impact or Paleoindian hunter-gatherer overkill. The start of the decline also predated the Clovis period by over 1,500 years and thus rules out the rapid spread of the Clovis culture being a factor in the extinctions. However, it did coincide roughly with the start of the Bølling-Allerød Interstadial, a warm period that began 14,700 years ago, suggesting a link to climate change.

The researchers then went on to consider tree pollen and charcoal data from the core sample, to investigate possible climate-induced changes in local vegetation that could have brought about the extinction. What they found was more or less the opposite of what might have been expected. There were no changes in the spruce-dominated forests until 13,700 years ago, which coincides with the disappearance of the local megafauna rather than the beginning of its decline. At that time, there was an increase in black ash, hop-hornbeam and ironwood, although spruce remained abundant.

The combination of these hardwood trees with spruce is not seen today and is known as a 'no-analogue plant community'. It had been thought that such communities arose through the impact of large herbivores on the landscape, but the results showed that the reverse was apparently true: the 'no-analogue' forests were a consequence of the extinction of the megafauna. The 'no-analogue' forests persisted until 11,900 years ago, eventually giving way to large numbers of pine and then oak as Holocene deciduous forests became established in the region. Charcoal levels are a reliable indicator of fires and show an increase in the 'fire regime' after the megafauna disappeared. Here, the implication is that increases in the vegetation previously consumed by the megafauna led to a corresponding increase in the frequency of natural fires.

The study found that there were clear links between climate change, the local extinction of the megafauna, and changes in the vegetation, but it refuted 'overkill', climate-induced habitat changes and extraterrestrial impacts as causes. It left unresolved the climatic versus human causation debate, but noted evidence for mammoth butchery in Wisconsin from 14,800 to 14,100 years ago, coincident in time with the decline of the megafauna at Appleman Lake. The study was publicised as supporting the human causation theory, but offered only modest circumstantial evidence in its favour.

A team led by biologist Susan Rule obtained comparable results in Australia. Again, the researchers used *Sporormiella* spore levels as a proxy for megafauna, along with pollen and charcoal levels to reconstruct vegetation, fires and climate change. The area under consideration was Lynch's Crater, a low-relief crater in Queensland. The crater once held a lake, but its interior is now a swamp fed by a stream that exits the crater to form a tributary of the North Johnstone River. Two core samples were analysed, spanning the periods from 130,000 to 24,000 years ago, and from 54,000 to 3,000 years ago. These dates span the whole of the Late Pleistocene, and were intended to document changes in both vegetation and *Sporormiella* spore levels as the climate fluctuated.

During arid periods, rainforest gave way to dry country vegetation, including eucalyptus and acacia. By 55,000 years ago, the lake had largely dried up to become a swamp and high *Sporormiella* spore counts suggest that megafauna were present on or around the swamp. But by 41,000 years ago, the *Sporormiella* counts had fallen to near zero, implying that the megafauna had gone extinct. This date is reasonably close to one obtained in an earlier continent-wide survey that had proposed a near-simultaneous extinction event across the whole of Australia 46,000 years ago.

The *Sporormiella* decline was followed roughly 100 years later by an increase in charcoal levels, and over the next 1,500 years rainforest was again replaced by grasses, eucalyptus and acacia – except unlike the earlier advances in dry country vegetation it was claimed that there was no link to climate change. Another difference is that the earlier vegetation changes had not been accompanied by *Sporormiella* declines. As with the findings of American study, extinction of megafauna preceded vegetation changes, and it was likewise suggested that once the megafauna were gone, reduced consumption of vegetation led to an increase in natural fires. These in turn led to the replacement of the fire-sensitive rainforest with more fire-tolerant grasses and vegetation.

Whereas the American researchers had largely hedged their bets as to the cause of the extinctions, their Australian counterparts came down firmly on the side of human causation. However, their conclusions were criticised by archaeologist Judith Field, who noted that contrary to what was claimed the period under consideration was one of climatic instability, and that there is evidence for increased aridity in Australia after 45,000 years ago. Field also questioned the assumption that the megafauna were present in such large numbers that their sudden disappearance would trigger the vegetation changes described in the report.

The argument as to the global cause of the extinctions continues unabated. Two studies published just weeks apart in 2015 reached quite differing conclusions. The first, published by an Australian team, found that the extinctions had clustered around abrupt warm climatic episodes known as Dansgaard-Oeschger events, and suggested that human impact was no more than an exacerbating factor. The second study, conducted at the University of Exeter, linked the extinctions to the dispersal of modern humans around the world, with climate change as only a secondary factor. Overall, it is very hard to make a convincing case for either climate change or human predation being solely responsible for the Late Quaternary extinctions on a worldwide basis, and it is likely that different factors operated in different places and at different times.

Irrespective of the role humans played in the extinctions, their subsequent activities from the early Holocene onwards has meant that a return to the biodiversity of the Pleistocene is impossible. Throughout the Pleistocene, world-wide human populations were undoubtedly fairly low, and such population growth that did occur was probably due to the colonisation of previously uninhabited regions. Humans at this point were still just one of many species of large mammal inhabiting the Earth, subject to the same constraints on population growth as other species. In 8000 BC, the world population is estimated to have been around five million, but by the start of the Christian era it had increased to around 300 million. These figures represent a 60-fold increase in 8,000 years, or a doubling every 1,350 years. A population of large mammals can only sustain such a growth rate if food is abundant and natural enemies few. In the case of humans, food was now being produced by agriculture rather than being obtained by hunter-gathering, and humans have no natural enemies save their own kind. Surprisingly, this growth rate was not sustained, and by AD 1650 the world population had reached just 500 million. The conventional explanation for this slowdown is the devastating bubonic plague pandemics that repeatedly swept Eurasia during this period.

However, this may not be the real explanation. All living things are ultimately dependent on the Sun for energy and growth, either directly in the case of photosynthesising plants, or indirectly in the case of animals. In both cases, what is happening is that solar energy is being converted into biomass, meaning that Earth's total biomass is limited by the amount of energy it receives from the Sun. Before any extinction, the available solar energy is shared between many large species. If the bulk of these species are wiped out, then an energy surplus will be created. Extinctions such as that of the dinosaurs were followed by explosions in biodiversity as new species evolved to exploit this surplus, but the aftermath of the Late Quaternary extinction saw a very different outcome.

After the Ice Age, agriculture emerged in many parts of the world, enabling far larger human populations to be supported than were sustainable by hunter-gathering. Instead of remaining available for a reestablishment of large mammal biodiversity, the solar energy surplus was taken up by humans to raise crops and livestock. The Earth's large animal biomass regained pre-crash levels just before the Industrial Revolution, but instead of a plurality of species it was dominated by humans and the large mammals raised by humans for food. The same energetic constraints nevertheless applied, and it is likely that the population slowdown occurred as the total human and food animal biomass approached the glass ceiling that had hitherto limited the size of Earth's megafauna population.

Biologist Anthony Barnosky has suggested that the addition of fossil fuels to the global energy budget enabled the human population to break through the glass ceiling. The use of fossil fuels for heating goes back thousands of years, but their use for mechanical power had to await the invention of the steam engine. Without mechanical power, the food production and distribution that supports current global populations would not be possible. If Barnosky is correct, a global population more than an order of magnitude greater than Earth's natural carrying capacity is now being supported by a non-renewable resource. Even without the effects of global warming caused by $CO_2$ emissions, this is a distinctly worrying prospect.

# 32: The Radiocarbon Revolution

*Radiocarbon dating forced archaeologists to revise their timescales of human prehistory not once but twice.*

The need for an archaeologist to determine the age of prehistoric material is fairly obvious, but until the invention of radiocarbon dating there was no clear-cut way to do so. Archaeologists relied on the written records of ancient Mesopotamia and Egypt for a chronology of pre-literate Europe. Artefacts traded between the literate and pre-literate world could be dated from the written records of the former, but for the most part it was necessary to make the assumption that elements of Mesopotamian and Egyptian culture had 'diffused' westwards across Europe via the Aegean cultures of Crete and Mycenae. This principle was known as *Ex Oriente Lux* ('Light from the East'), and it was at the forefront of archaeological thinking for decades. For example, it was generally accepted that the megalithic tombs of Western Europe had been inspired by the pyramids of ancient Egypt and the *tholos* tombs of Minoan Crete. Similarly, it was thought that Stonehenge could not have been built without Mycenaean know-know, and must therefore date to no earlier than 1550 BC. Not only was the premise of uncultured Europeans dubious, but such methods of dating still ultimately relied on written records, which did not exist anywhere in the world until after 3500 BC.

Before the middle of the last century, it is unlikely that many archaeologists would have thought of a solution to their dating problems that lay in the realms of nuclear physics. At that time, the physical sciences were not a field with which they were expected to be familiar. Nevertheless, the announcement of the first radiocarbon dates in 1949 caused great excitement in the archaeological community. While few understood the underlying science, the possibilities were obvious. It was only necessary to recover a small quantity of organic material from any site, and its age could be determined.

Radiocarbon dating is actually only one of a number of dating techniques that rely on the decay of radioactive materials. Known generally as radiometric dating, all share the concept that radioactive material present in a sample can be used as a 'clock' to determine its age. The material decays at a known rate and by measuring the amount still present in the sample, its age can be calculated. The decay rate of a radioactive element is usually quoted as the 'half-life', i.e. the time it will take half of the atoms present in a sample to decay. Radiometric dating came into use during the early twentieth century, only about a decade after researchers had demonstrated the existence of radioactive decay. The problem was that early methods relied on elements such as uranium, which has very long half-life. They gave good results for rocks that were millions or even billions of years old, but could not be used to date anything more recent. While of great value to geologists, these methods were practically useless to archaeologists.

Radiocarbon ($^{14}C$) is an unstable isotope of carbon that decays to nitrogen with a half-life of just 5,730 years, making it ideal for dating artefacts on an archaeological timescale. Given that this is an infinitesimally short time in comparison to the age of the Earth, it might be expected for the terrestrial supply to have long since decayed. In fact, radiocarbon is constantly being produced by the action of cosmic rays upon nitrogen in the upper atmosphere, and thus can be found in small proportions in atmospheric carbon dioxide ($CO_2$).

All living things absorb carbon: plants by photosynthesis of atmospheric carbon dioxide, and animals by eating plants or other animals. Consequently, all living tissues contain small amounts of radiocarbon. Once a plant or animal dies, it ceases to absorb fresh carbon, and the proportion of radiocarbon in its tissues begins to fall in comparison to that of living organisms. By measuring the proportion of radiocarbon still present, the time since death occurred can be established. The technique was invented by the American chemist Willard Libby and it earned him the Nobel Prize for Chemistry in 1960.

Radiocarbon dating can only be used for human, animal or plant remains – the ages of stone tools and other inorganic artefacts can only be inferred if organic material can be recovered from the same archaeological context. Another drawback is that it is only useful for artefacts and remains that are no more than 50,000 years old. Beyond that age, the quantity of radiocarbon remaining is too small to be measured, even with modern techniques such as accelerator mass spectrometry (AMS). Despite these limitations, radiocarbon dating was eagerly embraced by archaeologists.

Not everybody was happy, though. In 1954, before many radiocarbon dates were available, British archaeologist Stuart Piggott published *The Neolithic Cultures of the British Isles*, which he hoped would become the standard work on the subject. He set the beginning of the British Neolithic to around 2000 BC, but soon afterwards much earlier radiocarbon dates began to show up. His reaction was to dismiss a date of 2600 BC for the Late Neolithic site of Durrington Walls as 'archaeologically unacceptable'. Less contentious was a date of 1720 BC for Stonehenge, obtained in 1959 from an antler pick. It was on the early side, but given the uncertainties of measurement, it was not overly problematic. As more and more radiocarbon dates came in, a picture began to emerge of a revised timeline of later European prehistory that could be just about accommodated within the traditional diffusionist framework. At the same time, radiocarbon dating was able to establish a chronology for events that predated the invention of writing. Agriculture in Southwest Asia was believed to have originated around 4500 BC, but this date was little more than guesswork. Radiocarbon dating established that the beginning of the Southwest Asian Neolithic lay thousands of years before that date. In little over a decade, a radiocarbon revolution had transformed the study of prehistory.

By the early 1960s, the veracity of radiocarbon dates was accepted by nearly all archaeologists – but then came a second shock. The problem this time arose from dendrochronology, a method of dating based on the analysis of tree-rings. As is well known, the annual growth of trees results in a series of tree-rings from which the age of a tree can be determined, often to the exact calendar year. A crucial point is that in addition, the density and thickness of each ring provides a permanent record of the climatic conditions under which it grew. By matching tree-ring patterns in ancient timber to core samples from living trees, the age of the former can be determined. Once accurately dated, tree-ring patterns in the ancient timber can be matched to those of even older timber, which in turn can be used to date material that is older still. In this way, tree-ring chronologies can be built up that in many cases go back thousands of years.

By itself, this was not a problem, but in the mid-1960s researchers used radiocarbon dating to obtain dates for wood from the bristlecone pine, a remarkably long-lived species of coniferous tree found in mountainous regions of the Southwestern United States. They found that there were significant discrepancies between these dates and those obtained by dendrochronology. From 1200 BC, radiocarbon dates were increasingly underestimating the age of samples, and by 4000 BC the discrepancy was amounting to as much as 800 years. It turned out that one of Libby's key assumptions was wrong. He believed that the cosmic ray flux that produces radiocarbon in the upper atmosphere remains constant, and that the percentage of radiocarbon in a living organism thousands of years ago was no different to that of today. In fact, we now know that the cosmic ray flux varies considerably over time. The tree-ring studies showed that 6,000 years ago, the concentration of radiocarbon in the atmosphere was much higher than it is today and samples from that period have more radiocarbon than Libby had believed. Unless this extra radiocarbon is taken into account, a sample from this period will appear to be younger than it actually is.

The solution was to use dendrochronology to calibrate the radiocarbon dates. Charts known as calibration curves are based on samples with ages that can be measured by independent means. Dendrochronology now goes back almost 14,000 years, but modern calibration curves also use data obtained from stalagmites and stalactites, coral, and microscopic shelled marine creatures known as foraminifera. The INTCAL series of calibration curves now extend across the whole usable range of radiocarbon dating, but they are constantly being refined. Accordingly, dates are often left uncalibrated in scientific literature and quoted as radiocarbon years before present (BP), or YBP uncalibrated. 'Present' is taken to be 1950, and readers can obtain calibrated dates using calibration curves compiled long after an article was published.

The first calibration curves appeared in 1967, and the consequences were far reaching. A second radiocarbon revolution followed as Stonehenge was found to be much older than the Mycenaean civilisation, and other elements of European culture were also shown to predate their supposed antecedents. Far from being uncivilised bumpkins, the Europeans could claim a long list of independent achievements that their supposedly more advanced cousins to the East would not have scoffed at. *Ex Oriente Lux* and diffusion were dead and buried, and archaeologists scrambled to come up new paradigms with which to make sense of our prehistoric past.

# 33: First farmers

*Agriculture brought about a revolutionary transformation of human societies – but how and why did it start?*

Humans are neither the only nor the first species learn how to produce food as opposed to hunt or forage. Ants were raising crops in the form of fungus and herding aphid 'cattle' tens of millions before humans learned the trick. Archaic humans obtained food by hunting and gathering for nearly three million years and even *Homo sapiens* got by without agriculture until the end of the last Ice Age.

The transition from hunter-gathering to agriculture was characterised by the Australian archaeologist V. Gordon Childe as the 'Neolithic Revolution'. When introduced in 1865 by the Victorian archaeologist Sir John Lubbock, the term 'Neolithic' ('New Stone Age') simply referred to the polished stone tools that appeared in the later stages of the Stone Age, but Childe redefined it as a revolutionary economic phenomenon analogous to the Industrial Revolution. Producing as opposed to collecting food requires far less land to support the same number of people. The result was that populations grew and more complex societies emerged. Agriculture has sustained the last 10,000 years of human population growth, and without it the rise of civilisation as we know it would not have been possible.

The transition did not happen everywhere at once, emerging in only a few parts of the world before spreading out at varying speeds from these primary centres. Between 9600 and 2000 BC, agriculture arose independently in Southwest Asia, China, the Highlands of New Guinea, the Andes, Mesoamerica, the Eastern Woodlands of the United States, and possibly one or two other places. Although the specifics differed, these developments all involved gradually assembling a 'package' of domesticated crops and/or animals. In Southwest Asia, for example, the package comprised sheep, goats, cattle, pigs, wheat, barley and legumes (peas, lentils, etc.). This could only happen if there were plant and animal species suitable for domestication.

Domesticated species are raised in a human-managed environment and have often undergone biological change in comparison to their wild counterparts. These changes make them more useful to humans, but in some cases, as with many domesticated crops, the domesticated form is incapable of reproducing without human intervention. The best-known example of biological change is that of the cereals, which include wheat, barley, millet, sorghum, rice and maize. Ears of wild cereals are held together by small, brittle structures known as rachis that shatter when ripe, so that the grains can disperse. Unless wild cereals are harvested before they fully ripen, much of the grain will be lost as sickle reaping or uprooting by hand causes the rachis to shatter. This does not happen with domesticated cereals, because the rachis are toughened and the ears remains intact until harvested.

It is not difficult to see how modern selective breeding and genetic modification could rapidly produce non-shattering varieties, but how were cereals domesticated by Neolithic farmers? Could they have known about selective breeding? Possibly, but it is thought more likely that the process was unintentional, at least in the early stages. Plants with non-shattering rachis occur in the wild from time to time as a result of genetic mutations and although incapable of reproducing in the wild, they would have been more likely to be successfully harvested by early farmers than ordinary plants. Provided they were cultivating wild cereals as opposed to simply harvesting them from wild stands, farmers would have thus been unintentionally selecting for non-shattering varieties. Over successive cycles of harvesting and sewing, seed stock held for replanting would have become progressively enriched with non-shattering varieties until the wild, shattering variety disappeared altogether.

In 1990, archaeologist Gordon Hillman and botanist Stuart Davies set out to demonstrate that by using harvesting methods available to early farmers, wild wheat and barley could have been domesticated within a few centuries, or possibly even decades. They considered a range of harvesting methods likely to have been used by early cereal cultivators but found the only method that would lead to domestication was to use sickles or uprooting to harvest the crop, and to harvest before it had fully ripened. Beating or shaking ears of grain into collecting baskets would favour the collection of the shattering variety, and in any case would only be effective for harvesting a fully-ripened crop.

However, it was entirely possible that some early farmers might have adopted harvesting methods that did not lead to domestication. Even where they did, the earliest presence of domesticated crops in the archaeological record would not identify the point at which hunter-gatherers began crop management practices, as these might have begun much earlier. Fortunately, there are three other strong archaeological indicators of crop management. These are: the presence of seeds in quantities greater than could have been harvested from local stands of wild cereals; the presence of the seeds of commonly-occurring weeds mixed in with the grain; and evidence of storage facilities.

Animal domestication probably involved a greater element of human selection than did plant domestication. Early pastoral herders might have bred from smaller and more docile animals, so one possible indicator of domestication is a reduction in size of herded animals in comparison to their wild counterparts. Unfortunately, the rule does not always hold good. Herders tend to cull young males but keep females alive until they have passed their reproductive peak. Since females are usually smaller than males, this can give the illusion that the domesticated animals are smaller. A more reliable approach is to look for archaeological assemblages of animal remains that are dominated by young males and older females.

The earliest 'experiments' with agriculture are now known to have occurred during a period known as the Epipalaeolithic, which preceded the Neolithic and spanned the latter part of the last Ice Age. Following the Last Glacial Maximum, global climates steadily warmed. The Natufian culture emerged in the Levant around 12,900 BC, slightly before the upturn, but as conditions improved they flourished. The Early Natufian period saw the appearance of village communities living in circular, semi-subterranean houses in the woodlands of the Mediterranean coast and Jordan Valley, where there were abundant stands of wild cereals. These were harvested using sickles, as has been implied from the tell-tale presence of sickle gloss on microliths used as hafted elements in sickles. Sickle gloss is a polish that occurs when a blade is regularly used to cut plant stems, and it is produced by silica present in these stems. Experiments using flint blades have shown that a smoother, brighter gloss develops when sickles are used to harvest semi-ripe cereals. This gloss is similar to that seen on Natufian microliths, suggesting that they harvested their cereals before they had fully ripened and before the rachis could shatter.

The Natufians did not initially domesticate the wild cereals that they harvested. Grain harvested when semi-ripe is still viable, and enough will fall to the ground during harvesting to re-seed a stand of wild cereal. Research has shown that within three years of harvesting, a wild stand will grow back to its original density. Evidently this was sufficient for the Natufians' needs and there was no need to sow fields with their own seed stock. Thus the process leading to domestication was not set in motion.

But around 10,900 BC, the Earth was plunged into renewed cold and aridity. The Younger Dryas was the final cold period of the last Ice Age, and it brought over a millennium of drought. The woodlands and cereals on which the Natufians relied retreated, and many of them abandoned village living and returned to a more mobile lifestyle. At the site of Abu Hureyra in Syria, the surrounding landscape became an arid and almost treeless steppe, and availability of wild foods declined rapidly. Rather than abandon the settlement, the villagers struggled to keep it viable as woodland fruits, then lentils, and then wheat and rye disappeared. Eventually, the villagers began to cultivate wild wheat and rye. Long after these cereals had ceased to be available in the wild, they persisted in reduced quantities in the archaeological record of Abu Hureyra. They were accompanied by weeds of types normally found on arable land, which as noted above is a clear indicator of cultivation practices. By 10,700 BC, these practices had resulted in the appearance of domesticated rye, and other crops soon followed. Unfortunately for the villagers, even domesticated crops could not support Abu Hureyra through the continuing drought. Eventually, the village was abandoned and the domesticated rye, unable to reproduce without human intervention, died out. Rye never became a major part of the agricultural package that later emerged in Southwest Asia. In comparison to wheat, rice, maize and barley, rye remains a relatively minor agricultural crop to this day.

Curiously, as many Natufian groups were forced to abandon village life, in the foothills of the Taurus and Zagros mountains groups were establishing villages for the first time. Hallan Çemi Tepesi is a Late Epipaleolithic village in southeastern Turkey where there is evidence that villagers kept herds of pigs. Analysis of pig remains from the site suggest that fewer than a third of the animals reached an age of three years old, which is a similar figure to that from sites where domesticated pig remains have been found. It was also found that the pigs' molar teeth were mid-way in size between those of wild and domesticated pigs. Such a reduction is regarded as a sign that pigs are in the early stages of domestication.

These early experiments with agriculture were only a foretaste of what was to come. Eventually, around 9600 BC, the Younger Dryas came to an abrupt end. Temperatures rose between 5 and 10 degrees Celsius in less than a decade, and in centuries that followed they carried on rising. The Holocene climate was not only warm and wet; it was also very stable, without the rapid oscillations between warm and glacial conditions that characterised the Late Pleistocene. It was these unstable conditions that had previously made agriculture all but impossible. There is archaeological evidence that within a few hundred years, agricultural practices had become widespread.

The early Neolithic in Southwest Asia was characterised by an absence of pottery. This was first noted by British archaeologist Kathleen Kenyon in the 1950s, when she excavated the Neolithic layers of the ancient site of Jericho. The lack of pottery was a surprise and refuted V. Gordon Childe's view that it was a prerequisite for agriculture. Kenyon divided the early Neolithic into a Pre-Pottery Neolithic A (PPNA) and a Pre-Pottery Neolithic B (PPNB), which are thought to have run from 9600 to 8500 BC and from 8500 to 6500 BC respectively. Both crops and animals were domesticated during the PPNA, but agriculture was only a component of an economy that still entailed a degree of hunting. A fully-fledged mixed-farming economy did not emerge until the PPNB. PPNA settlements were larger than their Natufian predecessors, although the houses were very similar. However, the PPNB saw a shift to the multi-roomed rectangular constructions that have largely characterised human dwellings ever since. PPNB houses were typically two-storeyed, with the lower storey used as a storage area and the upper storey as main living-quarters.

At the PPNA sites of Gilgal and Netiv Hagdud in the Jordan Valley, several hundred thousand grains of barley and oats have been found. Although not domesticated, it is apparent that they were being cultivated. It would not have been possible to harvest cereals in such large quantities as local stands would have been exhausted within a few years. At Jerf el-Ahmar in Syria, wheat and rye remains have been found associated with the remains of weeds commonly associated with agriculture. Again, these cereals were not domesticated, but they must have been under cultivation.

At the site of Dhra', which lies to the south of the Dead Sea, excavations have revealed the remains of at least four purpose-built communal granaries. Dating from around 9300 BC, the granaries are located between residential buildings. The latter were also used for food-processing, with grindstones set into the floors. The granaries are the first large, dedicated food-storage facilities known anywhere in the world. They were circular, about 3 m (10 ft.) across, built with dried mud walls, and some also had outer retaining walls of stone. Although no roofing materials have been found, they were probably topped with a flat roof of wood, reeds and dried mud for protection against rain. Inside was wooden sloping floor, supported above the ground by stone pillars to aid air circulation and to keep away insects, rats and mice. The slope aided the runoff of any rainwater that penetrated the roofing. Grain was probably stored in baskets, stacked upon the floor.

From around 8500 to 6500 BC, domesticated forms of barley, lentils, peas, chickpeas, bitter vetch, and flax spread throughout Southwest Asia, along with domesticated sheep, goats, cattle and pigs. Though it was assembled in a rather piecemeal and haphazard manner, the 'agricultural package' that finally emerged was potent and adaptable, and it enabled farming to spread rapidly to Europe, Central Asia, the Indian subcontinent, and North Africa.

But why did agriculture start at all? That might seem a strange question given its apparent advantages and indeed the view that it started for no other reason than it was 'a good idea' was popular with Victorian scholars and remained so until well into the last century. It was finally challenged by Canadian anthropologist Richard Lee, who showed that present-day hunter-gatherers in the Kalahari Desert have very little trouble in finding enough to eat and that foraging was actually less time-consuming than farming. Later work suggested that the adoption of agriculture was accompanied by a decline in health and life expectancy. Early farmers faced increased incidence of anaemia, bone disease, tuberculosis, leprosy and malnutrition. Living in close proximity to livestock exposed farmers to smallpox, influenza, tuberculosis, malaria, bubonic plague, measles and cholera, all of which crossed the species barrier from farm animals to humans. In the crowded, unsanitary conditions of early farming settlements, these diseases flourished. Diet was generally poorer than that of hunter-gatherers, and there was a dramatic impact on adult stature. In Greece and Turkey, at the end of the Pleistocene, men averaged 1.78 m (5 ft. 10 in.) and women 1.68 m (5 ft. 6 in.) in height, but with the coming of agriculture, these figures dropped sharply. By 4000 BC men were averaging 1.60 m (5 ft. 3 in.) and women 1.55 m (5 ft. 1 in.). Not until classical times did average height begin to increase, but it has still not reached hunter-gatherer levels.

With these issues in mind, anthropologists considered the possibility that the shift to agriculture might have been driven by population pressures. The improving climate conditions towards the end of Pleistocene resulted in population growth, which in turn led to a shift in diet from large game to more readily available small game, seafood and cereals. Increasingly crowded into smaller territories by their neighbours, hunter-gatherer groups adopted a sedentary lifestyle, leading to further population increases. Women living in nomadic groups must space out birth intervals to four years or more, because a mother can carry only one infant or slow toddler when a group moves camp; but this is not an issue for women living in sedentary communities. Eventually, people were forced to cultivate cereals, simply to feed the growing numbers. Animal domestication soon followed as game animals declined in numbers. Another factor might have been risk management. Early Holocene climates were never completely stable and periods of plenty might have been punctuated by mild downturns in the climate. Such periodic fluctuations in food supplies might have led to early experiments with agriculture.

Other theories abound, including the 'competitive feasting' model proposed by Canadian archaeologist Brian Hayden, who suggests that among larger, more complex hunter-gatherer groups, one way to maintain prestige was to stage an extravagant feast. This would only be possible among sedentary communities living in relatively rich environments, where the necessary food surpluses could be acquired and stored.

There is no overall consensus on how and why agriculture arose. It is unlikely that the same explanations were applicable to each and every case, although it is likely that the emergence of more sedentary communities was an important factor. Regardless of how and why it started, agriculture would go on to serve as the economic foundation upon which the modern world would be built.

# 34: First came the temple

*A spectacular complex of stone circles, erected thousands of years before Stonehenge.*

Standing on the limestone ridge of Göbekli Tepe ('Potbelly Hill') near the city of Şanlıurfa in southeastern Turkey is a remarkable complex of monumental dry-stone walled enclosures. Each surrounds a pair of T-shaped limestone monoliths, carved with bas-reliefs of animals. Up to twelve smaller T-shaped pillars are set into each wall, often linked to one another by stone benches. Four such enclosures have so far been excavated, but geomagnetic surveys have indicated that at least twenty exist. The 11,000-year-old complex predates Stonehenge by almost seven millennia, and is thought to be the world's oldest temple.

The site was noted by a survey team in 1963, but it was largely ignored until 1994 when it came to the attention of German archaeologist Klaus Schmidt. Believing it to be a Neolithic site, he began excavating there the following year and continued his work there up until his death in 2014. At the lowest level of the site, Layer III, Schmidt discovered the pillared enclosures, which are circular or oval in shape, and sunken into the ground. The pillars range in height from 3 to 5 m (10 to 16 ft.) and weigh up to 10 tonnes. They were quarried from limestone plateaus close to the site, where a number of incomplete pillars were left *in situ*. One of these weighs over 50 tonnes, larger than any of the finished pillars so far excavated. Many of the pillars are carved with bas-reliefs of animals, including snakes, wild boar, foxes, lions, aurochs, wild sheep, gazelle, onager, birds, various insects, spiders, and scorpions. The images are often life-sized, and semi-naturalistic in style. Some pillars exhibit pairs of human arms and hands, which might represent stylised anthropomorphic beings although it is not clear whether they represent gods, shamans, ancestors, or possibly even demons. There are also a number of mysterious abstract symbols that have been interpreted as pictograms.

Pictograms are graphic symbols used to convey information. They are widely used in present-day road and other public signage to denote traffic lights, pedestrian crossings, speed cameras, etc. Often they depict a physical object, though they can be entirely abstract as, for example the 'Radiation Hazard' trefoil symbol. They can also combine pictorial and abstract motifs; for example the use of a circle containing an image struck out with a diagonal bar to denote interdiction. Pictograms formed the basis of the earliest writing systems before later usage extended them into the logographic systems of ancient Mesopotamia, Egypt and China. If the Göbekli Tepe symbols were indeed pictograms, then the origins of writing may go back into the early Neolithic, thousands of years before the appearance of cuneiform and hieroglyphic script.

No evidence of any form of dwellings have been found at the site and there is little doubt that Göbekli Tepe was a ritual centre. Unlike Stonehenge, the PPNA people who built Göbekli Tepe lacked a mixed farming economy, refuting the view that large projects could only be realised by fully-established farming communities. *"First came the temple, then the city"*, as Schmidt put it. How are we to interpret this temple?

One possibility is the site was used by a number of tribes or clans and the animals depicted in the various enclosures are the totemic emblems of these various groups. Each would travel to the site to perform rituals in its own particular enclosure, although it is likely that all the groups shared a common underlying belief system. It is possible that animals depicted in each enclosure could provide clues as to the origins of particular groups. For example, wild boar depiction seen in one of the four excavated enclosures suggests a group originating from the north, where pigs account for up to 40 percent of the animal remains found at PPNA sites. Another has a combinations of wild boar, aurochs and cranes. This suggests a junction of steppe with river valley; conditions which occur along many water courses in the Euphrates and Tigris region. Another possibility is that the site was associated with shamanistic practices, as has been suggested for the painted caves of Upper Palaeolithic Europe. The totemic and shamanistic explanations are not necessarily mutually exclusive.

However, there are important differences between the Upper Palaeolithic cave paintings and Göbekli Tepe. Whereas the cave paintings were the works of a few talented artists, a project on the scale of Göbekli Tepe would have required large numbers of labourers and craftsmen. In addition to coordinating their activities, there would have been significant logistical problem of providing food, water and shelter for all these people.

Could such an undertaking would have been carried out by a few shamans and their communities, none of which were even fully-fledged agriculturists? The answer, on the face of it, seems to be 'no'. It is difficult to believe that the monument was not constructed by a hierarchical, stratified society, with powerful rulers. The shamans might have had more in common with priests. The link between rulers and religion, so prevalent in later times, might have already started to take shape. However, there is an element of doubt. It has long been assumed that only powerful chiefdoms would have had the resources to carry out major projects such as Stonehenge, but this view has been challenged. It has been suggested that hierarchical societies were not a precondition for complex undertakings, and that people regarded working on such projects as ritual acts that formed part of their social customs and traditions.

Eventually, around 8000 BC, the Layer III enclosures at Göbekli Tepe complex were filled in and buried with debris. Animal remains and stone artefacts mixed in with the soil suggest that the filling material came from a typical Late PPNA settlement refuse dump. The actual settlement has not yet been found, but the amount of debris involved suggests that it could not have been very far away. Subsequently, a far less impressive Layer II complex was constructed over the first, comprising rectangular pits with smaller pillars, averaging about 1.5 m (5 ft.) in height.

Just why was original complex filled in and replaced? A possible clue comes from the site of Nevali Çori, 30 km (18 miles) away. The site has lain under water since the construction of the Atatürk Dam across the Euphrates, but it was extensively excavated before it was flooded. It was first occupied at the start of the PPNB around 8500 BC and occupation continued through three phases until 7600 BC. The settlement comprised 29 houses and a 'cult building' where rituals were practiced. The 'cult building' dates to the site's second and third phases. It was approximately square, measuring 13.9 by 13.5 m (45 ft. 7 in. by 45 ft. 4 in.), and was accessed by two downward steps. A stone bench ran all the way around the interior, broken by pillars similar to those at Göbekli Tepe and again surrounding a central pair, although they resembled the Hebrew letter ד (daleth) rather than the letter T. It seems very likely that there was a connection between the two sites.

The houses at Nevali Çori were rectangular multi-roomed and two-storeyed, rather than the circular and single-roomed dwellings that had characterised the PPNA. The new architecture of the PPNB is thought to reflect a shift from the community to the household as the basic economic unit. Increased settlement sizes led a greater need for privacy and a growing emphasis on personal goods and ownership. At the same time, communal granaries gave way to dedicated storage areas within individual houses. This significant shift in social systems would almost certainly have been reflected in belief systems, and this could be the explanation for the rebuilding of the Göbekli Tepe temple complex. In Sumerian times, it was believed that temples were residence of the gods, and Sumerian temples were built to the same basic plan as domestic residences. The implication is that this belief had a Neolithic origin and that the change in architectural practice between the PPNA and PPNB necessitated rebuilding the temple complex in a rectangular style.

# 35: Unlikely partners

*The domestication of the world's most popular and at the same time unlikely pet.*

Of all the relationships humans have formed with animals, the most unlikely is that with cats. Geneticists have shown that the domestic cat (*Felis silvestris catus*) is descended from the Near Eastern Wildcat (*Felis silvestris lybica*), a subspecies of the widely-distributed Old World Wildcat. Unlike every other species domesticated by humans, the Old World Wildcat is a solitary rather than a herd animal. In a herd, some animals are dominant, but most are subordinate. Neolithic farmers exploited the dominance hierarchy of herd animals so that they transferred their submissive behaviours to humans – but this was not possible with cats.

Another no-no is that cats are territorial, and they are far more likely to become attached to places than to people. Furthermore, they are obligate carnivores, meaning that they have difficulty digesting anything other than proteins. Unlike horses, cattle or sheep, you cannot feed a cat hay and oats or leave it in a field to graze. Even when these difficulties are overcome, the benefits are questionable. Cats cannot be trained to perform specific tasks, and even as mousers they are less effective than dogs or ferrets.

The question, then, is why would Neolithic farmers have actively sought out wildcats as pets? The answer, probably, is that they didn't. Fossilised remains of rats, mice and sparrows at late pre-agricultural Natufian sites in the Levant suggest that commensal species wasted little time in exploiting the new niche that opened up when humans first began to live in permanent settlements. The word 'commensal' means 'eating at the same table as' and while this was not literally true, these pests have been firmly associated with human settlements ever since. While the appearance of commensals was undoubtedly a nuisance for humans, it was a major opportunity for cats.

A likely scenario is that the domestication of the cat occurred in two stages. The first stage occurred soon after the appearance of commensals in human settlements. To cats, human settlements offered a reliable source of food. Initially commensals themselves, their presence was tolerated by humans rather than actively sought out as domestic pets. In time, though, villagers came to value cats as mousers and pets, and began to provide shelter and additional food for them. Cats who were able to tolerate humans were at an advantage to those who shunned them, and thus the process leading to domestication was set in motion.

Curiously, evidence in support of this model has been slow to emerge. The earliest evidence for an association between humans and cats was reported in 2004 from the Neolithic site of Shillourokambos, 6 km (3.5 miles) from Limassol in southern Cyprus. In one of the numerous burials excavated at the site, an eight-month-old cat was found buried, accompanied by human remains and extensive grave goods. The latter included axes, ochre, flint tools and sea shells, suggesting the burial of a high-status individual. There is no doubt that the cat was intentionally buried, and it seems likely that it was killed on the death of its owner.

Humans have been living in Cyprus since around 10,500 BC, but the first farmers did not arrive until 8500 BC. Shillourokambos was one of the earlier farming settlements on the island, with occupation beginning at 8400 BC. The cat burial is rather later, and dates from about 7350 BC, although cats reached Cyprus at the same time as the first farmers. Their introduction must have been a response to the arrival of mice, which probably reached Cyprus as stowaways in boats bringing farmers and supplies from the mainland. It is interesting to note that foxes were introduced to Cyprus around 8000 BC, suggesting that farmers tried a number of small predatory species to combat the problem. During the early stages of settlement in Cyprus, it is possible that cats were seen as just another introduced predator, and the close relationship between them and humans did not develop until several centuries later.

Although this relationship was apparently established by the time of its burial, the Shillourokambos cat was not domesticated. It was within the upper half of the size range of the present-day Near Eastern Wildcat and was far larger than even the largest historical or present-day domestic cats. Until recently, the earliest evidence for domesticated cats was in Egyptian Middle Kingdom art from around 2000 BC; for the crucial period from 7000 to 2000 BC there was nothing. An archaeological discovery in Predynastic Egypt has now changed this picture.

The remains of six cats were found were found in a circular pit in an elite graveyard at the ancient city of Hierakonpolis. The grave-yard is thought to date to the Naqada IC-IIB period from 3800 to 3600 BC. The six cats included an adult male, a young adult female and four kittens. The cats had apparently been sacrificed and buried as part of a funerary ritual. The slightly differing ages of the kittens suggest that two came from one litter and the other two from an-other, but the adult female was too young to have been the mother of either pair. The male, on the other hand, could have fathered ei-ther or both pairs of kittens, but we have no way of knowing if this was actually the case. To take all of these animals from the wild would have necessitated four separate captures, which would be dif-ficult if required at short notice for sacrificial purposes. Further-more, the slightly different ages of the kittens suggest that at least one pair was born outside the natural reproductive cycle of Egyptian wild cats, where there is a single birth season in spring. It therefore seems likely that the cats were bred in captivity or at least in close association with humans.

An early domestication of cats was also claimed in China. The discoveries were made at the Neolithic village of Quanhucun in Shaanxi Province, where cat remains dating to around 3500 BC were found. The site is associated with farmers of the Yangshao Culture, who grew millet as a staple crop. Unlike the Shillourokambos cat, the Quanhucun cats were within the size range of modern domestic cats. That rats and mice were a threat to grain stores at Quanhucun was demonstrated by the presence of ancient rodent bones on the site, and burrows leading into the grain storage pits were also dis-covered. The farmers tried to keep their grain safe by storing it in specially-designed ceramic vessels, but this measure was evidently unsuccessful. Stable isotope data indicates that the rodents still man-aged to feed on the millet, though they in turn were eaten by the cats. Interestingly, the isotopic results indicate that one of the cats ate less meat than the others: possibly it was unable to catch mice and the villagers fed it grain instead. If so, it suggests that at least some of the cats were seen as more than just working animals. An-other cat had survived into old age, suggesting that it too led an eas-ier life than it would have done in the wild.

However, China lies well beyond the geographical range of the Near Eastern Wildcat, so the origin of the Quanhucun cats was un-clear. Could they represent a local domestication from an East Asian subspecies of the Old World Wildcat? The answer turned out to be 'no'. An assessment of the remains by a second group of researchers found that the Quanhucun cats were not domesticated Near Eastern Wildcats but leopard cats (*Prionailurus bengalensis*), a small wildcat native to the region. The Quanhucun cats represent an experiment in the domestication of an entirely different species of wildcat, but it was evidently unsuccessful. By 500 BC, domesticated Near Eastern Wildcats had reached China, and it is from these that all present-day Chinese cats are descended.

From these beginnings, the cat has gone on to become the world's most popular pet. During the historical period, cats have been worshipped as gods, associated with witchcraft, and are widely-supposed have multiple lives (usually nine, but fewer in some traditions). Yet to this day, cats are known for their detachment from human affairs. In reality, they are very little changed from their wild counterparts. It is certainly safe to say that cats have far fewer hang-ups about humans than do humans about cats.

# 36: Best friends

*Tracing the origins of the long partnership between dogs and humans.*

The dog possesses many attributes that make it a more plausible companion for humans than the cat, although it remains the only large carnivore ever to have been domesticated. Its wild ancestor, the Grey Wolf (*Canis lupus*), is a highly intelligent social animal. The range of tasks a dog can be trained to carry out is enormous, as evidenced by the large number of breeds of working dog. Dogs are used for herding livestock, hunting, controlling rodents, pulling sledges and other vehicles, guide dogs for the blind, guarding, policing, rescue work, detecting drugs and explosives, as well as their role as pets. The dog has certainly earned its label as 'man's best friend'.

Like the cat, the origins of the domestic dog are uncertain, although the broad details are now reasonably well understood. In *The Origin of Species*, Darwin speculated that because of the enormous variation in size and shape between dog breeds, the dog must have had more than one wild ancestor. Dogs, wolves, coyotes and jackals can all interbreed, so this suggestion was perfectly feasible at the time. In the 1990s, however, genetic studies confirmed that the domestic dog's wild ancestor was the Grey Wolf, and it is now classified as the subspecies *Canis lupus familiaris*. The ability of dogs to interbreed with wolves might in some cases be theoretical rather than actual: it is difficult to imagine a Chihuahua mating with a wolf. Despite the variability of dog breeds, however, the skull of a dog can always be distinguished from that of a wolf by the shorter, broader muzzle.

It is not difficult to envisage how domestication occurred. Like cats, wolves were probably attracted to human settlements, which offered excellent opportunities for scavenging. The inhabitants would have come to value them as companions, and begun to tame them. Tamed wolves could have been used for hunting, or as guard dogs to warn of approaching strangers. Once isolated from the native lupine population, these animals became subject to artificial rather than natural selection. The more sociable and docile wolf pups would have been the ones most likely to end up being kept as pets. Over many generations, physical changes occurred such as the shortening and broadening of the muzzle. The key questions are just where, when, and on how many occasions did domestication occur?

Dogs do not become well established in the archaeological record until fairly late in pre-agricultural times, and they did not spread beyond the natural range of the Grey Wolf until the arrival of agriculture. However, fossils have been found of 'proto-dogs' that lived over 30,000 years ago, predating the Last Glacial Maximum. The remains of these dog-like animals were found at three widely-separated Upper Palaeolithic cave sites: Goyet Cave in Belgium, Razboinichya Cave in the Altai Mountains of southern Siberia and Předmostí in the Czech Republic. Goyet was first occupied by Neanderthals 100,000 years ago, but during the Upper Palaeolithic, modern humans took up residence. Finds from the cave include the 36,000-year-old skull of what appears to be an early dog rather than a wolf. The skull is broader and wider than that of a wolf, though the lower jawbone and teeth are much larger than those of a modern dog. The dog was about the same size as a shepherd dog and probably resembled a Siberian husky. Stable isotope data suggests that its diet included muskox, reindeer and horse. The Razboinichya dog dates to around 33,000 years ago and it more closely resembles the Greenland dogs of a thousand years ago than it does a wolf. At Předmostí, three skulls have been identified as dogs rather than wolves on the basis of their short skull lengths, short snouts, and wide palates and braincases relative to wolves. The Předmostí dogs date to around 27,000 years ago.

Do these remains represent the earliest ancestors of modern dogs, or were they independent and ultimately failed experiments with domestication? In the case of the Goyet and Razboinichya dogs at least, this does appear to be so. Comparisons between DNA obtained from their remains and that of modern dogs indicates that they died out and did not contribute to later dog lineages. It has been suggested that the social disruption caused by the intense cold of Last Glacial Maximum might have interrupted the domestication process and prevented the emergence of fully domesticated dogs at that time.

Geneticists believe that modern dogs were domesticated just once, from a single population of wolves, and that all present-day dogs are descended from this ancestral population. These include Australian dingos and pre-Columbian New World dogs. Genetic studies have shown that dingoes are descended from a founding population of domesticated dogs that lived around 5,000 years ago in East Asia. It is likely that a small group of these dogs were brought to Australia by Austronesian settlers, and that a feral population subsequently became established. Ancient DNA from the remains of pre-Columbian New World dogs shows that they are closely related to Eurasian dogs, suggesting that the first Americans brought domesticated dogs with them from Siberia rather than domesticating dogs locally from New World wolves.

But early attempts to use genetics to pinpoint the origin of modern dogs were hampered by the long history of cross-breeding between dogs from different parts of the world, ancient and recent interbreeding between dogs and wolves, and intensive inbreeding within certain dog breeds. Genetic studies variously located the centre of domestication in Southwest Asia, Southeast Asia, or Europe, and indicated that the timing lay anywhere between 32,000 and 16,000 years ago.

One problem with these studies was the underlying assumption that dogs are descended from a still-existent population of wolves. This view was called into question by a study that showed that no single present-day wolf population is any more closely related to dogs than any of the others. A possible explanation for this result is that dogs were domesticated from a now-extinct wolf population that diverged from present-day wolf populations before any of these diverged from one another. Such a population existed in Eastern Beringia during the Late Pleistocene. Fossil remains suggest that compared to modern wolves, they were more specialised for preying on relatively large animals and for scavenging. Ancient mitochondrial DNA obtained from fossil remains indicates that these wolves were genetically distinct from modern wolves. To test the theory that dogs could be descended from this population, researchers sequenced ancient DNA from a 35,000-year-old wolf bone fragment found during an expedition to the Taimyr Peninsula in Siberia. It was found that the Taimyr wolf belonged to a population that was genetically close to the common ancestor of present-day dogs and wolves, and that the split occurred somewhere between 27,000 and 40,000 years ago. This only tells us when the ancestral populations split – the actual domestication of dogs might have occurred much later. The researchers also found that dogs later interbred with the Taimyr wolves in northern latitudes. Modern Arctic breeds including the husky and the Greenland sledge dog have the highest percentages of Taimyr wolf ancestry in their genetic makeup.

A criticism of these earlier studies is that they only considered small portions of the genome, so in 2015 researchers obtained whole genome sequences from 58 canines around the world including grey wolves, indigenous dogs from East Asia, village dogs from Nigeria and a diverse range of dog breeds from across the world. The researchers found significantly higher genetic diversity in dogs from Southeast Asia, suggesting that this is where domestic dogs originated. It was estimated that these basal dogs diverged from wolves 33,000 years ago, confirming an Ice Age origin for present-day domestic dogs even if the contemporary Goyet and Razboinichya dogs had gone extinct. The researchers also managed to unravel the subsequent career of these early dogs. 15,000 years ago, one group began a migration to Southwest Asia, Africa and Europe, reaching the latter 10,000 years ago. Subsequently, one of these 'out of Asia' lineages migrated back to the East, cross-breeding with endemic Asian lineages in northern China, and ultimately migrating to the New World. Although this dispersal was probably associated with humans, the initial spread of domesticated dogs from Southeast Asia might in part have been driven by environmental factors, such as the retreat of glaciers towards the end of the Ice Age.

Geneticists have also compared the genomes of dogs with those of wolves in order to identify genetic changes associated with the domestication process. Differences were found in a gene known as AMY2B, which is linked to the production of the enzyme amylase. Amylase is present in the saliva of a number of mammals, including humans, and its role is to catalyse the metabolic breakdown of starches into sugars. It was found that the AMY2B gene was 28 times more active in dogs than it is in wolves. These changes enabled dogs to thrive on starchy diets, relative to the carnivorous diet of wolves, and they were probably an adaptation to living in farming communities. However, it was later found that the enhanced AMY2B amylase gene is not present in dingoes and very early dog breeds such as huskies, consistent with the view that dog domestication preceded agriculture. Nevertheless, it was agriculture that eventually enabled dogs to spread beyond the original range of the Grey Wolf, and assured them of the prominent role they have played in human affairs to this day.

# 37: The forked mound

*Why did thousands of people choose to live in a vast hive-like settlement in middle of a spacious and otherwise unpopulated plain?*

The great mound of Çatalhöyük has been described as a proto-city, but in all respects other than sheer size, it bears little resemblance to a town or city. There are no public buildings or spaces, and no obvious town centre. Despite its size, there are no streets or approaches at ground level. Instead, the rectangular houses directly abut one another honeycomb style, forming a contiguous mass. Lacking windows or even front doors, they were accessed via a trapdoor in the roof. The only way of getting about was to walk over the flat roofs of neighbouring houses, with ladders being used to get in and out of the houses and the settlement itself. Located on the Konya Plain in central Anatolia, Çatalhöyük was first occupied in 7400 BC and it remained in use until around 6000 BC. It reached 13.5 ha (33 acres) in extent, with an estimated population that ranged from 3,000 to 8,000 people. Çatalhöyük was strikingly different to any other farming settlement of the Southwest Asian Pre-Pottery Neolithic B period (PPNB), although it was something of a late-comer.

The emergence of a fully-fledged mixed farming economy during the PPNB resulted in significant population increases, which were reflected in much larger settlement sizes. The Early PPNB saw a three-fold increase in average settlement size compared to the preceding PPNA, and by the Late PPNB, the increase was ten-fold and settlement populations were averaging over 3,000. Some sites such as 'Ain Ghazal, on the outskirts of Amman, Basta, south of Petra, and Çatalhöyük became very large indeed. Of these 'mega sites', perhaps the most notable is Çatalhöyük. The site comprises two mounds: the larger East Mound comprising the Neolithic occupation, and a later, smaller West Mound. Some 18 levels of occupation have been identified in the East Mound, corresponding to roughly one level every 70 to 80 years, and there are some 21 m (69 ft.) of occupation debris.

Çatalhöyük was known to locals long before it came to the attention of archaeologists. The name means 'forked mound' in Turkish and refers to the path from the town of Çumra to the south, which divides into three at the site. One path goes to the east, another to the west, and the other passes between the two mounds and continues to the town of Karkin. British archaeologist James Mellaart first noted the mound at a distance in 1952, but he was unable to reach the site itself until 1958. At this time, he was excavating the site of Hacilar and it was not until 1961 that he commenced operations at Çatalhöyük. Mellaart worked at the site until 1965, and discovered spectacular painted walls, burials and figurines. He believed that Çatalhöyük had been the cult centre of an earth mother goddess that was a forerunner to the Classical-era Anatolian deity Cybele. Despite the considerable interest in Mellaart's findings, his excavations were followed by a lengthy hiatus. It was not until 1993 that a team lead by his former student Ian Hodder returned to Çatalhöyük to commence a still-ongoing program of excavation, site conservation and research that was able to take advantage of the many techniques developed in the intervening years.

The Konya Plain lies in the middle of the Anatolian Plateau at an elevation of 1,000 m (3,300 ft.), and the average annual rainfall is just 350 mm (14 in.). Although the rainfall was higher in the Early Holocene, drought conditions still prevailed during the summer. However, the region benefitted from alluvial fans formed by rivers flowing onto the plain, and from marshlands and seasonal lakes. Çatalhöyük lies in the centre of the largest of the fertile alluvial fans, the Çarsamba Fan, on the southern margin of the plain. Archaeologists have determined that there were a number of settlements on the plain both before Çatalhöyük was established and after it was abandoned – but that none were contemporary with it. Why would this have been? What was it that drew people into a single, densely-packed community in the middle of an open plain where resources were widely-available?

The obvious explanation is that the region had fallen under the control of a powerful central authority that compelled everybody to move into the one, centralised settlement. The problem is that is that, as noted, Çatalhöyük has few attributes of a city or town other than size. Not only are there no public buildings or spaces; it also lacks granaries and other communal storage facilities, administrative buildings, and elite residences. It more or less devoid of any form of internal differentiation, and the basic social and economic unit was the house. Nevertheless, there would have been a communal dimension to life in Çatalhöyük: a settlement of such great size would certainly have required collective organisation for matters such as drainage, water supply, disposal of waste, and allocation of land for farming and herding, although it is likely that decisions were made by a group of elders rather than a chief or king. It is been suggested that the settlement was divided into two equivalent paired halves and that each functioned as a moiety, a type of society in which members of one half are obliged to marry into the other.

Architecturally, the houses were all very similar. They were built with mud brick walls, supported by timber posts. Despite the proximity of the houses to one another, people built and maintained their own walls; party walls were very rare. Internally, they comprised a main room for living, working, cooking, eating and sleeping. From the main room, low openings provided access to smaller storerooms. Running around the walls were low platforms, which served as benches and work surfaces. Many burials have been found under the floors of houses, typically below platforms by the northern wall. The use of space within the houses was rigidly controlled. There were specific parts of the houses where it was or was not permissible to carry out various activities or store particular items. Thus ovens, artwork, obsidian caches, and buried ancestors all had their allotted places. It is possible that even the parts of the house in which people could sit and work was dictated by age and sex. The entry ladder was usually set into the south wall of the house, and led down into the main living area. Situated directly below the ladder was an oven, so the trapdoor entrance doubled as a chimney. Many activities were probably carried out on the roofs of the houses when the weather was suitable, and there might also have been pens for livestock.

The inside walls and floors of the houses were plastered, along with some interior features such as basins and bins. The soft lime-rich mud plaster required regular resurfacing, typically on an annual basis. Successive layers of plaster on the walls built up to as much as 7.5 cm (3 in.) thick, and in one case a wall was found to have 450 layers of plaster. The walls were richly decorated with paintings and moulded reliefs, mainly of wild animals including leopards, bulls, deer, goats and vultures. Leopards were frequently depicted in pairs standing head to head. There are also portrayals of human figures, including hunting scenes in which hunters are wearing leopard skins. Often, skulls and horns of bulls and other animals were plastered and set into the walls or placed on pillars. Most of these wall decorations are found on the north walls of houses, opposite the entrance ladder. Houses had a useful life of around 70 to 80 years before they had to be demolished and rebuilt. This entailed dismantling the roof and removing the main structural timber supports. The walls were then dismantled to leave rubble, which was levelled and the new house constructed on top.

In 1962, during the original excavation of the site, Mellaart discovered a mural which he subsequently described as the world's oldest map. The 3 meter (9 ft. 10 in) wide mural was painted on the northern and eastern walls of a room described as Shrine 14. At the bottom of the mural a pattern of around 80 square cells, arranged in a honeycomb fashion, which has been interpreted as a bird's eye view of the settlement. Above is a portrayal of a twin-peaked mountain, closely resembling the now-dormant volcano Mt Hasan 130 km (80 miles) northeast of Çatalhöyük. It was suggested that eruptions of Mt Hasan were of significance to the inhabitants of Çatalhöyük because they collected obsidian from its vicinity (although not from the volcano itself), or that they witnessed a violent eruption and that the volcano subsequently became associated with their belief systems. This interpretation was challenged on the grounds that there was no independent evidence that Mt Hasan was ever active during the period that Çatalhöyük was occupied. However, in 2013, a team of geologists collected pumice samples from the summit and flanks of Mt Hasan and dated them using (U-Th)/He zircon geochronology, a radiometric dating technique widely used for dating volcanic material. They established that the volcano erupted at some time between 7600 and 6320 BC, which corresponds fairly closely to the time that Çatalhöyük was occupied and strengthens the case that this is what the mural depicts.

In contrast to the crowded settlement in which they lived, the people of Çatalhöyük exploited a wide area for the various resources they required. Many of the materials required for building and tool-making were not locally available. The pine and juniper timbers used for house building came from mountainous regions to the south and to the west and obsidian, used for tool-making and trade, could only be obtained from the vicinity of Mt Hasan. Analysis of wheat remains suggest that they were cultivated in well-drained soils rather than the marshy lands around the site. Domesticated crops included wheat, peas, lentils and vetch. However, wild vetch was still collected, and other wild foods included almonds, acorns and hackberries. Animal remains suggest that the Çatalhöyük people herded domesticated sheep and goats, and eggshell remains found on the site hint that ducks and geese were kept in small numbers. Cattle account for under 25 percent of the animal remains, and they are thought to be wild aurochs rather than domesticated cattle. Stable nitrogen isotope analysis of human remains show that cattle were not a major part of the diet; however they do appear to have been an important element in communal feasting. Unlike the remains of sheep and goats from the site, aurochs bones were not processed for marrow and grease. They also occur in sizeable concentrations, suggesting events where large quantities of meat was eaten. It is notable that images, reliefs and plastered skulls of bulls form a major part of the artwork, but there are very few depictions of sheep and goats. The implication is that there was an ideological distinction between the wild and the domesticated.

There is little doubt that ritual played a major role in life at Çatalhöyük, but the belief systems of its inhabitants might have had its roots in much earlier times. As we have already seen, David Lewis-Williams has proposed that the universal belief in a three-tiered cosmos is rooted in the very structure of the human brain, and that the painted caves of Upper Palaeolithic Europe were seen as the entrails of a nether realm. Along with archaeologist David Pearce, Lewis Williams has proposed that Çatalhöyük was a 'built cosmos' reflecting a similar belief system. Descent into houses, limited light, and the need to crawl through small openings between rooms were akin to the experience of moving through the limestone caves used for rituals in the Upper Palaeolithic. Limestone caves occur in the Taurus Mountains, not far to the south of Çatalhöyük. That people from Çatalhöyük explored the caves is clear from the pieces of stalactite and limestone concretions have been found at the site. Some were partially carved although others, resembling breasts, udders and human figures, were left un-carved. The ladders used to access the houses might have been associated with trans-cosmological travel, while burials below the floor were associated with the subterranean realm. The plastered skulls of bulls and other animals might have been shamanistic spirit helpers. Walls were 'permeable' boundaries beyond which other realms lay; their three-dimensional imagery reflected that of Upper Palaeolithic caves.

This 'built cosmos' theory could explain why Çatalhöyük comprised an agglomeration of houses with no streets or spaces. From settlements across the Konya Plain, people were drawn to this vast mound. Their ideology was powerful, but oppressive. Archaeologist Steven Mithen believes that every aspect of life in Çatalhöyük had become over-ritualised. The bulls and other artwork imply an ideology so oppressive that it stifled any independence of thought and behaviour. In stark contrast to hunter-gatherers, the people of Çatalhöyük seemed to have feared and despised the wild.

# 38: A tale of three cemeteries

*What cemeteries can tell us about the diverse social conditions of Mesolithic Europe.*

Humans have intentionally buried their dead since long before the emergence of *Homo sapiens*, but dedicated places of burial – cemeteries – are a far more recent development, reflecting the appearance of larger, more settled communities. In Europe, the first cemeteries appeared during the Mesolithic, the period of prehistory that followed the end of the last Ice Age and preceded the arrival of agriculture from Southwest Asia. Although agriculture did not arise indigenously in Europe, the region was certainly no cultural backwater, and the Mesolithic saw increases in population and social complexity, and technological advance. Microliths came into use for a wide range of applications, ranging from weapon tips to vegetable graters and drill bits. Other innovations included controlled burning of vegetation to stimulate plant growth, hunting methods adapted to the new, post-glacial landscape, and the use of nets and substantially-built boats for fishing. Settlements varied considerably in size, suggesting that Mesolithic societies were diverse in their size and complexity.

The first Mesolithic cemeteries appeared in Spain around 7400 BC. Their appearance might have linked to increasing populations and a perceived need by groups to mark out their territories though the presence of ancestors. Cemeteries were mainly located in coastal areas or near lakes and rivers, where large populations could be supported. They vary considerably in size: most contain no more than between twenty to sixty burials, but some were much larger. From them, much knowledge about Mesolithic society has been inferred. Three of note are Skateholm in Sweden, Hoëdic and Téviec in France, and Oleneostrovski Mogilnik in the Russian autonomous republic of Karelia.

Skateholm is associated with the Late Mesolithic Ertebølle culture, and is located by a now dried-up lagoon on the coast of southern Sweden. People were attracted by its immense diversity of plants, fish, seabirds and marine mammals, together with an adjacent forest in which deer and pigs could be hunted. Despite its size,

Skateholm was not a year-round settlement. Estimates of the age at death for wild boar remains suggest that they were killed during the winter only. Although fish remains have been found in large quantities, there are very few cod, mackerel, or garfish. These fish come inshore to breed during the summer months, and would have been caught in large numbers if people had been present at that time of year.

There are two cemeteries at the site, located 150 m (490 ft.) apart and known as Skateholm I and Skateholm II. Skateholm I dates approximately to 5000 BC, and Skateholm II is about 300 years older. Skateholm I is the larger of the two, with 61 burials as opposed to 22. In both cemeteries, multiple burials were rare and most individuals were buried singly. In contrast to a modern cemetery, the graves at Skateholm I are randomly positioned and there is no consistency in the way people were buried. Some were buried sitting, others lying either face up or face down, and others with knees drawn up beneath the chest. In some cases, remains were cremated. Equally varied were the grave goods, which tools, pendants made from the teeth of elk and aurochs, bones, boar tusks, and deer antlers. The implication is that Skateholm was not a closely-knit community and its residents were largely-independent family units, each with its own burial practices. In some cases, dogs were accorded the same ritual treatment as humans and buried with grave goods, emphasising their importance to hunters in Mesolithic times.

No fewer than four individuals had depressed skull fractures consistent with blows from a blunt instrument, and a further two had been struck by flint arrowheads which were found with their remains. While the latter could have been the result of accidents while hunting large game, the skull injuries cannot be explained by anything other than violence. Skateholm was a very attractive site, but it would not have been able to support all comers. It is quite likely that the frequent need to beat off marauders was the main and possibly only factor unifying the family groups living there.

The cemeteries of Hoëdic and Téviec hint at a far more hierarchical society than that of Skateholm. They are now located on two small islands in the Bay of Quiberon, Brittany, although in Mesolithic times they would have been well inland. The sites date to approximately 6200 BC, and on the basis of similarities in tool typology, they are thought to have been roughly contemporaneous. A total of nineteen graves holding the remains of 37 adults and children have been identified at the two sites, though it is likely that other graves were submerged by the rising sea levels. Between them, Hoëdic and Téviec account for two-thirds of known Mesolithic burials in France.

A notable feature of the two sites is that many were interred in multiple burials, in contrast to Skateholm and most other Mesolithic sites. It may be assumed that these each contained members of a single descent group and that lineal ties were important to these people. Many of the burials took place in complex structures comprising graves lined with stone slabs, surmounted by small cairns. Graveside hearths at many burial sites suggest elaborate funerary practices involving ritual feasting. Grave goods included a variety of stone tools, bone pins, awls, items made from antler and boar tusk, red deer teeth and marine shell necklaces and bracelets.

Also notable is that some but not all of the child burials were accompanied by grave goods. This has been interpreted as evidence for a hereditary, ranked society, in which status was acquired by virtue of birth rather than by achievements in life. In such a society, children of high-ranking parentage would be likely to have richer burials than those of ordinary parentage. Conversely, in a meritocracy, children would be unlikely to have accrued significant wealth.

Oleneostrovski Mogilnik ('Red Deer Island') contrasts with both Skateholm and Hoëdic/Téviec. Located in a former quarry on one of Lake Onega's many islands, it is the largest-known Mesolithic cemetery in sub-Arctic Europe. Since it was first excavated in the 1950s, it has revealed 170 burials in two burial clusters, one northern and one southern. It is likely that many more graves were destroyed by the quarrying activities, and the actual number might have been as high as 500. Over 7,000 items of grave goods have been found, including pendants, sculptured effigies of stone, wood or bone, hunting implements, and other tools. The pendants were made from the pierced teeth of bears, beavers and elks. No other type of animal teeth were used for making pendants, suggesting that these three species might have been of particular symbolic importance to the Oleneostrovski Mogilnik people.

Graves were typically rectangular, aligned east-west, with bodies facing east – but there were exceptions. Two men and two women were interred in vertical graves consisting of a funnel-shaped shaft, and it has been suggested that the four were shamans. There was a considerable variation in grave goods, and there is little doubt that the Oleneostrovski Mogilnik people lived in a large, socially-complex society. The sculptured effigies occurred frequently, but those in the northern cluster were invariably carvings of elks, and those in the southern cluster were of either snakes or humans. The two burial clusters might have represented a division of the Oleneostrovski Mogilnik society, possibly a moiety where members of one half are obliged to choose marriage partners from the other half.

Some graves contained over 400 items of grave goods, but around 20 percent contained none at all. Some items were gender-specific: bone points, pins and harpoons, and stone adzes occur in male burials, while ornaments made from carved beaver teeth are found with female burials. A small number of graves contained slate knives and daggers, which are thought to have been prestige items. The Oleneostrovski Mogilnik people used flint as their principle raw material, and presumably had to procure slate by trading with regions where it was produced. The slate grave goods might have been associated with burials of traders involved with the regional exchange network.

The pierced animal tooth pendants might have been an indication of an individual's wealth. Those made from bear teeth were found with the prestigious slate knives and daggers, suggesting that they were regarded as more valuable than those of beaver and elk teeth. Unlike Hoëdic and Téviec, child burials were rare, and it was found that individuals in the prime of life were wealthier in terms of numbers of pendants than were the young and the old. In addition to commodities such as slate, the grave goods might also have reflected an individual's hunting abilities. As these declined with age, individuals became less able to hold on to their wealth. Oleneostrovski Mogilnik appears to have been a meritocracy, but one in which there was no way to save for retirement.

# 39: Doggerland: a prehistoric Atlantis

*The rich hunting grounds that sank beneath the North Sea.*

In September 1931, the Lowestoft trawler *Colinda* under the command of Captain Pilgrim E. Lockwood was fishing on the Leman and Ower Banks, 40 km (25 miles) off the Norfolk coast. When the nets was hauled in, the crew found a large lump of moorlog (peat) among the catch, which when broken up yielded a Mesolithic-era point made from red deer antler. Possibly used as a harpoon or fish spear, it measured 21 cm (8 ¼ in.) in length, with barbs carved on one side. A now-submerged plain between the east of England and mainland Europe had been predicted by geologist Clement Reid in 1913, but the *Colinda* discovery was the first direct evidence for its existence.

A year after the discovery, botanist Harry Godwin from the University of Cambridge persuaded Lockwood to take him to the find spot to obtain further peat samples. Godwin was a pioneer in the then-new field of pollen analysis. The results showed that the site had once been a woodland similar to those of the northeast coast of England and the northern coast of mainland Europe in the period immediately following the last ice age. The implication was that much of what is now the North Sea had then been a part of contiguous landmass of birch, pine, hazel and oak woodland, occupied by hunter-gatherers. In 1936, archaeologist Grahame Clark, a colleague of Godwin at Cambridge, claimed that the region had been the heartland of the Mesolithic Maglemosian culture of northwestern Europe.

The world was intrigued, but the difficulties of investigating what was effectively a *terra incognita* meant that it was largely ignored by mainstream archaeologists. The tendency was for archaeologists to think of it as a land bridge over which people and animals passed rather than a habitable landscape in its own right. It was not until 1998 that archaeologist Bryony Coles attempted to recreate the late glacial and early Holocene landscapes of what she named 'Doggerland', after the sandbank familiar to anybody who has ever listened to the BBC's Shipping Forecast. Subsequently, a team at Birmingham University led by archaeologist Vincent Gaffney at mapped the lost land using seismic survey data collected by oil companies during decades of exploration of the sea bed for new deposits of oil and gas. Their investigations revealed ancient river courses, hills, lakes and marshland.

What is now Dogger Bank was a range of hills, separated from the North Yorkshire Moors by lowlands through which flowed a greatly-extended River Ouse. The northeastern flank of the Dogger Hills was skirted by the Elbe and its tributaries, which drained into the Norwegian Trench between Doggerland and Scandinavia. To the south, a large, previously-unknown river drained the Dogger Hills region into a freshwater lake known as Outer Silver Pit. The river was named the Shotton River after Frederick Shotton, a former Professor of Geology at Birmingham whose wartime research into the geological makeup of the Normandy beaches helped pave the way for the D-Day landings. Even during the coldest part of the last Ice Age, Doggerland was not entirely icebound, as the ice sheets covering Britain and Scandinavia never met in the middle. The regions free of ice were inhospitable polar desert and arctic tundra, but as the ice retreated this was replaced by temperate forest. A large freshwater basin formed in the centre of Doggerland, into which flowed the Thames from the west and the Rhine from the east. Its lagoons, marshes and mudflats would have hosted a rich variety of wildlife.

By 7500 BC, Doggerland was possibly the richest hunting ground in Mesolithic Europe, with abundant game, fish and migrating wildfowl. The climate of what is known as the Boreal period was highly favourable and slightly warmer than today. Since the *Colinda* discovery, other Mesolithic artefacts have been dredged up by North Sea fishermen, confirming that there was a widespread human presence in Doggerland. Ironically, the *Colinda* harpoon itself has proved to be something of an enigma. In form, it closely resembles those found at the Mesolithic site of Star Carr in North Yorkshire, suggesting a cultural connection, but radiocarbon dating has established that it is around three thousand years older than the peat in which it was found. The peat dates from around 7000 to 7900 BC, an age consistent other peat samples from the same depth. Assuming the date of the harpoon is correct, the implication is that it was reworked from an implement that was already three thousand years old and dated to a time when the region was still arctic tundra. Possibly it originally belonged to Late Upper Palaeolithic hunter-gatherers from the south, who made an expedition north for game, furs and seasonal wildfowl.

But Doggerland's days were numbered. On the coast, the landscape began to change as sea levels rose, transforming woodlands and grasslands into salt marsh. Further inland, the rising water table caused lakes to appear in what had been hollows. The average annual rise in sea level was not enormous and has been estimated at somewhere between 2.3 to 4.0 cm (0.9 to 1.6 in.) per year – but the resulting impact on the landscape would have been clearly perceptible over the course of a lifetime. Sometimes, violent storms or particularly high tides would have effected permanent changes in the space of a few hours.

Doggerland was facing a double whammy. Globally, sea levels were rising as meltwater added to the oceanic volume, but a secondary effect was also coming into play known as forebulge. During the Ice Age, the great mass of the British and Scandinavian ice sheets had forced the underlying land downwards, but this in turn forced the land beyond the ice sheets to move upwards due to the viscosity of the Earth's upper mantle. Now, as the ice melted, the land underneath rebounded upwards and Doggerland sank downwards.

By 6200 BC, all that remained of Doggerland was a low-lying, marshy island that was about the size of Wales, and Britain and Ireland were now insular. It is disputed as to whether any permanent settlements remained by this time, though people probably still came to Doggerland to hunt and fish. But then came an event known as the Storegga Slide. One of the largest landslides ever known, it occurred underwater at the edge of the Norwegian continental shelf and was caused by the collapse of sedimentary debris that had accumulated during the Ice Age. An estimated 290 km (180 miles) of coastal shelf collapsed, triggering a tsunami of comparable magnitude to the one that struck Japan in 2011. The Norwegian coast closest to the landslide was struck by a wave 10 to 12 m (32 to 40 ft.) high, and at the Shetlands the tsunami exceeded 20 m (65 ft.). The impact on the eastern coast of Scotland was less severe, but the wave still exceeded 3 to 5 m (10 to 16 ft.). Dogger Island experienced a 5 m (16 ft.) wave, which largely inundated it. Very few people would have survived.

Although it is not known just when Doggerland finally disappeared beneath the North Sea, it is thought that the Storegga Slide marked the end of a Mesolithic presence there. None of the Mesolithic artefacts that have been found there postdate the tsunami. Strangely, though, two Neolithic axes have been recovered from the

Brown Banks region of the North Sea. Even if vestiges of Doggerland survived as an archipelago of small islands at this late stage, it
is unlikely that they would have been colonised by Neolithic farmers.
It is probable that the axes were lost by explorers or accidentally
dropped from a boat – but we cannot rule out the possibility that
they were intentionally left as ritual offerings by people whose legends told of a once-bountiful land that had vanished below the
waves: a prehistoric Atlantis.

# 40: Lurches and longhouses

*Did the Neolithic transition in Europe represent the spread of farmers or merely knowledge of farming?*

Textbooks about Neolithic Europe are dominated by cultures named for pottery styles; thus there are the Trægtbægerkultur (Funnel-necked Beaker Culture), Linearbandkeramik (Linear Pottery) Culture, Cardial Ware Culture, Stichbandkeramik (Stroke-ornamented ware) Culture, and so on. The names reflect the late nineteenth century view that material culture was a basis for identifying distinct ethnicities and groups in the archaeological record of prehistoric societies, and the preponderance of German names reflects the pre-eminence of German archaeologists such as Gustaf Kossinna in the field at that time. This 'pots equals peoples' view fell out of favour in the 1960s, when archaeologists began to appreciate that the ideas and artefacts could be spread by trade and other long-distance social interactions, and didn't necessarily correspond to waves of migration. Nevertheless, many prehistoric European cultures are named for their pottery styles to this day.

Thus the cultural phenomenon that emerged in western Hungary around 5600 BC is named Linearbandkeramik (Linear Pottery) Culture (usually abbreviated to LBK) on account of its pottery with incised banded decoration. However, the most distinctive feature of the LBK was not its pottery but its settlements of massive timber-built longhouses, which sometimes measured up to 70 m (230 ft.) in length. The longhouses were typically situated in small groups in forest clearings on river terraces, where there was ready access to water and rich loess farmland. One of the most important LBK sites is Langweiler, located in the Merzbach Valley on the Aldenhovener Plateau of western Germany. Here there is evidence for 160 longhouses in eight distinct settlements, as well as a cemetery and three enclosures. The latter were sited away from the houses and might have been used for social or ritual activities by the whole community. The longhouses were periodically rebuilt in the same place in uninterrupted occupation sequences that could span several centuries. At Langweiler 8, the largest of the settlements, occupation spanned fourteen episodes of rebuilding over the course of four hundred years – roughly the length of the Roman occupation of Britain. The Langweiler complex comprises a single 'settlement cell' and it might have maintained contacts with similar units 20 to 50 km (12 to 30 miles) for exchanging breeding stock and possibly marriage partners.

From its Hungarian origins, the LBK spread rapidly to the Rhineland by 5300 BC and the Paris Basin thereafter, its dispersal probably aided by boats along the rivers of Central Europe. The LBK also spread eastwards as far as Ukraine and Moldova. Clearly, the LBK represents a success story – but just *how* was it spreading? One of the most hotly-debated topics in European prehistory is the process by which farming spread across the continent from Southwest Asia. Were the often highly-sophisticated Mesolithic peoples simply replaced by incoming farmers in all cases; or did they at least sometimes learn about agriculture from farmers, and adopt it themselves? The two viewpoints are known as demic diffusion and cultural diffusion respectively.

The demic diffusion view was promoted in the 1970s and 1980s by Italian geneticist Luigi Luca Cavalli-Sforza and his collaborator, American archaeologist Albert Ammerman. Using mathematical models, they showed that the archaeological record was consistent with a continuous 'wave of advance' of Neolithic farmers across Europe. As population pressures grew, farmers spread out into previously-unfarmed regions. Further expansion occurred as these regions in turn filled up, and so on. Based on the radiocarbon data available at the time, Cavalli-Sforza and Ammerman proposed an average rate of expansion of 1 km (0.62 miles) per year, though this ranged from as little as 0.7 km (0.43 miles) per year in the Balkans to as much as 5.6 km (3.5 miles) per year in Central Europe. The pair later backed up their conclusions with a genetic study based upon blood group data.

Both radiocarbon dating and genetic techniques have advanced considerably since the 1980s, and newer data has shown that the true picture is rather more complex than the scenario proposed by Cavalli-Sforza and Ammerman. Genetic studies have shown that modern Europeans retain a significant genetic heritage from the Upper Palaeolithic, suggesting that the hunter-gatherers did not simply die out. Reassessment of the radiocarbon data, using the larger body of information now available, has suggested that the average expansion rate was 1.3 km (0.8 miles) per year. While this overall picture is not too dissimilar to the earlier results, there is considerable local variation in the rate at which the transition from hunter-gathering to farming occurred. In some places it happened rapidly, suggesting that one population did indeed replace another, but in others the Mesolithic radiocarbon record tails off only gradually, with a significant overlap with that of the early Neolithic. In such places, it is likely that transition to agriculture was brought about by the spread of ideas rather than people.

Archaeologist Peter Rowley-Conwy suggests the true picture was one of sporadic rather than continuous movement. Often it involved 'leapfrog' migrations, where farmers occupied available farmland just beyond their neighbours. Incoming farmers interacted with local hunter-gatherers in a number of ways. Sometimes the hunter-gatherers simply lost their separate identity and were assimilated to varying degrees into the Neolithic farming communities. On other occasions, the farmers were themselves ultimately assimilated by the locals into an indigenous or 'start-up' Neolithic farming culture. Such interactions would have meant that migrating farmers carried with them a varying mixture of European and Southwest Asian genes. Rowley-Conwy suggests that the wave of advance is better described as a series of local and disparate 'lurches of advance'.

The speed with which the LBK expanded and its cultural homogeneity is more suggestive of a spread of colonising farmers than indigenous hunter-gatherers taking up farming – but what of the latter? Did the hunter-gatherers die out altogether, or did some of them throw in their lot with the LBK farming communities? Stable isotope analysis of dental enamel strontium obtained from LBK burials at cemeteries at the German sites of Flomborn, Schwetzingen and Dillingen has found that some of those buried were not local to the sites. Their strontium isotopic ratios were too high to be consistent with local geology, suggesting that they had originated from upland regions, where ratios are higher. In many cases, the burial orientation and grave goods of the outsiders differed from those of local people, hinting at some form of social differentiation. Notably, the majority of the outsiders were women, suggesting that men from the farming communities sometimes married women from indigenous hunter-gatherer groups. Such a pattern has been recorded ethnographically. Forager women do marry into farming communities, but the reverse is very rare as women from farming communities regard it as marrying down.

A slightly different picture was seen at the site of Vaihingen near Stuttgart. Unlike the other sites, outsiders were just as likely to be men as they were women, though there were again hints of social differentiation. In this case, the outsiders were more likely to be buried in a ditch near the site than within the settlement itself. The strontium data in this case suggests that the outsiders might have been nomadic pastors, who ranged cattle in a neighbouring limestone region where the strontium isotopic composition was significantly different to that near the site.

By 5000 BC, the picture of straightforward assimilation of hunter-gatherers was beginning to change. By now, the LBK had begun to differentiate into a number of regional successor groups, which are mainly classified on the basis of their pottery types although they continued to build longhouse settlements. One such group was the Villeneuve-Saint-Germain (VSG) culture, located on the western limits of the LBK expansion in northwestern France. Instead of giving rise to later, related cultures, it disappeared within 200 to 300 years, to be replaced by a less distinctive farming culture that had arisen among indigenous hunter-gather communities. Thus in this case, the pioneer farmers were eventually assimilated by indigenous people who had taken up agriculture for themselves. Some post-LBK groups simply disappeared. One of these was located on Poland's Baltic coast near the mouth of the Vistula. Sites associated with the Stroke Ornamented Pottery culture suggest that agriculture arrived around 5000 BC, but the area soon reverted to a hunter-gatherer economy implying that the colonisation by Neolithic farmers was ultimately unsuccessful.

Three sites dating to the later part of the LBK have provided chilling evidence that relations between settlement cells were not always harmonious. A mass grave known as the Death Pit at Talheim, Germany, was discovered in 1983 and held the remains of 34 individuals, including sixteen children and adolescents and seven women. Most of the bodies showed traces of violence, and analysis of the injuries inflicted enabled the murder weapons to be identified. Eighteen of the victims had been struck with the cutting edge of a polished stone adze; fourteen had been struck with a blunt instrument – probably the side of an adze; and three had been wounded by arrows. Most had received head injuries on the rear of the skull, suggesting that they were attempting to flee from their attackers. The polished stone 'shoe-last' adze is a characteristic LBK tool used for felling trees and for woodworking. They have been found in LBK graves of elderly males and were probably regarded as high-status items. That they doubled as weapons in the Talheim massacre suggests that the perpetrators were raiders from a neighbouring LBK settlement rather than local hunter-gatherers, though we can only speculate as to the motive for the attack.

The Talheim incident was not the even the worst example of internecine violence between LBK communities. At the site of Schletz, Austria, the remains of 67 individuals were found in an enclosure that was probably built as a defensive structure. Bodies had been thrown into a ditch surrounding the enclosure, and others were found in a well within the settlement itself. It suggests that the settlement was eventually overrun, possibly after a desperate defence, and its occupants killed. Again, the victims were mainly killed with blows to the head from stone adzes, ruling out a clash with local hunter-gatherers.

Possibly the most disturbing find was a mass grave discovered by chance during road building work at Schöneck-Kilianstädten, Germany, in 2006. In 2015 it was reported that the grave had held the remains of at least 26 individuals including 13 predominantly male adults, one young adult and twelve children, mostly aged no more than six years old. The youngest was just six months old. The bodies had been tossed unceremoniously into the burial pit without any of the customary grave goods, or grouping by family. The skulls all showed signs of violence, but around half of the shin bones recovered from the grave had been freshly broken. While the bodies could have been mutilated after death, a more sinister possibility is that individuals were tortured before they were killed. These three sites, widely separated geographically but not in time, paint a grim picture of widespread violence during the later stages of the LBK.

Despite the undoubted success of agriculture, the forager lifestyle was remarkably persistent. As late as the fourth millennium BC, some forager groups were apparently still living alongside farming communities. Blätterhöhle is a cave site near Hagen in North Rhine-Westphalia that was used as a burial ground: once during the Mesolithic between 9210 and 8340 BC, and again during the Late Neolithic from 3986 to 2918 BC. The remains of 450 individuals have been recovered from the cave. Researchers analysed stable carbon, nitrogen and sulphur isotope ratios of the bones and teeth of 25 individuals, and obtained ancient mitochondrial DNA from 25 of them; five from the Mesolithic occupation and 20 from the Late Neolithic occupation. Mitochondrial DNA, as we have seen, tracks maternal lineages.

The five Mesolithic-era individuals all belonged to mitochondrial haplogroup U, which is typical of pre-Neolithic hunter-gatherers in central, eastern and northern Europe. What was unexpected was that twelve of the Neolithic-era individuals also belonged to haplogroup U. Among Late Neolithic farmers, U is rare, and its presence suggested a surprising persistence of Mesolithic maternal ancestry. The remaining eight individuals belonged to more typical Neolithic haplogroups.

The stable isotope analysis indicated the existence of three distinct groups. The first, comprising the Mesolithic-era individuals, had subsisted on a diet of wild foods typical of that found at other inland Mesolithic sites. The other two groups were both from the Late Neolithic, but they differed from one another. One group had subsisted on a diet of domesticated animals typical of German Neolithic sites, but the diet of the other group was unusual for the period and was low in plant and animal protein and high in freshwater fish. The members of this second Neolithic group all belonged to mitochondrial haplogroup U, whereas members of the first Neolithic group were a mixture of Mesolithic and Neolithic haplogroups. The conclusion is that a fisher-forager community had persisted into the Late Neolithic and was living alongside a group of farmers. That both groups used the Blätterhöhle cave site at the same time implies that they were near-neighbours. But, it seems, they were not equal communities. No Neolithic mitochondrial haplogroups were found among the fisher-foragers; but the Mesolithic haplogroup U was present among the farmers. As was the case at Flomborn, Schwetzingen and Dillingen, women were marrying into the farming community, but none were going the other way.

The LBK was just one of many cultures that arose in Neolithic Europe, but it demonstrates that the spread of agriculture was far more complex than a monolithic wave of advance that either assimilated or eliminated all in its path. Despite the rapidity of the transition from hunter-gathering to farming – just three and a half millennia – the genes of our Mesolithic and Upper Palaeolithic ancestors endure to this day.

# 41: Drawing down the Moon

*The enigmatic recumbent stone circles of northeastern Scotland.*

Stone circles, rows, standing stones, chambered tombs and other megalithic monuments dot the landscape of Brittany, Britain, and Ireland, and provide the most visible reminder of the Neolithic period of Atlantic Europe. Although sites such as Stonehenge, Avebury and Carnac are household names, most are far less conspicuous and are known only to locals and amateur enthusiasts. Although the larger monuments were undoubtedly major undertaking, the majority of circles and rows were probably erected and used by local farming communities.

As to just why they were built, such a question is perhaps naïve given the great variety of monuments. They were also built over a considerable period of time: for example, the Avebury stone circle was built around 3000 BC; the neighbouring Silbury Hill dates to around 2400 BC; but the hilltop West Kennet Long Barrow is much earlier than either, dating to 3600 BC. In some cases, monuments evolved considerably over their lifetime: for example, it has long been known that Stonehenge encompassed three major phases of construction, which are now known to have spanned the period from 3100 to 1600 BC.

Inevitably, though, these enigmatic monuments have attracted more than their fair share of pseudo-scientific speculations involving ancient knowledge, lost civilisations, aliens and the like. Many attempts have been made to apply astronomical explanations, although the field of archaeoastronomy has been described by archaeologist Clive Ruggles as one "...*with academic work of high quality at one end but uncontrolled speculation bordering on lunacy at the other*".

We can be fairly certain that the movements of sun, moon and stars were of interest to prehistoric societies. Long before Neolithic times, people would have been aware of the link between the seasons and the sun's annual movements and that particular constellations were always prominent at the same time of the year. It is almost certain that such phenomena have been embedded in the cosmologies of human groups for as long as humans have been behaviourally modern. But to what extent were such concerns responsible for the construction of the megalithic monuments?

The best-known astronomical alignment is that of the Heel Stone at Stonehenge on the summer solstice sunrise, which was first noted by the antiquarian William Stukeley in the 1720s. Another is the 'roof-box' at Newgrange in County Meath, Ireland, which allows the light of the rising sun to fall on the back of the chamber for a few days on either side of the winter solstice. The roof-box serves no other obvious function, so the alignment is unlikely to be coincidental. Though neither Stonehenge nor Newgrange were 'observatories' as such, they incorporated powerful astronomical symbolism into their design – but could this also have been the case for other, far less high profile monuments?

The Grampian region of northeastern Scotland is dotted with so-called recumbent stone circles, where a single massive stone has been placed on its side between two tall upright flanker stones as part of the overall circle. This 'recumbent' stone is usually by far the largest stone in the circle, and the most important part of the monument. The stones in the remainder of the circle are often graded in height, rising towards the flanker stones. The recumbents and flankers are generally of different colour and material to the other stones in the circle. For example, at the site of Easter Aquhorthies, near Inverurie, the recumbent is red granite, the flanker stones are light grey granite, and the remaining stones are pinkish porphyry. It was often necessary, therefore, to obtain the recumbent stone from some distance away, although locally-available stone was used for rest of the monument. Given that the recumbents averaged 24 tonnes in weight, transportation would have been a significant undertaking.

The circles themselves are not large, typically measuring from 18 to 24 metres (60 to 80 ft.) in diameter. Dating to around 3000 BC, they typically occupy small territories of around 10 sq. km. (3.8 sq. miles), suggesting that they served small groups of subsistence farmers. Around a hundred are known, though it is likely that many more have been dismantled over the centuries. Small quantities of cremated human remains have been found, but these are thought to be associated with ritual offerings rather than graves. No prestigious artefacts have been found at any of these sites, suggesting the stone circles were built and used by small, egalitarian societies.

The circles were always placed on artificially-levelled sites on the summits of low hills with a clear view of the horizon. When viewed from the centre of the circle, the low recumbent stone and its tall flankers focus the viewer's attention on the portion of the horizon so framed. The recumbent and flankers were invariably placed on the SSW (202°30') side of the circle, covering about a quarter of the horizon from WSW (247°30') to SSE (157°30') as viewed from the centre. Such consistency that cannot be due to chance, and suggestions of an astronomical connection go back to the early part of the last century. The obvious interpretation is that these monuments were intended to enable the observation of celestial bodies on or above the stretch of horizon framed by the recumbent and its flanker stones. But what was being observed?

A popular explanation is that the intended alignment was on the setting of the midsummer full Moon. As it passed low over the recumbent stone and shed light into the stone circle, the Moon might have provided the backdrop for rituals. The problem is that the Moon's movements are rather more complex than those of the Sun, so trying to prove this theory is not as straightforward as ones involving the winter or summer solstitial Sun.

The elevation of the noontime Sun above the horizon (known astronomically as the 'culmination') depends on the time of the year, reaching a maximum at the summer solstice and a minimum at the winter solstice. The solstices also correspond to the southernmost and northernmost sunrises and sunsets of the year. The Moon behaves in a similar manner, except the cycle takes a month to complete rather than a year. 'Month' in this context is the 27.32 days it takes for the Moon to complete a single orbit of the Earth (the 'sidereal' month) rather than the 29.53 days that it takes to go through a full set of phases (the 'synodic' month). The two 'types' of month differ because the phase is determined by the Moon's position in the sky relative to the Sun. At the same time as the Moon is going around the Earth, the Earth is going around the Sun, so the Moon has to travel a bit further to return to the same position in the sky relative to the Sun. The upshot is that the culmination of the full Moon (and indeed all other phases) varies with the time of year. In winter, the full Moon rides high in the sky, but in summer it never gets very far above the horizon.

A further complication is that unlike the Sun, the Moon's southern and northern rising/setting limit are not fixed and increase and decrease cyclically between 'major standstill' and 'minor standstill' over the course of 18.61 years, a period known as the lunar nodal cycle. At 'major standstill', the differences between the culmination of the midwinter and midsummer full Moons are at their greatest, and in Scotland the latter barely rises above the horizon. It is this phenomenon, when the Moon would appear to 'roll' along the top of a recumbent stone, that many believe that the recumbent stone circles were intended to capture. Cup-shaped hollows on the recumbents, the flankers and adjacent stones might mark the points where the Moon rises and sets on these occasions.

Not everybody accepts this theory. Some argue for the midwinter sun, or that frequent use of red stones suggests an interest in red stars such as Betelgeuse and Aldebaran. Planetarium software has been used to suggest a connection with the constellation Orion, showing that at the time the circles were in use, it would have set within the recumbent frame on the night of the winter solstice. Another suggestion that intended axis of alignment was parallel to rather than perpendicular to the recumbent.

It is unlikely that we will ever know the full intentions behind the construction of these monuments, but they testify to a shared ritual tradition among people who had no central controlling authority. Similarly, we can only speculate on the nature of the rituals that took place, but the recumbent stone circles have ensured that their eerie echo reverberates to this day.

# 42: Of rice and men

*Seeking 'The Birthplace of Asian Rice'.*

Rice provides a fifth of the world's caloric intake, and is the predominant staple food for almost 2.5 billion people. There are 22 wild and two cultivated species of rice, and over 100,000 varieties are recognised. The cultivated species are *Oryza sativa* (Asian rice) and *Oryza glaberrima* (African rice), both of which originated from wild forms in humid tropical regions. Asian rice is grown world-wide, but African rice is grown mainly in West Africa. African rice has lower yields than its Asian counterpart, but it is hardy and it matures faster than Asian rice.

The wild precursor of Asian rice was *Oryza rufipogon*, a plant with edible red grains known as wild rice or red rice. Modern rice growers in the United States regard *Oryza rufipogon* as a 'noxious pest' because it competes with the domesticated strains, but sheds most of its grains before harvest and thus contributes very little to yields. There are two principle varieties of Asian rice, known as *japonica* (short grained) and *indica* (long grained). Just when and where domestication occurred has long been disputed. It is not just of historical and scientific interest: there would be considerable prestige associated with successfully claiming the title of 'The Birthplace of Asian Rice'. But the wide geographical range of *Oryza rufipogon* has led to competing claims from locations as far apart as the Ganges Valley, the southern slopes of the Himalayas, the coastal swamp regions of Southeast Asia, and the Yangtze region of China.

Archaeological evidence favours the latter possibility. Rice cultivation did not become widespread in India until around 2500 BC, although there is limited evidence for much earlier usage. The lakeside site of Lahuradewa in Uttar Pradesh dates to 6500 BC and the presence of rice there has been inferred from the remains of grains and husks, and from pottery tempered with rice husks. What remains unclear is whether the rice was cultivated or simply harvested from locally-occurring wild stands. Similarly, there is no strong evidence for rice cultivation in Southeast Asia until 2300 BC.

On the other hand, China was one of the primary centres of independent agricultural development. Millet was cultivated in the

Middle and Lower Yellow River valleys to the north and rice in the Middle and Lower Yangtze River valleys to the south. It has been suggested that millet and rice agriculture were independent developments, but it is more likely that they were linked and that the Yellow and Yangtze regions were part of a single sphere of interaction. A third centre of agricultural development was located in the southernmost part of the country, along the Zhu Jiang (Pearl) River.

The earliest rice remains in China have been recovered the cave sites of Xianrendong and Diaotonghuan in Jiangxi Province, and Shangshan in Zhejiang Province. All three sites date to around 8000 BC, although at this stage the rice might simply have been collected from wild stands rather than cultivated. The earliest site at which actual rice cultivation has been definitely identified is Jiahu in Henan Province, which was occupied from 7000 to 5800 BC. The site is located in the Upper Huai River region, which lies well to the north of the Yangtze, and beyond the range of wild rice. Thus the rice was certainly being cultivated, though it is disputed as to whether or not it was domesticated. Domesticated pigs were also present, but the archaeological evidence suggests that rice and pork were only dietary supplements and that the people of Jiahu subsisted mainly on hunting and wild plant foods.

Shortly after this, stronger evidence for partial domestication of rice begins to emerge from two Lower Yangtze sites in Zhejiang Province: Kuahuqiao and Tianluoshan. At Kuahuqiao, which dates to around 5750 BC, rice has been interpreted as being in an early stage of domestication. Forty percent of the rice has been identified as domesticated *japonica* and the remainder as wild. However, the rice appears to have been harvested before it had fully ripened – which would be necessary to avoid grain losses from shattering only if it had not yet been domesticated. On the other hand it is possible that the Kuahuqiao farmers were continuing to follow ancient harvesting practices, unaware that they were now no longer necessary. In any case, the small amount of rice found at the site in relation to other plant foods suggests that it was still only comprised a minor part of the Kuahuqiao villagers' diet.

Tianluoshan provides evidence for the oldest-known paddy fields – a technology that would eventually revolutionise rice agriculture. A study of rice remains dating from 4900 to 4600 BC shows that the Tianluoshan rice consisted of a high proportion of the shattering wild type. During that time, however, the percentage of the non-shattering variety increased from 27 to 39 percent. Meanwhile rice as a proportion of all the plant remains trebled from 8 to 24 percent. But although rice was clearly increasing in importance, even at the end of this period it was not fully domesticated, and it accounted for less than a quarter of the plant remains. Nevertheless, the farmers had apparently begun to utilise paddy field farming. Among the Tianluoshan rice remains were found a number of weeds that are associated with wet rice cultivation and found in present-day paddy fields.

Archaeological evidence is not the only line of enquiry, and geneticists have also attempted to unravel the early history of rice. Researchers have compared the genetic makeup of domesticated rice with wild strains of Asian rice from many locations, with the idea that the wild strain or strains giving the closest match will mark the spot or spots where domestication occurred. Studies at first indicated that there were two entirely separate domestications: *japonica* in southern China and *indica* within a region south of the Himalaya mountain range, probably eastern India, Myanmar, or Thailand.

Subsequent research seemed to confirm that *indica* and *japonica* came from separate stock, but it was also found that the two share a number of genes associated with non-shattering and other features of domestication. It soon became clear that these genes first appeared in *japonica* rice and only later found their way into *indica*. The simplest explanation is that *japonica* was the original domesticated strain, but it was later hybridised with either wild or semi-domesticated rice in northern India to produce the modern white-grained *indica* variety. This would accord with the archaeological evidence, but there was a surprise when geneticists obtained genome sequences from over four hundred geographically-widespread strains of wild Asian rice and from just over a thousand cultivated *indica* and *japonica* varieties to construct a comprehensive map of rice genome variation.

The results suggested that the initial domestication of rice occurred in the middle reaches of the Zhu Jiang (Pearl) River, in the Guangxi autonomous region. This region lies well to the south of the Yangtze and is located in the southernmost part of the country. As already noted, it was the third centre of Chinese agricultural development – but its major crops included roots, taro and other tubers. There is no archaeological evidence for early rice cultivation in the region. It is possible that the Pearl River farmers simply did not keep large stores of rice, unlike their Yangtze counterparts further north. It is clear, though, that our understanding of the earliest history of rice farming is incomplete.

The best hope of solving the riddle is to recover DNA from ancient rice, which might enable researchers to determine just when and where the major genes associated with domestication emerged. Unfortunately, most rice remains from archaeological sites are charred, and attempts to obtain ancient DNA from them have so far proved unsuccessful. However, generic sequencing techniques are improving all the time, and we may be hopeful that in the near future such efforts are rewarded. When they are, we will be able to gain further insight into one of the most crucial episodes in Asian prehistory.

# 43: An unlikely success story

*The origins of the world's most important cereal crop.*

Maize is the most widely produced cereal crop in the world. World-wide production was 831,358,000 tonnes for the period 2010-11, according to figures released by the US Department of Agriculture. Of this, the United States accounted for 316,165,000 tonnes, or just below 40 percent. In addition to its familiar guises of sweetcorn, popcorn and flour, an increasing amount of maize production is now used for biofuel production, especially in the United States where the figure exceeds 40 percent. Other maize products include corn oil, corn syrup and animal feed. But possibly the most startling fact about maize is that it was ever domesticated at all.

Archaeologists were long baffled by the sudden appearance of maize in the archaeological record. Unlike wheat, barley or rice it has no obvious wild relative; there is no wild cereal with anything resembling its massive cobs. As long ago as the eighteenth century, it was noticed that the seedlings of a wild Mesoamerican cereal known as teosinte resemble those of maize. The name means 'grain of the gods' in the indigenous Mexican Nahuátl language, but there is very little godlike about ears of teosinte. In contrast to a 1,000-grained ear of maize, they contains no more than twelve grains and these are enclosed in a hard, woody shell known as the cupulate fruitcase. Teosinte is certainly not the type of plant that early farmers might have been expected to cultivate, and view that it was the wild ancestor of maize fell out of favour during the first half of the twentieth century. Some even believed that it was more closely-related to rice than maize.

Dog corn, a plant intermediate between teosinte and maize was thought to be a more promising candidate, but by 1928 this had been shown to be a natural first-generation cross between the two. Significantly, however, dog corn is fertile, which implied a close genetic relationship between teosinte and maize. Geneticists Rollins Adams Emerson and George Beadle at Cornell University investigated further and found that each has ten chromosomes, and that these are so similar that teosinte and maize are effectively the same species. Emerson and Beadle believed that they had solved the problem of maize ancestry, but by the late 1930s further studies suggested that the genetic differences between teosinte and maize were too great to be accounted for by domestication. Botanist Paul Mangelsdorf claimed that teosinte was a recent species derived from hybridisation between maize and a wild grass known as *Tripsacum*. This theory gained widespread acceptance despite a chromosomal incompatibility between the two species and a complete lack of evidence for natural hybridisation even though they often grow in close proximity.

After retirement in 1968 from a distinguished career that saw him share the Nobel Prize in 1958 for his work in genetics, Beadle returned to the problem of maize ancestry and set out to determine the genetic differences between it and teosinte. The genetic sequencing techniques used in modern studies were still some way in the future, so Beadle began growing large populations of teosinte-maize crosses to see if he could obtain offspring equivalent to either teosinte or maize parents. The laws of genetic inheritance, as formulated by Gregor Mendel in the mid-nineteenth century, state that if there is a difference of one gene between two parents, each original type will show up in the second generation with a frequency of one in four; but for two different genes the frequency is one in sixteen, and for ten differences it is around one in a million. It followed that even for as few as ten genetic differences between teosinte and maize, the chances of finding one that resembled either of the original parents were pretty remote. However, by growing 50,000 second generation plants, there would be a reasonable chance of making such a find provided there were no more than six or seven major genetic differences. After several seasons of crossing, Beadle found that the occurrence of parental types was around one in 500, corresponding to about five major gene differences between teosinte and maize. There seemed to be absolutely no reason to suppose that cultivation by pre-Columbian farmers could not have brought about these changes.

With Beadle now vindicated, the next step was to try to locate the 'cradle of maize domestication' by identifying the strain of teosinte most closely related to domesticated maize. A number of molecular studies were conducted during the 1980s, and in 1990 botanist John Doebley concluded that only the teosinte subspecies *Zea mays* L. ssp. *parviglumis* gave a molecular overlap with maize. The best match was found with populations from the Central Balsas River watershed, which lies to the southwest of Mexico City. Doebley believed that the same series of mutations was unlikely to have occurred more than once and concluded, therefore, that maize was domesticated only once. In 2002, using modern genetic techniques, a team led by Doebley studied teosinte from across its entire geographical range and confirmed the earlier results, also suggesting that domestication had occurred around 7000 BC. However, further studies indicated that the process of domestication was fairly slow and that maize in its modern form might only have emerged within the last 2,000 years.

The confirmation that teosinte was the ancestor of maize brought archaeologists firmly back to the question that had made them doubt teosinte ancestry in the first place: why was a grain crop offering such limited rewards domesticated at all? One suggestion was that it was originally cultivated not for its grain but for its sugar-rich stems. Maize is closely related to sugarcane, and a maize stem typically contains 15 to 50 gm. (0.5 to 1.75 oz.) of sugars (sucrose, fructose, and glucose), or two to sixteen percent by weight. The sugar would have had many uses, including for brewing maize beer. Plant remains found at a number of cave sites in Mesoamerica and South America suggest that maize stems were on occasion chewed as a sugary snack. The practice declined after around 1500 BC, possibly as cobs became larger and maize became an increasingly important food staple. Critics of the theory noted that there is no archaeological evidence in the form of large quantities of crushed and discarded stems, but proponents argued that the chances of finding such remains are extremely low. Such activities would be more likely to take place out in the open than in caves where discarded maize stems might be preserved, and it is also probable that the stems would have been dried out and used as fuel rather than simply discarded.

The earliest archaeological evidence for domesticated maize has been found in the Central Balsas watershed, strengthening the case that domestication occurred there. Archaeological work at the Xihuatoxtla rock shelter site has revealed a long sequence of human occupation and plant exploitation reaching back to the early Holocene. Stone tools dating to around 6700 BC have been recovered, including flaked points, simple flake tools, and numerous milling stones. Starch grains were recovered from the milling stones and other stone tools, of which 90 percent were found to be from maize. The average grain size was larger than the size range for wild teosinte grains, consistent with domesticated maize. The irregular shape of the grains is similar to that of maize, but differs from the oval or bell shapes of teosinte grains. Archaeologists also recovered large numbers of maize phytoliths from the sediment samples. Phytoliths are microscopic silica bodies found in some plant tissues, and their size and shape can provide an indication as to the domesticated status of plant remains. The Xihuatoxtla maize phytoliths were consistent with those from domesticated maize. However, the phytoliths refuted the sugar stem theory. No phytoliths of the type found in both maize and teosinte stems were found, implying that the emphasis had always been on the cobs.

Until the discoveries in the Central Balsas region, the earliest evidence for domesticated maize was thought to be at the site of San Andrés, Tabasco, located 15 km (9 miles) inland from Mexico's southernmost Gulf coast. Archaeologists used pollen data to track the development of early Mesoamerican agriculture over the course of over two and a half millennia. Maize pollen was first seen around 5100 BC, but the grain sizes were consistent with wild teosinte. At the same time, an abrupt rise in charcoal particles suggests that forests were being cleared to make way for farm land. Larger pollen grains, consistent with domesticated maize, first appeared around 5000 BC and were common by 4000 BC. However, small teosinte pollen grains did not finally disappear until around 2500 BC, suggesting that full domestication was a fairly protracted process. Nevertheless, teosinte is not native to this region, so it must have been imported for the specific purposes of cultivation. As unpromising as it might seem as a grain crop, teosinte was clearly valued by early Mexican farmers.

Domesticated maize cobs do not show up in the archaeological record until rather later than the pollen evidence. At Guilá Naquitz Cave in the highlands of Oaxaca, archaeologists recovered three cob fragments dating to 4250 BC, all of which might have come from the same harvest. All three possessed non-shattering rachis, and were thus were unable to propagate without human intervention. One of the cobs had four rows of grain rather than just the two seen in wild teosinte. Although this was still a long way from the many rows of grain seen in a modern cob, it is clear that farmers were selecting for cobs with four or more rows of grain.

Maize phytoliths appear quite suddenly at Guilá Naquitz around 4250 BC, but have not been found in earlier occupation phases of the cave. Although *Cucurbita pepo* squash was cultivated there as long ago as 8000 BC, apparently neither wild teosinte nor maize were harvested for food prior to 4250 BC. It is a similar picture at the cave sites of San Marcos and Coxcatlán in Puebla, where domesticated squash was grown millennia before the arrival of maize around 3500 BC. Curiously, there is evidence that maize had spread south into Panama well before it was grown at Guilá Naquitz Cave. Analysis of starch grains recovered from plant processing tools show that it was present at a number of rock shelter and cave sites by 5800 BC, together with locally-growing wild yams, and arrowroot and manioc from South America.

By 2500 BC, maize production was becoming more intensive. Pollen data from sites in the Maya Lowlands of northern Belize has revealed evidence for forest clearance and widespread maize and manioc cultivation, although the more complex societies of the Maya did not start to emerge until after 1000 BC. From its Mesoamerican origins, maize spread south with some rapidity, with starch grains from charred cooking-pot residues at Loma Alta confirming its presence in Ecuador by 3300 and disputed phytolith data from Real Alto hinting at an Ecuadorian presence as early as 4400 BC. Similar evidence indicates that maize reached Peru by 2000 BC and Uruguay by 2800 BC. Meanwhile, in the northwards direction, fossil remains from open air sites and rock shelters in New Mexico and Arizona show that maize reached the United States no later than 2100 BC. The domestication of maize provided New World farmers with a highly productive cereal crop. It matures quickly, can easily be stored, and has evolved many high yielding varieties. Along with beans and squashes, maize became one of the 'Three Sisters' upon which New World agriculture was largely based.

# 44: Spreading the word

*The on-going search for the Indo-European homeland.*

What do Ancient Greek, Latin and Sanskrit have in common, other than that they are no longer spoken anywhere in the world? In 1786, Sir William Jones, a 40-year-old English judge serving in India, noted that the grammar and vocabulary of Sanskrit, the liturgical language of Hinduism, has much in common with that of Ancient Greek and Latin. All three are 'dead' languages, which were current at roughly the same time as each other. In an address to the Asiatic Society in Calcutta, Jones claimed that these similarities were not due to chance and that the three languages might have arisen "...*from some common source, which, perhaps no longer exists*". He also speculated that Gothic (the precursor of German), Celtic and Old Persian may share the same common origin.

The idea that an ancient link might have existed between languages spoken in places as far apart as Iceland and India was startling to say the least, but it soon became accepted as more and more language groups were added to what became known as the Indo-European language family. Jones suggested that the various ancient languages could all be traced back to a common homeland, setting in motion a debate that has continued ever since. The homeland has been located at just about every point on Earth, leading the American scholar J.P. Mallory to remark, "*One does not ask 'where is the Indo-European homeland?' but rather 'where do they put it now?'*".

That groups of languages can arise from a common origin was already accepted in Sir William Jones' day. It had long been realised that many European languages including French, Spanish, Portuguese, Italian and Romanian had all diverged from Latin after the fall of the Roman Empire. Languages are not static: that they evolve over time is apparent from the King James Bible:

*The Lord is my shepherd; I shall not want.*
*He maketh me to lie down in green pastures:*
*He leadeth me beside the still waters.*
*He restoreth my soul:*
*He leadeth me in the paths of righteousness for his name's sake.*

*Yea, though I walk through the valley of the shadow of death, I shall fear no evil:*
*For thou art with me; thy rod and thy staff they comfort me.*
*Thou preparest a table before me in the presence of mine enemies:*
*Thou anointest my head with oil; my cup runneth over.*
*Surely goodness and mercy shall follow me all the days of my life:*
*And I will dwell in the house of the Lord for ever.* – The 23rd Psalm.

Although the 'biblical' feel of the text may seem familiar, it only reflects the way people actually spoke in the early seventeenth century. Forms such as *thou art* (you are) were still in everyday use, and the *-eth, -est* inflections had yet to give way to the modern *-s* form (for example *makes* rather than *maketh*). Such changes come about as one generation's sloppy speech becomes the next generation's received version. English was once a fully-inflected language, and both nouns and pronouns used grammatical cases. Although pronouns retain cases (for example *he/him*), those for nouns fell into disuse. In addition, plurals were simplified: forms such as *foxas* (foxes), *tungan* (tongues) and *bec* (books) were once common before the modern *-s/-es* suffix came into use. Today, only a few archaic forms survive, such as *man/men, woman/women* and *child/children*.

Just as a language is not fixed in time, so it varies across regions. All languages are really collections of closely-related dialects. Until the fifteenth century, what became known as 'Standard' English was nothing more than the dialect that happened to be spoken in London, but the rise of the printing industry there meant that manuscripts usually appeared in this version. Consequently, it became accepted as 'standard' English, although the other dialects were equally valid. Similarly, in Roman times, different dialects of Latin were spoken in different parts of the Empire. After the fall of Rome, contacts between the various peoples reduced, and these differences became ever more marked. Eventually, the Latin dialects spoken in Italy, France, Spain, etc. diverged to such an extent that they became distinct languages, forming the present-day Romance group of languages.

Following the same chain of reasoning, it was logical to assume that similarities between the Indo-European languages could be explained by divergence from a single ancestral language, originally spoken by people from a single region. This hypothetical language became known as Proto-Indo-European (often abbreviated to PIE). But who were the speakers of this language, and when did they live?

Above all, how did the languages descended from their ancestral tongue come to be spoken across an area far greater in extent than the Roman Empire?

To answer these questions, linguists first needed to reconstruct PIE. The task of piecing together a prehistoric language might sound impossible, but by following a number of rules it is possible to reconstruct a long-dead mother tongue from its successor languages. For example, the word for *man* is *uomo* (Italian), *l'homme* (French), *hombre* (Spanish), *homem* (Portuguese) and *om* (Romanian). As can be seen, they are all very similar to one another. The similarity reflects the common etymological origin of these words, which all arose from the Latin word *homo*. Such words are known as cognates (the English words *man* and *men* are cognate with the German words *Mann* and *Mensch*).

In the early nineteenth century, linguists noticed that phonetic features in one language differ from those of another in a consistent way. For example, in Latin the *f-* sound in many words corresponds to the *b-* sound in Germanic languages. Thus *frater* in Latin becomes *brother* in English and *Bruder* in German. Another example is *th-* in English, which becomes *d-* in German. Thus *thank* becomes *danke* in German. If it is known what sound shifts have occurred among a group of daughter languages, it is possible to work backwards from a group of cognates to reconstruct a word in the original mother tongue.

Using this method, which is known as the comparative method, nineteenth century linguists were able to reconstruct many PIE words. For example, the word *sheep* is *avis* in Lithuanian, *ovis* in Latin, *ois* in Greek, *oveja* in Spanish and *ewe* in English. The reconstructed PIE word is *\*owis* (the asterisk denotes reconstruction). Other reconstructed words include *\*mehter* (*mother*), *\*phator* (*father*), *\*swesor* (*sister*), *\*bhrater* (*brother*), *\*dhughater* (*daughter*), *\*suhnus* (*son*), *\*tauros* (*bull*), *\*gwous* (*cow*), *\*uksen* (*ox*), *\*porkos* (*pig*), *\*kapros* (*goat*) and *\*kwon* (*dog*). The familiarity of these words stands out immediately. Even where the meaning isn't immediately obvious, it doesn't take much working out. For example, *\*kwon* is cognate with the English word *hound*.

The next step was to use the reconstructed words to make inferences about the Proto-Indo-Europeans, their homeland, and their way of life. One approach tried in the mid-nineteenth century was linguistic palaeontology. The basic assumption was that if a PIE word exists for something, then the Proto-Indo-Europeans must have been familiar with it, and inferences can therefore be made about their way of life. Unfortunately, the approach has its limitations.

PIE has words pertaining to wheeled vehicles including *wheel*, *axle*, *shaft* and *hub*. The wheel was invented around 3300 BC and if the existence of PIE words for it is taken at face value, then we get a date for when the language was spoken that is no earlier than then. This is consistent with the observation that Mycenaean Greek, Indo-Iranian and Anatolian separated from one another well before 2000 BC. However, archaeologist Colin Renfrew has challenged the widely-accepted inference that the Proto-Indo-Europeans must have had wheeled vehicles and argued that the universality of words relating to the wheel results from widespread linguistic 'borrowing'. He believes that innovations such as the wheel and wheeled vehicles spread so rapidly that the relevant vocabulary spread with them as loanwords. Subsequent sound-shifts in the borrowing languages would create the illusion that borrowed words were part of the proto-lexicon. A modern comparison would be the spread of the word *internet*, which is *Intāranēta* in Bengali (an Indo-European language), *aaintarnaat* in Burmese (Sino-Tibetan) and *aterineto* in Malagasay (Austronesian).

Another potential pitfall is to assume that because there is no reconstructed word for something, it was unknown to the Proto-Indo-Europeans. For example, PIE contains many words for domestic animals, but only a few pertaining to farming. This led some to suppose that the Proto-Indo-Europeans were nomadic pastors rather than farmers. The problem is that nomadic pastors are familiar with farming and their way of life involves interaction with farmers. Another example is that there are reconstructed words for *eye* and *eyebrow*, but no word for *eyelid*. It is nevertheless safe to assume that the Proto-Indo-Europeans were familiar with the latter.

We also run into difficulties when we attempt to make inferences about the social systems of the Proto-Indo-Europeans. For example, there are cognate words for *king* in many Indo-European languages, such as *raj* (Sanskrit), *rex* (Latin) and *ri* (Old Irish). Some have taken this to imply that the Proto-Indo-Europeans were ruled by a king, but if we look at the English cognate *ruler* we can see that this notion is suspect. The verb *to rule* can indeed mean to reign, but it also possible to rule on other matters, such as a point of law. Rules crop up in business, sport, science, and of course at school. Things can be 'ruled out'. Finally, it is possible to rule a straight line. The correspondence between straight lines and rules can be seen in the expression 'to keep on the straight and narrow', and this correspondence is also found in other Indo-European languages. Rather than a king, the reconstructed PIE word *reg* might have referred to a tribal head, or simply an arbiter of right and wrong.

Another field of study that has long attracted Indo-European scholars is the religion of the Proto-Indo-Europeans. The word for *god* is widely attested, for example *devas* (Sanskrit), *deus* (Latin), *dievas* (Lithuanian), *dia* (Old Irish) and *deity* (English). The reconstructed PIE word is *deiwos*. Rather more striking is the word *dyeus phater* (*sky father*), better known to anybody familiar with Greek or Roman mythology as Zeus or Jupiter. The obvious assumption is that the head honcho of the Proto-Indo-European pantheon was a brash thunderbolt-hurling alpha male – but the same god was less prominent in other religions such as Indic. It is likely that the pre-eminence of Zeus/Jupiter in Mediterranean religions was a later phenomenon involving the conflation of the Indo-European god with local weather deities.

By the end of the nineteenth century, it was becoming apparent that the Proto-Indo-European problem could not be solved with linguistic data alone, and scholars turned to archaeological evidence. In 1926, V. Gordon Childe proposed a homeland on the Pontic-Caspian steppes north of the Black Sea and Caspian Sea. This suggestion was later taken up by Lithuanian émigré Marija Gimbutas, who associated the Proto-Indo-Europeans with what she termed the Kurgan culture. The name comes from the Russian word for the Kurgan peoples' trademark barrows or burial mounds, and Gimbutas introduced it as a blanket term for a number of steppe cultures in eastern Ukraine and southern Russia. The Kurgan people were nomadic pastors who originated in the lower Volga basin and the lower Dnieper region around 4500 BC.

Drawing on both linguistic and archaeological evidence, Gimbutas envisaged the Kurgan people as a warlike male-dominated society, worshipping masculine sky-gods. They were a nomadic society, using ox-drawn wagons and horses for transport. Only a few permanent settlements have been found, as would be expected for nomadic people. They are known mainly from their mortuary practices, whereby the dead were interred in earthen or stone chambers, above which a burial mound was frequently erected. By contrast, the people of what Gimbutas termed 'Old Europe' were farmers, living in small family-based communities. Gimbutas characterised them as peaceful, matriarchal and possessing a mother goddess-centred religion. Geographically, Old Europe comprised the Balkan and Danube regions, the Adriatic coast of Italy, and Sicily.

Gimbutas claimed that between 4400 and 2800 BC, the Kurgan people mounted three invasions of Old Europe, Anatolia and the Caucasus, before moving eastwards towards India and along the steppe into Central Asia. The culture of Old Europe gave way to that of the Kurgan warriors and fine Old European ceramics and painted wares were replaced by cruder Kurgan material. Kurgan burials appeared, generally confined to males, and accompanied by arrows, spears, knives, horse-headed sceptres. Stone stelae have been found in the Alpine region depicting horses, wagons, axes, spears and daggers, all of which are valued by a warlike society. Similar evidence is seen in the South Caucasus, Anatolia and southern Siberia.

The Kurgan hypothesis has been widely accepted, but in 1987, Colin Renfrew put forward an entirely different model and suggested that the Proto-Indo-Europeans were Neolithic farmers. He drew on the 'wave of advance' model that has been proposed some years earlier by the Italian geneticist Luigi Luca Cavalli-Sforza and American archaeologist Albert Ammerman. As we have seen, the pair used mathematical models to show that the archaeological record of Europe indicated a 'wave of advance' of Neolithic farmers spreading out from Southwest Asia. As population pressures grew, farmers spread out into previously-unfarmed regions. Further expansion occurred as these regions in turn filled up, and so on. Renfrew claimed that it was the spread of agriculture that had distributed the farmers' language over such an enormous area. He proposed that the Proto-Indo-European expansion had begun in Anatolia before 6500 BC. From there, it had spread to Greece before moving in a north-westerly direction across Europe. Once farming had reached the Eurasian steppe, nomadic pastoralism developed and the pastors moved swiftly east across the steppes and into Iran and northern India.

Renfrew's model attracted considerable interest, although like any radical new theory it attracted its fair share of controversy. Many felt that the date of 6500 BC was too far early to be associated with PIE. Other critics focussed on genetic and archaeological evidence suggesting that indigenous hunter-gatherers had not simply disappeared but had in many cases taken up agriculture themselves. Renfrew later fine-tuned his model to take into account such regional effects, but the essential premise of farming and language dispersal remained.

To this day, it remains unclear as to which of the two rival hypotheses is correct. In the last decade, a statistical technique known as Bayesian inference has been applied to the problem. The technique is named for the eighteenth century mathematician Rev. Thomas Bayes and is a powerful but computational-intensive statistical method. In recent years, the method had been brought to the fore by the 'number-crunching' abilities of modern computers, which enable calculations that would once have taken weeks to be performed in a matter of minutes. Researchers obtained a date of between 7500 and 6000 BC for when the various Indo-European languages began to diverge from one another. This date is more consistent with Renfrew's model than with the Kurgan hypothesis, and in addition the studies suggested that the geographical homeland of PIE is Anatolia. However, this conclusion has been contradicted by a recent genetic study indicating a large-scale migration into Europe from the steppes between 3000 and 2500 BC, which is consistent with the Kurgan hypothesis. One possibility is that there are elements of truth in both models. It could be that the steppe migration was a secondary migration of people descended from the original Anatolian farmers. On this view, the latter spoke an early form of PIE known as Pre-PIE or Proto-Indo-Hittite. The steppe people spoke a later form of the language, known as Early Steppe PIE.

Regardless of its ultimate origin, PIE has been extraordinarily successful. Probably it was originally spoken by no more than a few tens of thousands, but it gave rise to languages now spoken by 45 percent of the world's population. It underwent further expansion after 1492, with the European colonisation of the New World. We should also note that if Renfrew is right, Neil Armstrong's first words from the surface of the Moon were spoken in a language that originated with the dispersal of farmers from Anatolia almost nine millennia earlier.

# 45: The copper awl

*Did the rich metalworking traditions of the Levant originate in the Balkans?*

The first use of metals by humans considerably predates the Bronze Age: copper is one of only a few metals that can occur naturally in the metallic state, and unlike gold and silver it is reasonably abundant. Such copper is described as 'native', and humans learned to make use of it long before the invention of metal smelting. As long ago as the eighth millennium BC, native copper was being hammered to make beads and other small objects at the Pre-Pottery Neolithic B site of Çayönü Tepesi in southeast Turkey. For several thousand years before then, beads made from copper ores such as malachite were prized for their distinctive green colour. The colour green was probably associated with plants and the environment (as is still the case today) and likely took on a greater significance with the advent of agriculture.

However, smelting ore to produce copper is a far more complex process in which ore is heated with charcoal and a sufficient air supply at a carefully-controlled temperature. The process generates carbon monoxide, which in turn 'reduces' the ore to metallic copper. Although the underlying chemistry is fairly straightforward, the practicalities are not, and the slightest mistake in the chain of operation will ruin the whole process. The pre-Bronze Age period when copper metallurgy was gradually coming into use alongside stone tools is referred to the Copper Age, Chalcolithic or Æneolithic; the latter two terms both mean 'copper-stone'. At some stage, it would have been noticed that the casting properties and hardness of the copper were improved when particular ores or combinations of ores were used. These contained quantities of arsenic and the result was arsenical bronze – an alloy of copper with arsenic. Tin bronze did not come into widespread use until 2200 BC, but over the next five hundred years it supplanted arsenical bronze throughout Europe and western Asia. The properties of tin bronze are only slightly superior to those of arsenical bronze, but it must soon have been realised that the use of tin avoided the adverse health issues associated with long-term exposure to arsenic.

Just when, where and how many times copper smelting was first invented is a key question for prehistorians. V. Gordon Childe believed that it was invented only once, in Southwest Asia. Given the importance of the region in the development of agriculture and the later rise of civilisation in Mesopotamia, this was not an unreasonable supposition. However, the matter remained unresolved: in the 1960s Colin Renfrew argued for multiple independent inventions throughout Eurasia, but the American historian Theodore Wertime contended that the necessary expertise could only have been invented once. At that time, and indeed for some time thereafter, there was insufficient data in the form of field and laboratory work to answer these questions.

There has been a long-running debate over how copper smelting is to be recognised in the archaeological record and whether early extraction processes would have left an archaeologically-visible signature in the form of vitrified slag. Copper ore may be reduced to metallic copper at relatively low temperatures of around 700 degrees Celsius, but the melting point of copper is 1,080 degrees Celsius. It has been suggested that early copper smelting entailed extraction from ore at low temperature and followed by melting at higher temperatures for casting into ingots or artefacts. Such a two-step process would leave very little in the way of vitrified slag, and would thus be difficult to detect. If on the other hand higher temperatures are used, only one step is required and slag is produced as a waste product. It has been argued that this latter process is more efficient, easier to control, and more likely to have been used. Even so, the presence of slag is not conclusive proof of smelting technology, because it can also be produced by re-melting metallic copper. However, chemical analysis can readily distinguish between the two cases. Smelting produces a slag that is rich in metals such as iron and manganese, whereas slag resulting from re-melting consists mainly of fused ceramic material contaminated with fuel ash with some copper metal and copper oxides.

The earliest such evidence found to date is from the site of Belovode in Serbia. The site is associated with the Vinča culture, which was current in much of the Balkan region for about 700 years from 5300 to 4600 BC. The culture is named for the site of Vinča near Belgrade and is associated with large implements made from high-purity copper, including hammer-axes, chisels and armbands. By analysing the impurities that were present, archaeologists determined that the 'geological provenance' of the metal was probably from deposits in Bulgaria, Macedonia and possibly Serbia. Unfortunately, there was very little evidence for smelting in the form of slag: only one piece, dating to around 4500 BC. All that changed in 1993 with the discovery of a major Vinča settlement at Belovode. The site was occupied from 5000 to 4650 BC and the Vinča culture occupation levels have yielding copper smelting slag, copper minerals and ores, and a droplet of copper metal, dating throughout the occupation. A geological provenance analysis suggested that manganese rich ores were used for smelting, whereas malachite was used for making beads. Radiocarbon dating of animal remains has been used to date the occupation levels and these are consistent with the dates for the Vinča culture elsewhere. The date of 5000 BC for smelting slag is 500 years earlier than anywhere else currently known in the Balkans and Southwest Asia.

The operative word, of course, is 'currently': these finds do not rule out the possibility of copper smelting technology of a comparable age elsewhere. By 4300 BC, the southern Levant was a major centre of metallurgy, a development that surely played an important part in the emergence of the first city-states a millennium later. Prestige items were being manufactured from copper by around 4300 BC. An elaborate tradition developed involving lost-wax casting of antimony or nickel-rich copper alloyed with arsenic to produce these objects. At the same time, more utilitarian objects such as axes, chisels and awls were produced by casting unalloyed copper in simple moulds. But was this metalworking tradition of independent origin?

The question remained unanswered until archaeologists recovered a badly-corroded copper awl at Tel Tsaf, a Middle Chalcolithic site in the Jordan Valley that was occupied between 5100 and 4600 BC. The settlement comprises a number of courtyard complexes of rectangular and rounded rooms, cooking facilities, and large numbers of grain silos. The latter are tall, barrel-shaped structures, built from mud bricks, measuring 2 to 4 m (6 ft. 6 in. to 13 ft.) in diameter with an estimated capacity of 15 to 30 tonnes of grain. Animal remains included large numbers of cattle and pigs. Together, these attest to the accumulation of food surpluses on a scale unprecedented for the region at that time. Artefacts from the site included elaborately painted pottery, over 2,500 beads made from ostrich eggshells, and another hundred made from stone. Many of the artefacts were of non-local origin, including obsidian items from Anatolia or Armenia, a shell from the Nile and pottery from northern Syria or Mesopotamia, indicating that the people of Tel Tsaf had access to long-distance exchange networks throughout Southwest Asia.

Four graves were found on the site, two inside and two adjacent to silos. The copper awl was discovered in one of the silo graves, which held the remains of a woman aged around forty. It is a 41 mm (1.6 in.) pin made from cast copper, with a maximum diameter of 5 mm (0.2 in.), narrowing to 1 mm (0.04 in.) near the tip. Other grave goods included an ostrich-shell bead necklace consisting of 1,668 beads. Corrosion made it impossible to be certain of the initial chemical composition of the awl, but analysis suggested it had comprised copper alloyed with 6 percent tin and 0.8 percent arsenic, with traces of lead and iron.

The presence of tin in the alloy suggests that the awl was not of local origin. Tin bronze artefacts are not found in the southern Levant until the Middle Bronze Age (second millennium BC), and natural tin bronze alloys do not occur in the region. The awl not only predates all previously-known metal artefacts in the southern Levant by several centuries, it also predates all known tin bronze items in the region by around 3,000 years. It therefore seems likely that the awl reached Tel Tsaf via long-distance exchange networks. Rather than being an indigenous development, metallurgy in the southern Levant probably arose from an earlier, non-local tradition that diffused from the north. At first, metal artefacts were imported and it was not until some centuries later that they were produced locally.

That the awl was found in what was clearly an elite grave suggests that at this stage, metal items were seen as rare and prestigious. The residents of the courtyard building where the grave was found evidently belonged to a family or group that exercised control over the local production and storage of grain and had access to long-distance trade. Possibly their wealth resulted from trade in luxury items obtained from places very remote from Tel Tsaf. Southwest Asia had been a primary centre where agriculture developed, and it would go on to host the world's first urban societies. However, the evidence from Belovode and Tel Tsaf suggests that it did not have a monopoly on innovation.

# 46: Ötzi the Iceman

*The life and violent death of Ötzi the Iceman.*

In September 1991, a German couple by the name of Helmut and Erika Simon were hillwalking in the Ötztal Alps on the border between Austria and Italy. They were making their way along the Tisenjoch Pass at an elevation of 3,210 metres (10,530 ft.) when they came across a frozen human body. Believing it to be that of a mountaineer, they alerted the authorities. After several days the body was recovered and taken to the University of Innsbruck, where it soon became clear that it had belonged to a man who lived and died in prehistoric times. Soon after death his body had become covered with ice, with the result that it became mummified and had deteriorated only slightly. Given the importance of the find, ownership immediately became an issue. Within a month, it was determined that the body had been found on the Italian side of the border, but it was agreed to allow the University of Innsbruck complete its scientific examination of what soon became known as Ötzi the Iceman. Radiocarbon dating has established that Ötzi had lived around 3250 BC, during the Chalcolithic period.

At the time of his death Ötzi is estimated to have been about 46 years old, stood 1.60 metres (5 ft. 3 in.) tall, and weighed about 50 kilograms (110 lb.). He was of slim build, with dark, wavy shoulder-length hair and a beard. Based on genetic data, it is thought that he had brown eyes and belonged to blood group O. The degree of preservation meant that the contents of his stomach and intestines could be analysed. The analytic work included DNA sequencing, which aided identification of much of the contents. His final meal, eaten around eight hours before his death, consisted of red deer meat, herbs and a processed cereal, possibly unleavened bread made from einkorn wheat. This had been preceded by a meal of ibis (mountain goat) meat.

Stable isotope analysis of Ötzi's dental enamel has provided information about where he spent his childhood, as even the adult dentition largely forms in the early years of life. Oxygen isotope data suggested that he lived south of the Alpine watershed, and lead and strontium data refined this to regions where the local geology is dominated by gneisses and phyllites: the Schnals, Vinschgau, Ulten, middle Eisack, and lower Puster valleys. The best overall match is Feldthurns, a Chalcolithic site on the terraces of the Eisack valley. The Vinschgau near Merano and the Ulten valley are also possibilities, although no Chalcolithic sites are known for the latter. The isotope data from Ötzi's bones suggests that in adult life, he relocated from his childhood home, possibly to the Vinschgau region. Alternatively, it was suggested that he was involved with what is known as transhumance, where livestock are moved between low-altitude settlements in the south and high-altitude summer grazing areas in the north. The practice continues to the present day, but later work established that it began no earlier than the Bronze Age, after Ötzi's time. Thus it appears that Ötzi spent nearly all of his life in an area several days walk to south of where his body was found.

Geneticists were able to sequence Ötzi's mitochondrial, Y-chromosomal and autosomal genomes. His mitochondrial DNA belongs to the haplogroup K1, which is fairly common in Europe and Southwest Asia, and has a high occurrence among Ashkenazi Jews. However, Ötzi could not be matched with any of the three present-day subgroups K1a, K1b and K1c. He was assigned to the Y-chromosomal haplogroup G2a4-L91, which is rare in mainland Europe, but common in southern Corsica and northern Sardinia. This result was consistent with autosomal data, which also indicated a connection with present-day inhabitants of Corsica and Sardinia. Sardinians, while part of the European gene pool, are genetically distinctive as a result of their isolation from mainland Europe, and it was suggested that their ancestral population might once have been more widespread. The possibility that this population could have left a faint genetic trace was conformed when comparisons with samples taken from over 3,700 male blood donors in Tyrol showed that 19 of them shared a rare genetic mutation of Ötzi's Y-chromosome.

Ötzi lacked the mutation associated with lactase persistence in adults, meaning that he was probably lactose intolerant. Most mammals lose the ability to digest the lactose sugar in fresh milk soon after weaning because the body stops producing lactase, the enzyme that breaks down lactose in the digestive system. This was also the case with humans in pre-agricultural times. However, among present-day populations in Europe, lactase production persists into adulthood with a frequency of around 80 percent. The failure to 'switch off' the production of lactase resulted from a chance mutation, which in hunter-gatherer societies conferred little benefit. With the advent of dairy farming, however, lactase persistence became highly beneficial and swept through the population, but studies of ancient DNA obtained from human remains at Neolithic sites suggest that it was still uncommon in Europe 5,000 years ago. Analysis of lipid residues taken from pottery vessels from sites in Southwest Asia and southeastern Europe has confirmed that the use of milk was already widespread by this time. However, it is believed that the lipid residues were from processed milk in the form of cheese, ghee, etc., rather than fresh milk. Such products could be stored for use throughout the year and would also have been a solution to the problem of lactose intolerance.

Researchers also obtained a genome of the common stomach bacterium *Helicobacter pylori* from Ötzi's stomach contents. *H. pylori* was carried by the first migrants from Africa, and is present in much of the world's population. Modern strains have been assigned to distinct populations according to their geographic origin. The European strain hpEurope is thought to have resulted from hybridization between two ancestral strains known as AE1 and AE2. AE1 is thought to have arisen in Central Asia and have evolved into the present-day strain hpAsia2, while AE2 is thought to have arisen in Northeast Africa. The hybridization was thought to have occurred in Southwest Asia as long as 50,000 years ago, with the recombined strain reaching Europe as populations expanded after the Last Glacial Maximum. Accordingly, it was believed that the *H. pylori* hosted by Ötzi would be similar to the present-day hpEurope strain. Instead, the researchers found that Ötzi was carrying a strain that most closely resembled hpAsia2, which is rare in modern Europeans. This unexpected result implied that the hybridisation with the African *H. pylori* strain actually occurred more recently than 5,000 years ago. The suggestion is that there was a Chalcolithic migration from Africa, and that the history of human settlement of Europe during this period is more complex than previously assumed. The *H. pylori* study is an example of how even unwanted guests can shed light on our prehistoric past.

While Ötzi would now be considered to be in no more than early middle age, by Chalcolithic standards he was elderly and his body was showing signs of considerable wear and tear. He was affected by osteoarthritis of the lumbar regions, knees and ankles and his teeth were in poor shape, with extensive cavities, severe wear of the dental enamel, and periodontal gum disease. The dental problems resulted from a diet heavy in cereals: the high level of carbohydrates caused tooth decay, and mineral grit resulting from milling of grain had abraded the surface of the teeth and led to the gum problems. Nor were these the extent of his health issues: He was genetically predisposed to a higher risk for coronary heart disease, and scans showed he had severe hardening of the arteries. Of the two finger nails found with his body, one showed three Beau's Lines. These are horizontal ridged indentations that indicate a period of illness, and are named for the nineteenth century French physician Joseph Honoré Simon Beau. In Ötzi's case, the episodes of ill health occurred 8, 13 and 16 weeks prior to his death, and they may indicate flare-ups of the same chronic disease. Genetic traces were found of the bacterium *Borrelia burgdorferi*, which is associated with Lyme disease; and eggs of the intestinal parasite whipworm (*Trichuris trichiura*) were present in his colon. In addition, his hair was found to contain high levels of arsenic, which would suggest that he was periodically involved with the smelting of copper ore.

But Ötzi's people apparently possessed an impressive medical knowledge. A number of tattoos had been applied to his arthritic lumbar region, right knee and both ankles. It has been suggested that the tattoos were an early form of acupuncture pain relief treatment, predating the earliest-known Chinese use of the technique by more than two thousand years. Ötzi also had in his possession a Chalcolithic first aid kit consisting of strips of hide to which were attached birch polypore (*Piptoporus betulinus*), a bracket fungus with an impressive array of medicinal properties. It has long been valued by practitioners of herbal medicine for its antibiotic, styptic (anti-bleeding) and antiseptic properties, and it contains substances that are toxic to parasitic worms.

Ötzi was well dressed for his arduous mountain journey. He was wearing a goatskin coat, loincloth and leggings, a calf leather belt and pouch, and a bearskin cap. His footwear consisted of deerskin shoes with an inner lining of hay, attached to a bearskin sole with leather straps. A strip of leather was also attached to the underside of the sole to give it a better grip. The shoes would have been warm and comfortable, but they would not have been entirely waterproof.

Tools recovered included a yew-handled copper axe, a flint-bladed knife complete with ash handle, a quiver containing fourteen arrows and a bowstring, an antler tool possibly used for sharpening arrows, a longbow made from yew, two birch bark baskets and a fire-starting kit comprising pyrites and tinder of various types. The longbow was unfinished, and twelve of the arrows were unfinished, untipped shafts. The other two were fletched and tipped, but were both broken.

The axe comprised a carefully smoothed yew haft around 60 cm (2 ft.) in length, with a forked shaft into which the blade was set with birch tar and tightly bound with thin leather straps. The 9.5 cm (3.75 in.) trapezoidal copper blade was produced by a combination of casting and cold-forging, and shows clear signs of use and re-sharpening. Experiments showed that a replica of the axe could fell a yew tree in 35 minutes without having to be sharpened. Copper implements were prestige items, often found in elite burials, suggesting that Ötzi was a high-status individual in his community.

Archaeologists also recovered parts of a backpack comprising a U-shaped frame of hazel wood measuring 2 m (6 ft. 6 in.) and two narrow connecting pieces of larch wood with notched ends measuring 38 and 40 cm (15 and 16 in.), originally bound together with grass string. Three large sections of matting made from woven alpine grass were originally thought to be a cloak, but are now thought to have been part of the backpack.

Behind this wealth of scientific information, there is a human story – the story of how Ötzi's body came to be entombed in ice on a lonely mountain pass, not to be discovered for more than 5,000 years. What were the circumstances of his death? At first, it was thought that he had simply been caught up in a winter storm and frozen to death. Another suggestion is that he was the victim of a ritual sacrifice, as is thought to have been the case for Lindow Man, a similarly-mummified male found in a peat bog near Wilmslow, Cheshire and believed to slightly predate the Roman occupation of Britain.

In July 2001, researchers studying new X-rays of Ötzi noticed a flint arrowhead lodged in his left shoulder and a re-examination of the body revealed an entry wound where he had been struck from behind. A subsequent investigation with high-resolution computerised tomography showed that the arrow had struck an artery below the left collarbone. The resulting massive loss of blood would almost certainly have been fatal and even with modern emergency techniques, the chances of survival would only be around 40 percent. At some stage, the shaft of the arrow had been pulled out, leaving the flint tip behind. This would have caused further damage, and if it happened while Ötzi was still alive it would only have hastened his death. Having established that Ötzi had died a violent death, investigators made a search for further evidence of a fight. They found injuries to his right hand, including a deep unhealed wound to the base of his thumb that must have occurred shortly before death. A further computerised tomography scan showed that he had sustained a skull fracture and a craniocerebral trauma, leading to major bleeding at the rear of his brain. It is not clear if this was the result of a blow from an attacker or if he fell forward and struck his head on the ground, possibly after being hit by the arrow. A possible scenario is that Ötzi fell face down, and his assailant attempted to retrieve the arrow.

This still leaves unanswered the question of who Ötzi was and why he was killed. His copper axe suggests that he was an individual of reasonably high status; the stable isotope data and other evidence suggests that he lived to the south of where he was found, possibly the Vinschgau region. In his final hours, he ate a meal, before becoming involved in a hand-to-hand knife fight, and finally being shot with an arrow and sustaining a major head injury. He clearly had enemies who pursued him up into the mountains and killed him. Just who these enemies were, and their motives, remain a matter for speculation. Further evidence may one day emerge from the mountains, but for now the death of Ötzi is a cold case in more ways than one.

# 47: The Nebra Sky disc

*The Nebra Sky disk was recovered from international black marketeers –*
*but what have we learned about this enigmatic Bronze Age artefact, and is*
*it even genuine??*

The Nebra Sky disk is a green patinated bronze disk measuring about 30 cm (12 in.) in diameter and weighing of 2.2 kg (4 lb 14 oz.). The disk is inlaid with gold symbols thought to represent either the sun or the full moon, a crescent moon, and stars. Two gold arcs (one now missing) were later added at the sides possibly to mark the summer and winter solstitial rising and setting of the sun; a third grooved arc at the bottom of the piece is a still later addition, and may represent a celestial barge of the type associated with the Egyptian sun god Ra. Thought to date to around 1600 BC, the disk features the oldest-known depiction of the cosmos anywhere in the world. In 2013, it was added to the UNESCO Memory of the World Register and described as one of the most important archaeological finds of the twentieth century.

The disk was part of a hoard discovered in 1999 on a hill near the town of Nebra in the German federal state of Saxony-Anhalt. Unfortunately, the circumstances in which it came to light were far from ideal and serve as a warning as to just how much harm can be caused by illegal treasure-hunting. Along with two gold-inlaid bronze swords, two axes, a chisel, and fragments of spiral bracelets, the disk was found by two unlicensed metal-detectorists whose excavation methods fell far short of acceptable archaeological practice. The disk was damaged by a pick during the excavation, inappropriate cleaning methods caused scratching and the loss of one gold star, and vital details about the context of the finds were not properly recorded. Worse still, rather than declaring the hoard – which by law was the property of Saxony-Anhalt – the finders sold it on the black market. Over the next two years, the disk changed hands several times, during which time its existence became common knowledge.

In May 2001, word of the disk reached Professor Harald Meller, director of the Saxony-Anhalt State Museum of Prehistory in Halle. Playing the role of a real-life Indiana Jones, Meller worked with the authorities, and together they planned a 'sting' operation to recover the disk. It took many months to bring the scheme to fruition, but in February 2002, posing as a prospective buyer of the disk, Meller arranged a meeting with black market sellers at the Hilton hotel in Basel. There, he was met by a man and a woman – but the police were on hand to arrest the couple the moment they produced the disk. Thanks to Meller's tireless efforts, the Sky disk had been recovered for science, and it is now on permanent display at the Museum of Prehistory.

The original finders were traced and eventually jailed, but in return for lighter sentences they revealed the discovery site. Archaeologists were then able to carry out the meticulous forensic work that should have been undertaken during the initial excavation: they found traces of corrosion products from the bronze artefacts, and soil from the site matches soil samples found fused to the disk and other artefacts. Despite this, the disk was so unlike anything that had previously found in Central Europe that many believed it was a fake. It was accepted as genuine only after an analysis of its patina. A method known as x-ray diffraction was used to identify it as being composed of malachite (crystalline copper carbonate hydroxide) and cassiterite (mineralised tin (IV) oxide, or stannic oxide). Such a patina is difficult to produce artificially and in any case would have resulted in smaller and lighter-coloured crystals than those making up the patina of the disk. These, by contrast, could only have grown over several millennia, and they also have a characteristic bubble-like appearance typical of a lengthy growth period. A further indication that the disk was buried for a long time is the presence of copper compounds on the gold inlays. It results from burial in the damp soil: the gold and bronze formed an electrochemical cell, causing copper ions to diffuse through the soil from the bronze and precipitate onto the surface of the gold.

Having confirmed that the disk was indeed very ancient, the next question was just how old was it? The other artefacts in the hoard provided strong indications. The axes and the chisel are of types that were characteristic in the region during the latter part of the Early Bronze Age, around 1600 BC. The swords, though not of a standard type, could be dated directly by applying radiocarbon dating to traces of birch bark pitch recovered from their hilts. A date range of 1600 to 1500 BC was obtained; consistent with the age attributed to the other pieces. This tells us roughly when the Sky disk was buried, but by this time it could already have been many decades or even centuries old. Studies have shown that it underwent a number of modifications between when it was made and when it was buried.

When it was new, the disk featured only the two major celestial bodies and stars. The two side arcs and the celestial barge are thought to have been added later. One star was moved slightly inwards to make way for the now-missing left hand arc, and X-ray imaging shows grooves used to inlay two stars that were removed when the right hand arc was added. The inlay grooves for fitting the arcs differ in style from those of the original gold appliques, and suggest a different craft worker was responsible. The celestial barge is probably a still later addition by a less skilled craft worker who was reluctant to move any of the stars. Instead, the barge has been rather clumsily fitted in between the stars, and the fringe engraved around the gold applique directly abuts one of them. A chemical analysis of the gold used for the appliques was carried out in Berlin and it confirmed that the disk had undergone these three phases of work. Trace impurities differed between the appliques added in each phase and also showed that the star displaced by the left hand arc was actually a new star and not a reuse of the original. In an even later change of use, holes were punched around the circumference of the disk, presumably to facilitate its attachment to something although it is not clear just what. Once again, it is apparent that this was a later development, because one of the holes slightly cuts into the base of the celestial barge. The left hand arc was already missing when the disk was buried; we do not know it was intentionally removed or if it simply fell off at some stage.

Subsequent geochemical studies determined the provenance of some of the metals used in the Sky disk and established that there must have been extensive Early Bronze Age trading links between Central Europe and Britain. The isotopic composition of the tin used in the bronze was found to be consistent with the bulk of tin ores found in Cornwall and trace impurities in the gold used in the first phase also indicated a Cornish origin; specifically placer gold from the Carnon River between Truro and Falmouth. Although Cornwall is mainly known for its tin and copper, it has also produced substantial quantities of gold. In 1808, the Carnon yielded the largest gold nugget ever found in England, weighing just under two ounces. However, the same study ruled out a Cornish origin for the copper in the Sky disk.

We thus know how and roughly when the Sky disk was made, but what was its purpose? Inevitably, many interpretations have focussed on astronomical phenomena, but it has also been suggested that it was used in shamanistic rituals. The stars on the disk do not correspond to any recognisable constellation although there is a cluster of seven stars which is claimed to represent the Pleiades or Seven Sisters, a small but distinctive grouping in the constellation of Taurus the Bull. The Pleiades is prominent in the traditions and folklore of many ancient and modern cultures, and it has been claimed that the Sky disk served a variety of calendrical functions based around conjunctions of the group with the spring evening crescent and autumnal full moons. In fact, other than there being seven stars in the Sky disk grouping, the likeness to the Pleiades is poor. The Sky disk grouping approximates to a hexagon with a seventh star at the centre, whereas the Pleiades resembles a small ladle. Given the level of craftsmanship that went into the Sky disk, it is difficult to believe that the Pleiades could not have been more accurately portrayed if that is what had been intended. The side arcs each subtend an angle of 82°30' and it has been claimed that this represents the movement of the sun's rising and setting points between the summer and winter solstices at the latitude of Nebra (51°17' N). In fact, the correspondence is not exact; the present-day figure is 79°00', although in 1600 BC it would have been 80°20'. Overall, it might be best to be wary of interpretations that see the Sky disk as encoding actual astronomical phenomena.

The various additions suggest that the meaning attached to the Sky disk changed over time. The celestial barge may represent the means by which the sun travelled through the underworld at night after setting in the west, so it could rise in the east the next morning. Eventually, a time might have come when nobody could remember the purpose of the Sky disk. As it had clearly been an object of great importance in the past, it was decided to bury it with prestige goods. The Nebra Sky disk bears a mute testament not only to a sophisticated metalworking tradition in Bronze Age Europe but also to the existence of complex long-distance trading relationships. Its ultimate meaning, though, remains mysterious.

# 48: The Egtved Girl

*The life and long-distance travels of a Danish national icon.*

Despite her high status, she did not live to her twentieth birthday, and we will probably never know the cause of her untimely death 3,400 years ago. The remains of the young woman known as the Egtved Girl are among the most prized relics of Danish prehistory, and take pride of place in the National Museum of Denmark's recently-renovated Prehistoric Galleries. To Danes, the Egtved Girl is a national icon – but in 2015 a multi-disciplinary investigation revealed that she wasn't actually born in Denmark.

The oak coffin in which she was buried was found in 1921 by archaeologists excavating the remains of a Bronze Age burial mound near the small Danish village of Egtved. The mound had been largely cleared during the nineteenth century, and a local farmer was planning to remove what was left. It was at this point that the coffin came to light. Made from a single tree trunk, it has since been dated very accurately by dendrochronology (tree-ring dating) to the summer of 1370 BC. The still-sealed coffin was taken to the National Museum of Denmark in Copenhagen, where it was opened and the Egtved Girl saw the light of day for the first time since the Bronze Age.

Rainwater had seeped through the acidic peat burial mound into the coffin, creating a waterlogged, acidic and oxygen-free environment. The Egtved Girl's skeleton had entirely dissolved, but her hair, tooth enamel, nails, parts of her brain and skin, and her clothing were still intact. The contours of her body could still be made out in the oxhide upon which it had rested, although of this only the hairs remained. She was 160 cm (5 ft. 3 in.) tall, with medium-length blonde hair. Based on the incomplete irruption of her teeth, she was between 16 and 18 years old when she died. She had not been buried alone and was accompanied by the cremated remains of a child aged between five and six years old, which were found wrapped in cloth.

Covered by a woollen blanket, she had been buried fully-clothed in a remarkably modern-looking knee-length corded woollen skirt and short-sleeved shirt. Figurines from the Bronze Age show women wearing similar clothing. Round her waist she wore a belt to which were attached a comb made from animal horn and bronze belt disc decorated with spirals. She wore bronze rings on each arm, and a single earring. By her head was placed a small box made from bark, containing a bronze awl and the remains of a hair net. A few bones from the young child were also found in the box. A bark bucket containing a thick brown residue was found in the coffin. When analysed, the residue was found to be the remains of what was probably beer sweetened with honey. Her elaborate burial marked her out as an individual of high status.

The Egtved Girl lived towards the end of the earlier Bronze Age in Europe, a time of great social change characterised by the rise of hereditary elites. Bronze was widely traded and used for the manufacture of weapons, tools and ornaments, all of which were regarded as prestige goods. The need to obtain copper and tin in order to make bronze acted as a stimulus to long-distance interaction. Sources of tin in particular were rare in Europe, and the metal was traded over very long distances. Following the rise of the first kingdoms in Egypt and Mesopotamia, state-level civilisations arose in Anatolia and the Aegean. Northern Europe was once thought to be a cultural backwater, inhabited by barbarous tribes, but we now know that this was not the case.

Artefacts such as the Trundholm sun chariot and the Nebra Sky disk attest to the cultural richness of the period. Archaeological evidence in the form of bronze swords, drinking cups and personal ornaments suggests the existence of a trade network of allied chiefdoms stretching from the Carpathian Mountains to southern Scandinavia. Through this network, highly-prized Baltic amber was traded southwards, with large quantities of bronze travelling the other way in payment. It has long been thought that inter-chief alliances were established though marriage with elite women from other chiefdoms, and the results from 2015 study of the Egtved Girl support this model.

Researchers carried out strontium isotope analysis of her hair, a molar tooth, a thumb nail and clothing. As we have seen, strontium has similar chemical properties to calcium and likewise is found in bones, teeth and hair, though in smaller amounts. Strontium isotope ratios are sensitive to local geology, so those obtained from body tissues can provide indications of where an individual was living at the time they formed. The adult first molars actually form during first three or four years of an individual's life, hence their strontium signature will match that of the region where they spent their early childhood. In the case of the Egtved Girl, the results suggested that she had been born and spent her first years in a region that was geologically very different to Denmark. The isotopic signature of the bones of the accompanying young child suggested that they, too, originated from outside Denmark.

By contrast, hair can be used to provide a 'rolling log' of an individual's recent movements. Local strontium isotopic ratios take about a month to show up in an individual's hair, and any changes of location will be reflected as the hair grows. By dividing the Egtved Girl's hair into four segments, researchers were able to track where she had spent the last two years of her life. They found that from fifteen to thirteen months before her death, she was staying in a place with a strontium isotope signature very similar to the one in the region where she was born. She then travelled to Denmark, where she stayed for about nine to ten months, before returning to her homeland for the next four to six months. There is no isotopic signature corresponding to her final journey to Denmark, so she must have died very soon after her arrival there. The thumbnail corresponded to the same time period as the most recent hair segment, and gave the same results.

The researchers were also able to apply the same 'rolling log' principle to study the Egtved Girl's diet. They focussed on stable isotope data for carbon and nitrogen: the relative abundance of the isotopes $^{13}C$ and $^{15}N$ are informative of the sources of protein eaten at the time body tissues form, for example plants, herbivores or seafood. The results indicated that she had eaten a seasonally-varying diet, with little or no seafood. The hair itself showed a number of contractions in its thickness, indicative of periods of restricted protein intake while she was travelling to and from Denmark. Another possibility was bouts of illness.

As with human hair, the strontium isotopic signature of the wool used to make the Egtved Girl's clothing provides an indication of where sheep were grazed. The wool was also found to be of non-Danish origin, but the isotopic signature showed a certain degree of variation which indicated that it had not all come from the same place. This in turn suggested that wool circulated over a wide area; a conclusion that was confirmed by a microscopic study that highlighted some differences in the processing of fleece to yarn. There had been extensive selection for wool fibre thickness, indicating that high-quality textiles had been used to make the clothing.

If the Egtved Girl was not from Denmark, where did she come

from? The researchers compared their results with isotopic ratios in regions adjacent to Denmark, looking for a region that could not only match the Egtved Girl herself but also account for the variation in the isotopic compositions of the textiles. The Black Forest and adjacent areas of southwestern Germany have strontium isotope signatures that overlap with the data obtained by the researchers, suggesting that the Egtved Girl, the child, and the garments all originated from there. It is possible that she was a high status individual from the Black Forest region who was married off to a Danish chief in order to secure an alliance. On the other hand, the two journeys to her homeland in just two years could indicate that she was a powerful woman in her own right.

The bronze belt disc that was buried with her has been associated with a Nordic sun-worshipping belief system of which the famous Trundholm sun chariot was also a part. The bronze disc mounted on the latter is gilded on one side only: the two sides have been interpreted as representing day and night. Accordingly, some have suggested that the Egtved Girl was a cultic priestess, although this is rather speculative.

Much about the Egtved Girl remains mysterious. What caused the deaths of her and young child buried with her? Could they both have fallen ill on their final journey to Denmark? What was the relationship between the two? In age, they differ by least ten but no more than thirteen years. They could just about be mother and child, or they could be siblings. Ancient DNA would certainly be informative, but attempts to obtain genetic material from the remains were unsuccessful.

Regardless of these considerations, the Egtved Girl provides evidence that periodic long-distance travel was a feature of the European Bronze Age. We have still much to learn about this relatively late era of the prehistoric past.

# 49: Early adopters

*The emergence of the world's first urban societies.*

The Neolithic Revolution was followed by what V. Gordon Childe termed the 'Urban Revolution', and it led to the rise of what we commonly refer to as 'civilisation'. The first true states – distant forerunners of today's nation states – were a consequence of the social changes brought about by the Neolithic Revolution. By 3000 BC, people in Mesopotamia were living in societies not too dissimilar to those of today. They lacked most of the refinements of a modern developed country, but the basics were in place including ruling elites, social differentiation, specialised professions, state bureaucracies, codified legal systems, and taxation. Over the next three thousand years, there were similar developments in Egypt, the Indian subcontinent, China, Mesoamerica, and the Andean region of South America.

Childe developed his ideas in the 1920s and 1930s before publishing his conclusions in 1950 in a seminal paper entitled *The Urban Revolution* in which he identified many of the traits now recognised as characteristic of states. These include a hierarchical, stratified society with a centralised ruling authority; the levying of taxes; formal systems of record-keeping; and a complex division of labour, with full-time specialists such as craftsmen, transport workers, merchants, officials and priests. Although the first cities appeared at this time, Childe regarded their appearance as just one aspect of the social changes from which state-level societies emerged. They were substantially larger and more densely-populated than even the largest Neolithic settlements, with temples, monumental buildings and other public works.

All of these developments arose from the preceding Neolithic Revolution. The substantial food surpluses that resulted from the new farming economies meant that for the first time in human history, it was possible for a society to support large numbers of full-time specialists who were not directly involved with food production. This in turn led to the emergence of increasingly complex societies, with correspondingly greater divisions of labour and wealth and from which eventually emerged the first states. Although the term 'Urban Revolution' has since fallen into disuse, and methods and concepts have advanced considerably since 1950, Childe's basic model influenced most of the later theories about state formation.

The world's first urban societies emerged in Mesopotamia from around 3500 BC, along with the invention of cuneiform script. Their rise was deeply rooted in two precursor cultures known as the Halaf and the Ubaid. The Halaf was a northern Mesopotamian culture, and lasted from 6000 to 5400 BC. The slightly later Ubaid was current between 5900 and 4200 BC, starting in southern Mesopotamia and later spreading into adjacent regions. These cultures were in turn based on the agricultural 'package' that had come together in Southwest Asia in Neolithic times, although there had been a number of technological advances since. The most important of these was the development of irrigation agriculture, which opened up the plains of what is now southern Iraq to new farming communities. Although Halaf and Ubaid societies were less rigidly stratified than state-level societies, many features of this period anticipated developments associated with later Mesopotamian society, including the building of temples; the use of stamp seals in economic administration; and extensive long-distance trade and exchange.

The Uruk period which followed saw the emergence of urban living as southern Mesopotamia was transformed into the most densely-populated region in Southwest Asia. The period is named for the city of Uruk, which became the dominant settlement in the region. Uruk was first settled around 4800 BC, probably beginning as two villages centred on shrines that later became major religious precincts of the Sumerian deities Anu and Eanna. The Uruk period is taken to have begun in 4200 BC, by which time the villages had merged into a single settlement that continued to expand. By 3100 BC, it had reached a size of around 100 ha (250 acres) – more than eight times the size of Çatalhöyük; by 2900 BC, it had attained 400 ha (990 acres, or 1.5 sq. miles) – rather larger than the financial district of present-day London. Unlike Çatalhöyük, Uruk was a genuine city – the first anywhere in the world, with a population probably in the tens of thousands. In contrast to the undifferentiated layout of Çatalhöyük, there were structures and places for specific activities, including temples, public spaces, craft production workshops, and housing.

The city would have been an imposing sight from afar, the temples of its two main religious complexes visible for miles around. Later texts suggest that these were dedicated to the sky god Anu and the goddess of war and love Eanna. In the Anu precinct, a series of successive temples spanning several centuries were built on terraces. The best preserved of these is the gypsum-plastered White Temple, which was set on a 13 m (42 ft.) high platform and was a forerunner of the ziggurats that later became so prominent in Mesopotamia. The Eanna precinct contains several monumental mud brick structures, which were probably used as temples. The Mesopotamians regarded temples as residences of the gods, so they were often constructed on the same general plan as a domestic residence albeit on a much larger and grander scale. In the Late Uruk phase of the Eanna precinct, the largest structure, Temple D, measured 80 by 50 m (260 by 165 ft.), comparable in size to a medium-sized present-day cathedral. Other buildings in the religious precincts were probably residences of priests and officials, and communal meeting places.

The exact nature of the political system in Uruk is uncertain, but texts and artistic representations indicate the presence of both priests and kings. Every aspect of life in Uruk and other early Sumerian city-states was rigidly controlled by a bureaucratic administrative system. Stamp seals of type in use during the Halaf period gave way to the cylinder seals of officials and institutions. Their function was to impress the clay tablets used for administrative record-keeping and the sealings used to secure storerooms, containers, and bales of commodities. The scenes portrayed on the cylinder seals give an impression of overarching control and order. Some depict bound captives kneeling in front of a skirted figure holding a spear. Portrayals of warriors armed with spears suggest that life in Sumerian times was far from peaceful. The Warka Vase, a large carved stone vessel found in the Eanna precinct at Uruk, portrays a procession of naked men with offerings of agricultural produce for the goddess Eanna. Crude, mass-produced bowls have also been interpreted as evidence of the growth of state control. They are of a standard size that closely matches the volume of the daily food ration issued in later times to state-employed workers, and it is likely that they served as containers for daily rations issued to craft workers, potters, metallurgists, farmers and labourers working for the Uruk authorities.

Anthropologist Guillermo Algaze believes that the emergence of the Sumerian city-states was accompanied by a process of aggressive territorial expansion in order to gain control of key trade routes. Later written records suggest that the Mesopotamians exported fine textiles and other manufactured goods, in return for which received copper, tin, gold, silver, precious and non-precious stones, bitumen and timber. Southern Mesopotamia lacked these materials, which the ruling elite groups required in order to maintain their grip on power. According to Algaze, a network of outposts was established in order to ensure the continued availability of vital commodities.

Outposts were established at strategically-important locations in northern Mesopotamia, northern Syria, southeastern Anatolia, in the Zagros and Taurus highlands, and on the plains of southwest Iran. The largest, such as Habuba Kabira on the Euphrates, were urban in size. The 18 ha (45 acres) site was laid out in accordance with a masterplan, with carefully-planned streets and distinct residential, administrative and industrial quarters. Based on the material culture identified by archaeologists, there is little doubt that its inhabitants were Sumerian colonists. Smaller settlements were probably used as way stations between the larger outposts and Sumerian city-states to the south. Others, beyond the range of the large outposts, might have been diplomatic outposts used for building relations with local communities.

It the need for expansionism that might have been responsible for the transformation of the chiefdoms of the Halaf and the Ubaid cultures into full-blown states. Like agriculture, urban societies did not emerge from less complex societies because they were a 'good idea'. Although both are characterised by centralised ruling authorities, chiefdoms lack the administrative bureaucracies that are characteristic of states. While even a complex chiefdom will have only two levels of decision-making (local and central), states will have at least four levels. Furthermore, lower-level decision-making is divided up into specialised processes, so that nobody lower down the chain of command ever has enough power for insubordination to become a problem. By contrast, in a chiefdom society any delegation of chiefly authority to a subordinate entails a major handover of power, and the chief runs the risk of being deposed.

However, the risk of delegation of chiefly powers means that there is a limit to the amount of territory a chief can effectively control. Distant subjugated territories require the projection of chiefly authority in order to maintain control and channel the inward flow of tribute and surpluses. The solution was for chiefs to promote internal administrative specialisation among officials dispatched to the territories in order to restrict their authority and limit their scope for independent action. Such a bureaucracy is expensive to run, but the cost is more than offset by the new resources made available by conquest. In other words, the need for territorial expansion by a chiefdom forces its internal reorganization into a state.

Expansion continued through the relatively brief Jemdet Nasr period from 3100 to 2900 BC and into the Early Dynastic period from 2900 to 2350 BC. By this time, there were a large number of city-states in southern Mesopotamia, each of which controlled its own agricultural hinterland. The period is known as the Early Dynastic because for the first time, written sources provide a list of the kings and dynasties that ruled over the Sumerian city-states.

# 50: Writing

*Mesopotamian invention and use of writing, and the beginning of recorded history.*

Writing is something we tend to take for granted, but along with taxation and other state paraphernalia, it is something that humans got along without for most of their existence. The uses to which the first writing systems were put were various: in Egypt, for example, early hieroglyphic script was used for the veneration of pharaohs. In China, most of the earliest surviving texts are records of oracles. In Mesopotamia, however, the earliest use of writing was for the more humdrum purpose of keeping records.

The writing system used in ancient Mesopotamia is known as cuneiform script, from the Latin word *cuneus* meaning 'wedge' in reference to the wedge-shaped styli used for marking clay tablets. It is likely that the origins of this system are to be found in the clay tokens, stamped clay sealings and stone stamp seals that came into use during the Halaf period. Sealings are stamp-seal impressed lumps of clay, which were used to secure pots, baskets and other containers. Several hundred sealings were found in a storeroom at the Halaf site of Tell Sabi Abyad in northern Syria. The storeroom might have functioned as a safe deposit room where secured goods belonging to nomadic pastors was left while they were away from the site. More radically, it has been suggested that the sealed containers held tokens rather than actual goods, and that these were redeemed against goods and services at a later date. Around two hundred clay tokens have been found at the site, including small spheres, discs, cones and cylinders. In all, there were ten different types, each of which might have represented a different product or service – for example, specific amounts of cereals might have been represented by the spheres.

After the start of the Uruk period, tokens became increasingly widespread. Some were incised with markings and, based on later cuneiform script, are thought to have represented sheep, oil, metal ingots, honey, garments and other commodities. Other, unmarked tokens might have been used to represent the quantities involved in transactions. From around 3500 BC, officials began enclosing tokens in a clay sphere known as bulla to protect them from tampering. The bulla was then stamped with a cylinder seal to identify the official or location associated with the transaction. At some point, the officials began recording the contents of the bulla by impressing the tokens into its surface prior to sealing them up inside. This rendered the actual tokens redundant, and eventually clay tablets replaced bullae as a means of recording transactions.

Over 5,000 of these clay tablets have been found at Uruk. They are incised or impressed with signs, made with a stylus while the clay was still soft, and grouped together in rectangular boxes known as cases. The script is known as proto-cuneiform: the precursor of the cuneiform script that remained in use in Mesopotamia for thousands of years. The tablets are records of economic and administrative data rather than written texts. They record the commodities in question (barley, sheep, fields, etc.), quantities, accounting periods, nature of the transaction, parties involved, and names of officials and institutions. It is likely that proto-cuneiform signs were based on the earlier system of marked and unmarked tokens. Instead of the base 10 (decimal) counting system with which we are familiar, the Mesopotamians used different systems for different functions. A sexagesimal system (units of 1, 10, 60, 600) was used for counting items such as animals, people, fish, or implements, whereas a bisexagesimal system (units of 1, 10, 60, 120, 1,200) was used for grain and other items distributed as part of a rationing system. Time was reckoned using a calendar in which there were three ten-day weeks to the month.

Although 90 percent of the Uruk tablets were nothing more than accounting records, some word lists have also been found. These include lists of fish, birds, other animals, textiles and vessels, and they reflect the need of Sumerian officials for categorisation. The best-known of these category lists is the Standard Profession List, a catalogue of professions practiced at the time, ranked according to status. The earliest known version, dating to the Jemdet Nasr period, is damaged and cannot be read completely, but its format was followed in later versions and most of its contents have been deduced. The Standard Professions List gives us an insight into the hierarchical nature of Sumerian society, not only showing how the various professions were ranked within society, but also rankings within many of the professions themselves. The catalogue was not static, but evolved over time to reflect changes in society. Thus for example the profession of tax collector was first recorded during the Early Dynastic III period from 2600 to 2334 BC.

Such recording systems were very cumbersome in terms of the large number of symbols required (about 1,200) and they could do little more than record transactional data. The evolution of a system capable of recording the spoken word might have begun when somebody thought of encoding sounds with what is known as the rebus, or visual pun. English examples of the rebus include the pronoun I (*eye*) and the prefix be- (*bee*). The earliest example of rebus use in Mesopotamia dates to the Jemdet Nasr period. The sign for an arrow (known as TI and pronounced /ti/ in Sumerian) was used to represent the Sumerian words /til/ (*life*) and /ti/ (*rib*). Another early example, commonly used in archaic texts, is the sign for *reed*, GI, used to express the Sumerian verb /gi/ (*to render*). The system evolved over the course of several centuries as the range of concepts that could be represented was extended. Names were being rendered phonetically by 2700 BC, with grammatical affixes soon after. By 2400 BC, full texts were being recorded.

The Mesopotamian writing system that finally evolved was logosyllabic; that is to say it was a combination of logograms, syllabograms and determinatives. A logogram is a written symbol used to represent a word, but it do not tell us how that word is pronounced. For example, a picture of a cow may be used to represent a cow, but not the sound *cow*. The difference is illustrated by the logographic Arabic numerals 1, 2 and 3, which in English are pronounced *one*, *two* and *three*, but are pronounced *un*, *deux* and *trois* in French. Determinatives are used to add various types of information to a logogram, for example a currency sign in front of a number indicates that it represents a sum of money. A syllabogram is a symbol used to represent a specific sound comprising one or more syllables, but unlike a logogram it does not represent an actual word.

The Mesopotamians used logograms to express nouns, verbs and adjectives, and they used phonetic signs for suffixes, prefixes, particles, and for spelling out foreign names. The number of symbols required gradually fell, reaching 600 by 2800 BC. At the same time, the symbols themselves became progressively more stylised. The use of wedge-shaped styluses encouraged a style in which the symbols were made up of combinations of wedges and straight lines, and they eventually bore little resemblance to their original form. This classic Mesopotamian cuneiform remained in use for the next 2,500 years. It is found on the tablets of the Akkadian Empire, the Babylonians, and the Assyrians, and it only fell into disuse after the conquests of Alexander the Great between 336 and 323 BC. The last-known text dates to AD 75.

The extent to which the Mesopotamian writing system influenced those elsewhere remains disputed. It has been claimed that early Egyptian writing systems were sufficiently different from one another as to make independent development likely; then again it has been suggested that these differences are small and that the Mesopotamian system was re-engineered for the very different use it was put to in Egypt. To the east, the Harappan civilisation of the Indus Valley are known to have enjoyed trade links with Mesopotamia. The Harappans used what is thought to be a logosyllabic writing system. Archaeologists have recovered stamp seals, sealings, amulets and small tablets, but the script remains undeciphered, and its relationship to the Mesopotamian system – if any – remains unknown. Regardless of these considerations, it is the Mesopotamian invention of writing that brings us, via semi-mythical figures such as Gilgamesh, to the earliest dawning of recorded history and to the end of this work.

# Sources and Further Reading

## General reading

Barker, G., 2006. *The Agricultural Revolution in Prehistory: Why did Foragers become Farmers*. Oxford: Oxford University Press.

Bellwood, P., 2005. *First Farmers*. Oxford: Blackwell Publishing.

Diamond, J., 1991. *The Third Chimpanzee*. London: Random.

Dunbar, R., 2004. *The Human Story*. London: Faber and Faber.

Finlayson, C., 2009. *The humans who went extinct*. s.l.:Oxford University Press.

Klein, R., 1999. *The Human Career*. 2nd ed. Chicago: University of Chicago Press.

Lewin, R. & Foley, R., 2004. *Principles of Human Evolution*. 2nd ed. Oxford: Blackwell Science Ltd.

Mellars, P., 1996. *The Neanderthal Legacy*. Princeton, NJ: Princeton University Press.

Mithen, S., 2003. *After the Ice: A Global Human History 20,000 - 5,000 BC*. London: Weidenfield & Nicholson.

Oppenheimer, S., 2003. *Out of Eden*. London: Constable & Robinson Ltd.

Roberts, A., 2009. *The Incredible Human Journey*. London: Bloomsbury.

Scarre, C., 2005. *The human past*. 1 ed. London: Thames & Hudson.

Seddon, C., 2015. *Humans: from the beginning*. 1 ed. London: Glanville Publications.

Stringer, C., 2012. *The origin of our species*. 1 ed. London: Penguin.

Stringer, C. & Andrews, P., 2005. *The Complete World of Human Evolution*. London: Thames & Hudson.

Trigger, B., 2003. *Understanding early civilizations*. New York, NY: Cambridge University Press.

## 3: Finding the Missing Link

Langergraber, K. et al., 2012. Generation times in wild chimpanzees and gorillas suggest earlier divergence times in great ape and human evolution. *PNAS*, 25 September, 109(39), pp. 15716-15721.

Sarich, V. & Wilson, A., 1967. Immunological time scale for hominid evolution. *Science*, Volume 158, pp. 1200-1203.

Takahata, N. & Satta, Y., 1997. Evolution of the primate lineage leading to modern humans: Phylogenetic and demographic inferences from DNA sequences. *PNAS*, April, Volume 94, pp. 4811-4815.

## 4: Four legs good, two legs better

Burt, A., 1992. Concealed Ovulation and Sexual Signals in Primates. *Folia Primatologica*, Volume 58, pp. 1-6.

Diamond, J., 1991. *The Third Chimpanzee*. London: Random.

Hughes, J. et al., 2010. Chimpanzee and human Y chromosomes are remarkably divergent in structure and gene content. *Nature*, 28 January, Volume 463, pp. 536-539.

Hughes, J. et al., 2005. Conservation of Y-linked genes during human evolution revealed by comparative sequencing in chimpanzee. *Nature*, 1 September.Volume 437, pp. 101-104.

Lovejoy, O., 1981. The Origins of Man. *Science*, 23 January, Volume 211, pp. 341-350.

Lovejoy, O., 2009. Reexamining Human Origins in Light of Ardipithecus ramidus. *Science*, 2 October, Volume 326, pp. 74e1-74e8.

McHenry, H., 1992. How Big Were Early Hominids?. *Evolutionary Anthropology*, pp. 15-20.

Rodman, P. & McHenry, H., 1980. Biogenetics and the Origin of Hominid Bipedalism. *American Journal of Physical Anthropology*, Volume 52, pp. 103-106.

Suwa, G. et al., 2009. Paleobiological Implications of the Ardipithecus ramidus Dentition. *Science*, 2 October, Volume 326, pp. 94-99.

Wheeler, P., 1984. The Evolution of Bipedality and Loss of Functional Body Hair in Hominoids. *Journal of Human Evolution*, Volume 13, pp. 91-98.

# 5: Lucy

Brunet, M. et al., 1995. The first australopithecine 2,500 kilometres west of the Rift Valley (Chad). *Nature*, 16 November, Volume 378, pp. 273-275.

Crompton, R. T. et al., 2012. Human-like external function of the foot, and fully upright gait, confirmed in the 3.66 million year old Laetoli hominin footprints by topographic statistics, experimental footprint formation and computer simulation. *Journal of the Royal Society Interface*, Volume 9, pp. 707-719.

Haile-Selassie, Y. et al., 2015. New species from Ethiopia further expands Middle Pliocene hominin diversity. *Nature*, 28 May, Volume 521, pp. 483-488.

Johanson, D., White, T. & Coppens, Y., 1978. A new species of the genus Australopithecus (Primates: Hominidae) from the Pliocene of eastern Africa. *Kirtlandia*, Volume 28, pp. 1-14.

Leakey, M., Feibel, C., McDougall, I. & Walker, A., 1995. New four-million-year-old hominid species from Kanapoi and Allia Bay, Kenya. *Nature*, 17 August, Volume 376, pp. 565-571.

White, T. et al., 2006. Asa Issie, Aramis and the origin of Australopithecus. *Nature*, 13 April, Volume 440, pp. 883-889.

# 6: The technological ape

De Heinzelin, J. et al., 1999. Environment and Behavior of 2.5-Million-Year-Old Bouri Hominids. *Science*, 23 April, Volume 284, pp. 625-629.

Harmand, S. et al., 2015. 3.3-million-year-old stone tools from Lomekwi 3, West Turkana, Kenya. *Nature*, 21 May, Volume 521, pp. 310-315.

McPherron, S. et al., 2010. Evidence for stone-tool-assisted consumption of animal tissues before 3.39 million years ago at Dikika, Ethiopia. *Nature*, 10 August, Volume 466, pp. 857-860.

Semaw, S., 2000. The World's Oldest Stone Artefacts from Gona, Ethiopia: Their Implications for Understanding Stone Technology and Patterns of

Human Evolution Between 2·6-1·5 Million Years Ago. *Journal of Archaeological Science,* Volume 27, pp. 1197-1214.

Semaw, S. et al., 1997. 2.5-million-year-old stone tools from Gona, Ethiopia. *Nature,* 23 January, Volume 385, pp. 333-336.

Toth, N., 1985. The Oldowan reassessed: a close look at early stone artefacts. *Journal of Archaeological Science,* Volume 20, pp. 101-120.

Toth, N., Schick, K. & Savage-Rumbaugh, E., 1993. Pan the toolmaker: investigations into the stone tool-making and tool-using abilities of a bonobo (Pan paniscus). *Journal of Archaeological Science,* Volume 20, pp. 81-91.

Wynn, T. & McGrew, W., 1989. An ape's view of the Oldowan. *Man,* Volume 24, pp. 383-398.

# 7: You are what you eat

Balter, V., Braga, J., Télouk, P. & Thackeray, F., 2012. Evidence for dietary change but not landscape use in South African early hominins. *Nature,* 27 September, Volume 489, pp. 558-560.

Copeland, S. et al., 2011. Strontium isotope evidence for landscape use by early hominins. *Nature,* 2 June, Volume 474, pp. 76-78.

Sponheimer, M. & Lee-Thorp, J., 1999. Isotopic Evidence for the Diet of an Early Hominid, Australopithecus africanus. *Science,* 15 January, Volume 238, pp. 368-370.

Sponheimer, M. et al., 2005. Hominins, sedges, and termites: new carbon isotope data from the Sterkfontein valley and Kruger National Park. *Journal of Human Evolution,* Volume 48, pp. 301-312.

Strait, D. et al., 2009. The feeding biomechanics and dietary ecology of Australopithecus africanus. *PNAS,* 17 February, 106(7), pp. 2124-2129.

Teaford, M. & Ungar, P., 2000. Diet and the evolution of the earliest human ancestors. *PNAS,* 5 December, 97(25), pp. 13506-13511.

Ungar, P., 2004. Dental topography and diets of Australopithecus afarensis and early Homo. *Journal of Human Evolution,* Volume 46, pp. 605-622.

# 8: Food for thought

Aiello, L. & Wheeler, P., 1995. The expensive tissue hypothesis: the brain and the digestive system in human and primate evolution. *Current Anthropology,* Volume 36, pp. 199-221.

Antón, S., Potts, R. & Aiello, L., 2014. Evolution of early Homo: An integrated biological perspective. *Science,* 4 July, 345(6192), p 45.

Byrne, R. & Whiten, A., 1988. *Machiavellian Intelligence.* Oxford: Oxford University Press.

DiMaggio, E. et al., 2015. Late Pliocene fossiliferous sedimentary record and the environmental context of early Homo from Afar, Ethiopia. *Science,* 20 March, 347(6228), pp. 1355-1359.

Dunbar, R., 1998. The Social Brain Hypothesis. *Evolutionary Anthropology,* 7 December, 6(5), pp. 178-190.

Spoor, F. et al., 2015. Reconstructed Homo habilis type OH 7 suggests deep-rooted species diversity in early Homo. *Nature,* 5 March, 7541(519), pp. 83-86.

Tobias, P., 1987. The brain of Homo habilis: a new level of organization in cerebral evolution. *Journal of Human Evolution,* Volume 16, pp. 741-761.

Villmoare, B. et al., 2015. Early Homo at 2.8 Ma from Ledi-Geraru, Afar, Ethiopia. *Science*, 20 March, 347(6228), pp. 1352-1355.

# 9: Dating the Mojokerto child

Coqueugniot, H. et al., 2004. Early brain growth in Homo erectus and implications for cognitive ability. *Nature*, 16 September, Volume 431, pp. 299-302.

Curtis, G., Swisher, C. & Lewin, R., 2000. *Java Man*. New York, NY: Little, Brown and Company.

Ferring, R. et al., 2011. Earliest human occupations at Dmanisi (Georgian Caucasus) dated to 1.85-1.78 Ma. *PNAS*, 28 June, 108(26), pp. 10432-10436.

Morwood, M., O'Sullivan, P., Susanto, E. & Aziz, F., 2003. Revised age for Mojokerto 1, an early Homo erectus cranium from East Java, Indonesia. *Australian Archaeology*, Issue 57.

Spoor, F. et al., 2015. Reconstructed Homo habilis type OH 7 suggests deep-rooted species diversity in early Homo. *Nature*, 5 March, 7541(519), pp. 83-86.

Swisher, C. et al., 1994. Age of the earliest known hominids in Java, Indonesia. *Science*, Volume 263, pp. 1118-1121.

Wood, B., 2011. Did early Homo migrate "out of" or "in to" Africa?. *PNAS*, 28 June, 108(26), pp. 10375-10376.

Zhu, Z. et al., 2014. New dating of the Homo erectus cranium from Lantian (Gongwangling), China. *Journal of Human Evolution*.

# 10: The Movius mystery

Cameron, D. & Groves, C., 2004. *Bones, Stones and Molecules: "Out of Africa" and Human Origins*. London: Elsevier Academic Press.

Coolidge, F. & Wynn, T., 2009. *The Rise of Homo sapiens*. Hoboken, NJ: Wiley-Blackwell.

Dennell, R., 2014. Hallum Movius, Helmut de Terra and the Line than Never Was: Burma, 1038. In: K. Boyle, R. Rabett & C. Hunt, eds. *Living in the Landscape: Essays in honour of Graeme Barker*. s.l.:McDonald Institute for Archaeological Research, pp. 11-34.

Joordens, J. et al., 2014. Homo erectus at Trinil on Java used shells for tool production and engraving. *Nature*.

Klein, R., 2005. Hominin Dispersals in the Old World. In: C. Scarre, ed. *The Human Past*. London: Thames & Hudson, pp. 84-123.

Kohn, M. & Mithen, S., 1999. Handaxes: products of sexual selection?. *Antiquity*, Volume 73, pp. 518-526.

Lepre, C. et al., 2011. An earlier origin for the Acheulian. *Nature*, 1 September, Volume 477, pp. 82-85.

Lycett, S. & von Cramon-Taubadel, N., 2008. Acheulean variability and hominin dispersals: a model-bound approach. *Journal of Archaeological Science*, Volume 35, pp. 553-562.

Swisher, C. et al., 1994. Age of the earliest known hominids in Java, Indonesia. *Science*, Volume 263, pp. 1118-1121.

# 11: The gift of Prometheus

Berna, F. et al., 2012. Microstratigraphic evidence of in situ fire in the Acheulean strata of Wonderwerk Cave, Northern Cape province, South Africa. *PNAS*, 15 May, 109(20), pp. E1215-E1220.

Brain, C. & Sillen, A., 1988. Evidence from the Swartkrans cave for the earliest use of fire. *Nature*, 1 December, Volume 336, pp. 464-466.

Goren-Inbar, N. et al., 2004. Evidence of Hominin Control of Fire at Gesher Benot Ya'aqov, Israel. *Science*, 30 April, Volume 304, pp. 725-727.

Pickering, T., 2012. What's new is old: Comments on (more) archaeological evidence of one-million-year-old fire from South Africa. *South African Journal of Science*, 108(5/6), pp. 1-2.

Roebroeks, W. & Villa, P., 2011. On the earliest evidence for habitual use of fire in Europe. *PNAS*, 29 March, 108(13), pp. 5209-5214.

Weiner, S. et al., 1998. Evidence for the Use of Fire at Zhoukoudian, China. *Science*, 10 July, Volume 281, pp. 251-253.

Wrangham, R., 2009. *Catching Fire: How Cooking Made Us Human.* New York, NY: Basic Books.

# 12: Footprints at Happisburgh

Ashton, N. et al., 2014. Hominin Footprints from Early Pleistocene Deposits at Happisburgh, UK. *PLoS One*, February.9(2).

Bermúdez de Castro, J. et al., 1997. A Hominid from the Lower Pleistocene of Atapuerca, Spain: Possible Ancestor to Neandertals and Modern Humans. *Science*, 30 May, Volume 276, pp. 1392-1395.

Carbonell, E. et al., 2008. The first hominin of Europe. *Nature*, 27 March, Volume 452, pp. 465-470.

Falguères, C. et al., 1999. Earliest humans in Europe: the age of TD6 Gran Dolina, Atapuerca, Spain. *Journal of Human Evolution*, September, 37(3-4), pp. 343-352.

Fernandez-Jalvo, Y., Diez, J., Caceres, I. & Rosell, J., 1999. Human cannibalism in the Early Pleistocene of Europe (Gran Dolina, Sierra de Aterpuerca, Burgos, Spain). *Journal of Human Evolution*, Volume 37, pp. 591-622.

Parfitt, S. et al., 2010. Early Pleistocene human occupation at the edge of the boreal zone in northwest Europe. *Nature*, 8 July, Volume 466, pp. 229-233.

Parfitt, S. et al., 2005. The earliest record of human activity in northern Europe. *Nature*, 15 December, Volume 438, pp. 1008-1012.

Rosas, A. et al., 2006. Paleobiology and comparative morphology of a late Neandertal sample from El Sidron, Asturias, Spain. *PNAS*, 19 December, 103(51), pp. 19266-19271.

# 13: The Boxgrove people

Coolidge, F. & Wynn, T., 2009. *The Rise of Homo sapiens.* Hoboken, NJ: Wiley-Blackwell.

Dunbar, R., 2004. *Grooming, Gossip and the Evolution of Language.* 2nd ed. London: Faber and Faber Ltd..

Rightmire, P., 1998. Human Evolution in the Middle Pleistocene: The Role of Homo heidelbergensis. *Evolutionary Anthropology*, 6(6), pp. 218-227.

Stringer, C., 2006. *Homo Britannicus*. London: Penguin.

Stringer, C. & Andrews, P., 2005. *The Complete World of Human Evolution*. London: Thames & Hudson.

Wagner, G. et al., 2010. Radiometric dating of the type-site for Homo heidelbergensis at Mauer, Germany. *PNAS*, 16 November, 107(46), pp. 19726-19730.

# 14: The Berekhat Ram pebble

Barham, L., 2002. Systematic Pigment Use in the Middle Pleistocene of South-Central Africa. *Current Anthropology*, February, 43(1), pp. 181-190.

Coolidge, F. & Wynn, T., 2009. *The Rise of Homo sapiens*. Hoboken, NJ: Wiley-Blackwell.

Diamond, J., 1991. *The Third Chimpanzee*. London: Random.

Himelfarb, E., 2000. Prehistoric Body Painting. *Archaeology*, July/August.53(4).

Klein, R. & Edgar, B., 2002. *The Dawn of Human Culture*. New York, NY: John Wiley & Sons, Inc..

Marshack, A., 1997. The Berekhat Ram figurine: a late Acheulian carving from the Middle East. *Antiquity*, 71(272), pp. 327-333.

McBrearty, S. & Brooks, A., 2000. The revolution that wasn't: a new interpretation of the origin of modern human behaviour. *Journal of Human Evolution*, Volume 39, pp 453-563.

# 15: New Man's Valley

Bahn, P., 1999. Neandertal Finds. *Archaeology*, March/April.52(2).

Schmitz, R. et al., 2002. The Neandertal type site revisited: Interdisciplinary investigations of skeletal remains from the Neander Valley, Germany. *PNAS*, 1 October, 99(20), pp. 13342-13347.

# 16: Were they really dimwits?

D'Errico, F. et al., 1998. Neanderthal Acculturation in Western Europe?. *Current Anthropology*, Volume 39, pp. S1-S44.

Finlayson, C. et al., 2012. Birds of a Feather: Neanderthal Exploitation of Raptors and Corvids. *PLoS One*, September.7(9).

Higham, T. et al., 2014. The timing and spatiotemporal patterning of Neanderthal disappearance. *Nature*, 21 August, Volume 512, pp. 306-309.

Hublin, J. et al., 1996. A late Neanderthal associated with Upper Palaeolithic artefacts.. *Nature*, 16 May, Volume 381, pp. 224-226.

Mellars, P., 2005. The Impossible Coincidence. A Single-Species Model for the Origins of Modern Human Behavior in Europe. *Evolutionary Anthropology*, Volume 14, pp. 12-27.

Pearce, E., Stringer, C. & Dunbar, R., 2013. New insights into differences in brain organization between Neanderthals and anatomically modern humans. *Proceedings of the Royal Society B*, 7 May.280(1758).

Peresani, M. et al., 2011. Late Neandertals and the intentional removal of feathers as evidenced from bird bone taphonomy at Fumane Cave 44 ky B.P., Italy. *PNAS*, 8 March, 108(10), pp. 3888-3893.

Radovčić, D., Sršen, A., Radovčić, J. & Frayer, D., 2015. Evidence for Neandertal Jewelry: Modified White-Tailed Eagle Claws at Krapina. *PLoS One*, 11 March.

Rendu, W. et al., 2014. Evidence supporting an intentional Neandertal burial at La Chapelle-aux-Saints. *PNAS*, 7 January, 111(1), pp. 81-86.

Rodríguez-Vidal, J. et al., 2014. A rock engraving made by Neanderthals in Gibraltar. *PNAS*, 16 September, 111(37), pp. 13301-13306.

Solecki, R., 1975. Shanidar IV, a Neanderthal flower burial in northern Iraq. *Science*, Volume 190, pp. 880-881.

Sommer, J., 1999. The Shanidar IV "flower burial": A reevaluation of Neanderthal burial ritual.. *Cambridge Archæological Journal*, Volume 9, pp. 127-129.

Soressi, M. et al., 2013. Neandertals made the first specialized bone tools in Europe. *PNAS*, 27 August, 110(35), pp. 14186-14190.

Zilhão, J. et al., 2010. Symbolic use of marine shells and mineral pigments by Iberian Neandertals. *PNAS*, 19 January, 107(3), pp. 1023-1028.

# 17: The million dollar question

Condemi, S. et al., 2013. Possible Interbreeding in Late Italian Neanderthals? New Data from the Mezzena Jaw (Monti Lessini, Verona, Italy). *PLoS One*, March.8(3).

Currat, M. & Excoffier, L., 2011. Strong reproductive isolation between humans and Neanderthals inferred from observed patterns of introgression. *PNAS*, 13 September, 108(37), pp. 15129-15134.

Ding, Q. et al., 2013. Neanderthal Introgression at Chromosome 3p21.31 Was Under Positive Natural Selection in East Asians. *Molecular Biology and Evolution*, 13 December, 31(3), pp. 683-695.

Duarte, C. et al., 1999. The Early Upper Paleolithic Human Skeleton from the Abrigo do Lagar Velho (Portugal) and Modern Human Emergence in Iberia. *PNAS*, June, Volume 96, pp. 7604-7609.

Fu, Q. et al., 2015. An early modern human from Romania with a recent Neanderthal ancestor. *Nature*, 13 August, Volume 524, pp. 216-219.

Green, R. et al., 2010. A Draft Sequence of the Neandertal Genome. *Science*, 7 May, Volume 328, pp. 710-722.

Longo, L. et al., 2012. Did Neandertals and anatomically modern humans coexist in northern Italy during the late MIS 3?. *Quaternary International*, 9 May, Volume 259, pp. 102-112.

Neves, A. & Serva, M., 2012. Extremely Rare Interbreeding Events Can Explain Neanderthal DNA in Living Humans. *PLoS One*, October.7(10).

Sankararaman, S. et al., 2014. The genomic landscape of Neanderthal ancestry in present-day humans. *Nature*, 20 January, Volume 507, pp. 354-357.

Sankararaman, S. et al., 2012. The Date of Interbreeding between Neandertals and Modern Humans. *PLoS Genetics*, October.8(10).

Vernot, B. & Akey, J., 2014. Resurrecting Surviving Neandertal Lineages from Modern Human Genomes. *Science*, 28 Fenruary, Volume 343, pp. 1017-1021.

Wall, J. et al., 2013. Higher levels of Neanderthal ancestry in East Asians than in Europeans. *Genetics*, May, Volume 194, pp. 199-209.

# 18: The fate of the Neanderthals

Banks, W. et al., 2008. Neanderthal Extinction by Competitive Exclusion. *PLoS One*, December.3(12).

Cameron, D. & Groves, C., 2004. *Bones, Stones and Molecules: "Out of Africa" and Human Origins*. London: Elsevier Academic Press.

Churchill, S. et al., 2009. Shanidar 3 Neandertal rib puncture wound and paleolithic weaponry. *Journal of Human Evolution*, Volume 57, pp. 163-178.

Diamond, J., 1991. *The Third Chimpanzee*. London: Random.

Finlayson, C. et al., 2006. Late survival of Neanderthals at the southernmost extreme of Europe. *Nature*, 19 September, Volume 443, pp. 850-853.

Higham, T. et al., 2014. The timing and spatiotemporal patterning of Neanderthal disappearance. *Nature*, 21 August, Volume 512, pp. 306-309.

Mellars, P. & French, J., 2011. Tenfold Population Increase in Western Europe at the Neandertal-to-Modern Human Transition. *Science*, 29 July, Volume 333, pp. 623-627.

Sahle, Y. et al., 2013. Earliest Stone-Tipped Projectiles from the Ethiopian Rift Date to .279,000 Years Ago. *PLoS One*, November.8(11).

Sala, N. et al., 2015. Lethal Interpersonal Violence in the Middle Pleistocene. *PLoS One*, 27 May.

Sepulchre, P. et al., 2007. H4 abrupt event and late Neanderthal presence in Iberia. *Earth and Planetary Science Letters*, Volume 258, pp. 283-292.

Villa, P. & Roebroeks, W., 2014. Neandertal Demise: An Archaeological Analysis of the Modern Human Superiority Complex. *PLoS One*, April, 9(4), pp. e96424.

Zollikofer, C., Ponce de Leon, M., Vandermeersch, B. & Leveque, F., 2002. Evidence for interpersonal violence in the St. Cesaire Neanderthal. *PNAS*, 30 April, 99(9), pp. 6444-6448.

# 19: An unexpected journey

Brumm, A. et al., 2006. Early stone technology on Flores and its implications for Homo floresiensis. *Nature*, 1 June, Volume 441, pp. 624-628.

Brumm, A. et al., 2010. Hominins on Flores, Indonesia, by one million years ago. *Nature*, 1 April, Volume 464, pp. 748-753.

Dennell, R. & Roebroeks, W., 2005. An Asian perspective on early human dispersal from Africa. *Nature*, 22/29 December, Volume 438, pp. 1099-1104.

Eckhardt, R., Henneberg, M., Weller, A. & Hsüc, K., 2014. Rare events in earth history include the LB1 human skeleton from Flores, Indonesia, as a developmental singularity, not a unique taxon. *PNAS*, 19 August, Volume 111(33) pp. 11961-11966.

Ferring, R. et al., 2011. Earliest human occupations at Dmanisi (Georgian Caucasus) dated to 1.85-1.78 Ma. *PNAS*, 28 June, 108(26), pp. 10432-10436.

Gabunia, L. et al., 2002. Découverte d'un nouvel hominidé à Dmanissi (Transcaucasie, Géorgie).. *C.R. Palévol*, Volume 1, pp. 243-253.

Gabunia, L. et al., 2000. Earliest Pleistocene Hominid Cranial Remains from Dmanisi,Republic of Georgia: Taxonomy, Geological Setting, and Age. *Science*, 12 May, Volume 228, pp. 1019-1025.

Henneberg, M., Eckhardt, R., Chavanaves, S. & Hsüc, K., 2014. Evolved developmental homeostasis disturbed in LB1 from Flores, Indonesia, denotes

Down syndrome and not diagnostic traits of the invalid species Homo floresiensis. *PNAS*, 19 August, Volume 111(33) pp. 11967-11972.

Jacob, T. et al., 2006. Pygmoid Australomelanesian Homo sapiens skeletal remains from Liang Bua, Flores: Population affinities and pathological abnormalities. *PNAS*, 5 September, 103(36), pp. 13421-13426.

Jungers, W. et al., 2009. The foot of Homo floresiensis. *Nature*, 7 May, Volume 459, pp. 81-84.

Kaifu, Y. et al., 2015. Unique Dental Morphology of Homo floresiensis and Its Evolutionary Implications. *PLoS One*, 10(11).

Kubo, D., Kono, R. & Kaifu, Y., 2013. Brain size of Homo floresiensis and its evolutionary implications. *Proceedings of the Royal Society B*, 17 April.280(1760).

Lieberman, D., 2007. Homing in on early Homo. *Nature*, 20 September, Volume 449, pp. 291-292.

Lieberman, D., 2009. Homo floresiensis from head to toe. *Nature*, 7 May, Volume 459, pp. 41-42.

Montgomery, S., Capellini, I., Barton, R. & Mundy, N., 2010. Reconstructing the ups and downs of primate brain evolution: implications for adaptive hypotheses and Homo floresiensis. *BMC Biology*, 8(9), pp. 1-19.

Morwood, M. et al., 2005. Further evidence for small-bodied hominins from the Late Pleistocene of Flores, Indonesia. *Nature*, 13 October, Volume 437, pp. 1012-1017.

Morwood, M. et al., 2004. Archaeology and age of a new hominin from Flores in eastern Indonesia. *Nature*, 28 October, Volume 431, pp. 1087-1091.

# 20: The Denisovans

Abi-Rached, L. et al., 2011. The Shaping of Modern Human Immune Systems by Multiregional Admixture with Archaic Humans. *Science*, 25 August.

Cooper, A. & Stringer, C., 2013. Did the Denisovans Cross Wallace's Line?. *Science*, 18 October, Volume 342, pp. 321-323.

Krause, J. et al., 2010. The complete mitochondrial DNA genome of an unknown hominin from southern Siberia. *Nature*, 8 April, Volume 464, pp. 894-897.

Meyer, M. et al., 2013. A mitochondrial genome sequence of a hominin from Sima de los Huesos. *Nature*, 4 December.Issue Published online.

Meyer, M. et al., 2012. A High-Coverage Genome Sequence from an Archaic Denisovan Individual. *Science*, 12 October, Volume 338, pp. 222-226.

Prufer, K. et al., 2014. The complete genome sequence of a Neanderthal from the Altai Mountains. *Nature*, 2 January, Volume 505, pp. 43-49.

Rasmussen, M. et al., 2011. An Aboriginal Australian Genome Reveals Separate Human Dispersals into Asia. *Science*, 7 October, Volume 334, pp. 94-98.

Reich, D. et al., 2010. Genetic history of an archaic hominin group from Denisova Cave in Siberia. *Nature*, 23/30 December, Volume 468, pp. 1053-1060.

Reich, D. et al., 2011. Denisova Admixture and the First Modern Human Dispersals into Southeast Asia and Oceania. *American Journal of Human Genetics*, 7 October, Volume 89, pp. 1-13.

Sawyer, S. et al., 2015. Nuclear and mitochondrial DNA sequences from two Denisovan individuals. *PNAS*, 22 December, 112(51), pp. 15696-15700.

Stringer, C., 2012. What makes a modern human. *Nature*, 3 May, Volume 485, pp. 33-35.

Van den Bergh, D. et al., 2016. Earliest hominin occupation of Sulawesi, Indonesia. *Nature*, 14 January, Volume 529, pp. 208-211.

## 21: Claustrophobics need not apply

Berger, L., Hawks, J., de Ruiter, D. & Churchill, S., 2015. Homo naledi, a new species of the genus Homo from the Dinaledi Chamber, South Africa. *eLife*.
Dirks, P. et al., 2015. Geological and taphonomic context for the new hominin species Homo naledi from the Dinaledi Chamber, South Africa. *eLife*.

## 22: Enter *Homo sapiens*

Clark, J. et al., 2003. Stratigraphic, chronological and behavioural contexts of Pleistocene Homo sapiens from Middle Awash, Ethiopia. *Nature*, 12 June, Volume 423, pp. 747-752.
Coolidge, F. & Wynn, T., 2009. *The Rise of Homo sapiens*. Hoboken, NJ: Wiley-Blackwell.
Day, M., 1969. Early Homo sapiens Remains from the Omo River Region of South-west Ethiopia: Omo Human Skeletal Remain. *Nature*, 21 June, Volume 222, pp. 1135-1138.
Lieberman, D., 1998. Sphenoid shortening and the evolution of modern human cranial shape. *Nature*, 14 May, Volume 393, pp. 158-162.
Lieberman, D., 2008. Speculations About the Selective Basis for Modern Human Craniofacial Form. *Evolutionary Anthropology*, Volume 17, pp. 55-68.
McDougall, I., Brown, F. & Fleagle, J., 2005. Stratigraphic placement and age of modern humans from Kibish, Ethiopia. *Nature*, 17 February, Volume 433, pp. 733-736.
Oppenheimer, S., 2003. *Out of Eden*. London: Constable & Robinson Ltd.
Rightmire, P., 2009. Middle and later Pleistocene hominins in Africa and Southwest Asia. *PNAS*, 22 September, 106(38), pp. 16046-16050.
Shea, J., Fleagle, J. & Assefa, Z., 2007. Context and Chronology of Early Homo sapiens Fossils from the Omo Kibish Formation, Ethipoia. In: P. Mellars, K. Boyle, O. Bar-Yosef & C. Stringer, eds. *Rethinking the human revolution*. Cambridge: McDonald Institute, pp. 153-162.
Stringer, C., 2002. Morphological and Behavioural Origins of Modern Humans. In: T. Crow, ed. *The Speciation of Modern Homo sapiens*. Oxford: Oxford University Press, pp. 23-30.
White, T. et al., 2003. Pleistocene Homo sapiens from Middle Awash, Ethiopia,. *Nature*, 12 June, Volume 423, pp. 742-747.

## 23: Mitochondrial Eve

Behar, D. et al., 2008. The Dawn of Human Matrilineal Diversity. *American Journal of Human Genetics*, May, Volume 82, pp. 1130-1140.
Cann, R., Stoneking, M. & Wilson, A., 1987. Mitochondrial DNA and human evolution. *Nature*, 1 January, Volume 325, pp. 31-36.
Forster, P., 2004. Ice Ages and the mitochondrial DNA chronology of human dispersals: a review. *Philosophical Transactions of the Royal Society B*, Volume 359, pp. 255-264.

Henn, C. et al., 2011. Hunter-gatherer genomic diversity suggests a southern African origin for modern humans. *PNAS,* 28 March, 108(13), pp. 5154-5162.

Shi, W. et al., 2010. A Worldwide Survey of Human Male Demographic History Based on Y-SNP and Y-STR Data from the HGDP-CEPH Populations. *Molecular Biology and Evolution,* 27(2), pp. 385-393.

Underhill, P. et al., 2001. The phylogeography of Y chromosome binary haplotypes and the origins of modern human populations. *Annual of Human Genetics,* Volume 65, pp. 43-62.

# 24: Fluctuation

Brown, K. et al., 2012. An early and enduring advanced technology originating 71,000 years ago in South Africa. *Nature,* 22 November, Volume 491, pp. 590-593.

Clarke, J. & Plug, I., 2008. Animal exploitation strategies during the South African Middle Stone Age: Howiesons Poort and post-Howiesons Poort fauna from Sibudu Cave. *Journal of Human Evolution,* June, 54(6), pp. 886-898.

Crawford, M. et al., 1999. Evidence for the unique function of docasahexaenoic acid during the evolution of the modern human brain. *Lipids,* 34(Supplement), pp. S39-S47.

Henshilwood, C. & Marean, C., 2003. The Origin of Modern Human Behavior. *Current Anthropology,* December, 44(5), pp. 627-651.

Henshilwood, C. et al., 2001. Blombos Cave, Southern Cape, South Africa: Preliminary Report on the 1992-1999 Excavations of the Middle Stone Age Levels. *Journal of Archaeological Science,* Volume 28, pp. 421-448.

Jacobs, Z. & Roberts, R., 2009. Catalysts for Stone Age innovations. *Communicative & Integrative Biology,* 2(2), pp. 191-193.

Jacobs, Z. et al., 2008. Ages for the Middle Stone Age of Southern Africa: Implications for Human Behavior and Dispersal. *Science,* 31 October, Volume 322, pp. 733-735.

Lombard, M. & Pargeter, J., 2008. Hunting with Howiesons Poort segments: pilot experimental study and the functional interpretation of archaeological tools. *Journal of Archaeological Science,* Volume 35, pp. 2523-2531.

Mackay, A., 2011. Nature and significance of the Howiesons Poort to post-Howiesons Poort transition at Klein Kliphuis rockshelter, South Africa. *Journal of Archaeological Science,* Volume 38, pp. 1430-1440.

Marean, C. et al., 2007. Early human use of marine resources and pigment in South Africa during the Middle Pleistocene. *Nature,* 18 October, Volume 449, pp. 905-909.

McBrearty, S. & Brooks, A., 2000. The revolution that wasn't: a new interpretation of the origin of modern human behaviour. *Journal of Human Evolution,* Volume 39, pp. 453-563.

McBrearty, S. & Stringer, C., 2007. The coast in colour. *Nature,* 18 October, Volume 449, pp. 793-794.

Mellars, P., 2006. Why did modern human populations disperse from Africa ca. 60,000 years ago? A new model. *PNAS,* 20 June, 103(25), pp. 9381-9386.

Mithen, S., 2003. *After the Ice: A Global Human History 20,000 - 5,000 BC.* London: Weidenfield & Nicholson.

Mourre, V., Villa, P. & Henshilwood, C., 2010. Early Use of Pressure Flaking on Lithic Artifacts at Blombos Cave, South Africa. *Science,* 29 October, Volume 330, pp. 659-662.

Powell, A., Shennan, S. & Thomas, M., 2009. Late Pleistocene Demography and the Appearance of Modern Human Behavior. *PNAS*, 5 June, Volume 324, pp. 1298-1301.

Villa, P., Soriano, S., Teyssandier, N. & Wurz, S., 2010. The Howiesons Poort and MSA III at Klasies River main site, Cave 1A. *Journal of Archaeological Science*, Volume 37, pp. 630-655.

Wadley, L., 2007. Announcing a Still Bay industry at Sibudu Cave, South Africa. *Journal of Human Evolution*, June, 52(6), pp. 681-689.

Wadley, L., Hodgskiss, T. & Grant, M., 2009. Implications for complex cognition from the hafting of tools with compound adhesives in the Middle Stone Age, South Africa. *PNAS*, 16 June, 106(24), pp. 9590-9594.

Walter, R. et al., 2000. Early human occupation of the Red Sea coast of Eritrea during the last interglacial. *Nature*, 4 May, Volume 405, pp. 65-69.

Will, M., Bader, G. & Conard, N., 2014. Characterizing the Late Pleistocene MSA Lithic Technology of Sibudu, KwaZulu-Natal, South Africa. *PLoS One*, May, 9(5), p. e98359.

Wurtz, S. & Lombard, M., 2007. 70 000-year-old geometric backed tools from the Howiesons Poort at Klasies River, South Africa: were they used for hunting?. *Southern African Humanities*, December, Volume 19, pp. 1-11.

Yellen, J. et al., 1995. A middle stone age worked bone industry from Katanda, Upper Semliki Valley, Zaire. *Science*, 25 April, Volume 268, pp. 553-556.

# 25: Middle Stone Age graphic art

Henshilwood, C., 2007. Fully Symbolic Sapiens behaviour: Innovation in the Middle Stone Age at Blombos Cave, South Africa. In: P. Mellars, K. Boyle, O. Bar-Yosef & C. Stringer, eds. *Rethinking the human revolution*. Cambridge: McDonald Institute, pp. 123-132.

Henshilwood, C. et al., 2011. A 100,000-Year-Old Ochre-Processing Workshop at Blombos Cave, South Africa. *Science*, 14 October, Volume 334, pp. 219-222.

Henshilwood, C., d'Errico, F. & Watts, I., 2009. Engraved ochres from the Middle Stone Age levels at Blombos Cave, South Africa. *Journal of Human Evolution*, Volume 57, pp. 27-47.

Henshilwood, C. et al., 2002. Emergence of Modern Human Behavior: Middle Stone Age Engravings from South Africa. *Science*, Volume 295, pp. 1278-1280.

Texier, P. et al., 2010. A Howiesons Poort tradition of engraving ostrich eggshell containers dated to 60,000 years ago at Diepkloof Rock Shelter, South Africa. *PNAS*, 6 April, 107(14), pp. 6180-6185.

# 26: Going global

Armitage, S. et al., 2011. The Southern Route "Out of Africa": Evidence for an Early Expansion of Modern Humans into Arabia. *Science*, 28 January, Volume 331, pp. 453-456.

Atkinson, Q., Gray, R. & Drummond, A., 2008. mtDNA Variation Predicts Population Size in Humans and Reveals a Major Southern Asian Chapter in Human Prehistory. *Molecular Biology and Evolution*, 25(2), pp. 468-474.

Bowler, J. et al., 2003. New ages for human occupation and climatic change at Lake Mungo, Australia. *Nature*, 20 February, Volume 421, pp. 837-840.

Bulbeck, D., 2007. Where River Meets Sea: A Parsimonious Model for Homo sapiens Colonization of the Indian Ocean Rim and Sahul. *Current Anthropology*, 48(2), pp. 315-321.

Cohen, A. et al., 2007. Ecological consequences of early Late Pleistocene megadroughts in tropical Africa. *PNAS*, 16 October, 107(42), pp. 16422-16427.

Curnoe, D. et al., 2012. Human Remains from the Pleistocene-Holocene Transition of Southwest China Suggest a Complex Evolutionary History for East Asians. *PLoS One*, March.7(3).

Dennell, R., 2010. Early Homo sapiens in China. *Nature*, 25 November, Volume 468, pp. 512-513.

Dennell, R. & Petraglia, M., 2012. The dispersal of Homo sapiens across southern Asia: how early, how often, how complex?. *Quaternary Science Reviews*, Volume 47, pp. 15-22.

Forster, P. & Matsumura, S., 2005. Did Early Humans Go North or South. *Science*, 13 May, Volume 308, pp. 965-966.

Kittler, R., Kayser, M. & Stoneking, M., 2003. Molecular Evolution of Pediculus humanus and the Origin of Clothing. *Current Biology*, 9 August, Volume 13, pp. 1414-1417.

Kivisild, T. et al., 2003. The Genetic Heritage of the Earliest Settlers Persists Both in Indian Tribal and Caste Populations. *American Journal of Human Genetics*, Volume 72, pp. 313-332.

Lambeck, K. & Chappell, J., 2001. Sea Level Change Through the Last Glacial Cycle. *Science*, 27 April, Volume 292, pp. 679-686.

Liu, H., Prugnolle, F., Manica, A. & Balloux, F., 2006. A Geographically Explicit Genetic Model of Worldwide Human-Settlement History. *American Journal of Human Genetics*, 230-237 August, Volume 79, pp. 230-237.

Liu, W. et al., 2010. Human remains from Zhirendong, South China,and modern human emergence in East Asia. *PNAS*, 9 November, 107(45), pp. 19201-19204.

Liu, W. et al., 2015. The earliest unequivocally modern humans in southern China. *Nature*, 29 October, Volume 526, pp. 696-699.

Macaulay, V. et al., 2005. Single, Rapid Coastal Settlement of Asia Revealed by Analysis of Complete Mitochondrial Genomes. *Science*, 13 May, Volume 308, pp. 1034-1036.

Mellars, P., 2006. A new radiocarbon revolution and the dispersal of modern humans in Eurasia. *Nature*, 23 Febuary, Volume 493, pp. 931-935.

Metspalu, M. et al., 2004. Most of the extant mtDNA boundaries in South and Southwest Asia were likely shaped during the initial settlement of Eurasia by anatomically modern humans. *BMC Genetics*, 5(26).

Oppenheimer, S., 2003. *Out of Eden*. London: Constable & Robinson Ltd.

Petraglia, M. & Alsharekh, A., 2003. The Middle Palaeolithic of Arabia: Implications for modern human origins, behaviour and dispersals. *Antiquity*, 77(298), pp. 671-684.

Petraglia, M. et al., 2011. The Toba volcanic super-eruption, environmental change, and hominin occupation history in India over the last 140,000 years. *Quaternary International*, August, Volume 238, pp. 119-134.

Petraglia, M. et al., 2007. Middle Paleolithic Assemblages from the Indian Subcontinent Before and After the Toba Super-Eruption. *Science*, 6 July, Volume 317, pp. 114-116.

Rasmussen, M. et al., 2011. An Aboriginal Australian Genome Reveals Separate Human Dispersals into Asia. *Science*, 7 October, Volume 334, pp. 94-98.

Reyes-Centeno, H. et al., 2014. Genomic and cranial phenotype data support multiple modern human dispersals from Africa and a southern route into Asia. *PNAS*, 20 May, 111(20), pp. 7248-7253.

Rose, J., 2007. The Arabian Corridor Migration Model:archaeological evidence for hominin dispersals into Oman during the Middle and Upper Pleistocene. *Proceedings of the Seminar for Arabian Studies*, Volume 37.

Rose, J., 2010. New Light on Human Prehistory in the Arabo-Persian Gulf Oasis. *Current Anthropology*, December, 51(6), pp. 849-883.

Rose, J. et al., 2011. The Nubian Complex of Dhofar, Oman: An African Middle Stone Age Industry in Southern Arabia. *PLoS One*, November.6(11).

Shen, G. et al., 2002. U-Series dating of Liujiang hominid site in Guangxi, Southern China. *Journal of Human Evolution*, December, 43(6), pp. 817-829.

Soares, P. et al., 2009. Correcting for Purifying Selection: An Improved Human Mitochondrial Molecular Clock. *American Journal of Human Genetics*, 12 June, Volume 84, pp. 740-759.

Thangaraj, K. et al., 2005. Reconstructing the Origin of Andaman Islanders. *Science*, 13 May, Volume 308, p. 996.

Usik, V. et al., 2013. Nubian Complex reduction strategies in Dhofar, southern Oman. *Quaternary International*, Volume 300, pp. 244-266.

Wells, S., 2002. *The Journey of Man*. Penguin: London.

Williams, M. et al., 2009. Environmental impact of the 73 ka Toba super-eruption in South Asia. *Palaeogeography, Palaeoclimatology, Palaeoecology*, Volume 284, pp. 295-314.

# 27: The first Australians

Allen, J. & O'Connell, J., 2003. The long and the short of it: Archaeological approaches to determining when humans first colonised Australia and New Guinea. *Australian Archaeology*, Volume 57, pp. 5-19.

Bowler, J., 1998. Willandra Lakes Revisited: environmental framework for human occupation. *Archaeology in Oceania*, Volume 33, pp. 120-155.

Bowler, J. et al., 2003. New ages for human occupation and climatic change at Lake Mungo, Australia. *Nature*, 20 February, Volume 421, pp. 837-840.

Gillespie, R., 2002. Dating the first Australians. *Radiocarbon*, 44(2), pp. 455-472.

Hiscock, P., 2008. *Archaeology of Ancient Australia*. Abingdon: Routledge.

O'Connell, J. & Allen, J., 2004. Dating the colonization of Sahul (Pleistocene Australia-New Guinea): a review of recent research. *Journal of Archaeological Science*, Volume 31, pp. 835-853.

O'Connell, J. & Allen, J., 2007. Pre-LGM Sahul (Pleistocene Australia-New Guinea) and the Archaeology of Early Modern Humans. In: P. Mellars, K. Boyle, O. Bar-Yosef & C. Stringer, eds. *Rethinking the human revolution*. Cambridge: McDonald Institute, pp. 395-410.

Roberts, R., Jones, R. & Smith, M., 1990. Thermoluminescence dating of a 50,000-year-old human occupation site in northern Australia. *Nature*, 10 May, Volume 345, pp. 153-156.

Roberts, R. et al., 1994. The human colonisation of Australia: optical dates of 53,000 and 60,000 years bracket human arrival at Deaf Adder Gorge, Northern Territory. *Quaternary Science Reviews*, 13(5-7), pp. 575-583.

Roberts, R. et al., 1998. Single-aliquot and single-grain optical dating confirm thermoluminescent age estimates at Malakunanja rock shelter in northern Australia. *Ancient TL*, 16(1), pp. 19-24.

Smith, C. et al., 2003. The thermal history of human fossils and the likelihood of successful DNA amplification. *Journal of Human Evolution*, Volume 43, pp. 203-217.

Stringer, C., 2000. Coasting out of Africa. *Nature*, 4 May, Volume 405, pp. 24-27.

Summerhayes, G. et al., 2010. Human Adaptation and Plant Use in Highland New Guinea 49,000 to 44,000 Years Ago. *Science*, 1 October, Volume 330, pp. 78-81.

Thorne, A. et al., 1999. Australia's oldest human remains: age of the Lake Mungo 3 skeleton. *Journal of Human Evolution*, June, 36(6), pp. 591-612.

## 28: Deus ex Speluncam

Barton, M., Clark, G. & Cohen, A., 1994. Art as information: explaining Upper Palaeolithic art in western Europe. *World Archaeology*, 26(2), pp. 185-207.

Clottes, J., 2008. *Cave Art*. New York: Phaidon.

Lewis-Williams, D., 2002. *The Mind in the Cave:Consciousness And The Origins Of Art*. London: Thames & Hudson.

Mellars, P., 1994. The Upper Palaeolithic Revolution. In: B. Cunliffe, ed. *Prehistoric Europe*. Oxford: Oxford University Press, pp. 42-78.

Mellars, P., 2004. Neanderthals and the modern human colonization of Europe. *Nature*, 25 November, Volume 432, pp. 461-465.

Mellars, P., 2006. A new radiocarbon revolution and the dispersal of modern humans in Eurasia. *Nature*, 23 Febuary, Volume 493, pp. 931-935.

Mellars, P., 2009. Origins of the female image. *Nature*, 13 May, Volume 439, pp. 176-177.

Pike, A. et al., 2012. U-Series Dating of Paleolithic Art in 11 Caves in Spain. *Science*, 15 June, Volume 336, pp. 1409-1413.

Straus, L., 1995. The Upper Palaeolithic of Europe: An Overview. *Evolutionary Anthropology*, Volume 4, pp. 4-16.

## 29: Who was Kennewick Man?

Atkinson, Q., Gray, R. & Drummond, A., 2008. mtDNA Variation Predicts Population Size in Humans and Reveals a Major Southern Asian Chapter in Human Prehistory. *Molecular Biology and Evolution*, 25(2), pp. 468-474.

Bonatto, S. & Salzano, F., 1997. A single and early migration for the peopling of the Americas supported by mitochondrial DNA sequence data. *PNAS*, March, Volume 94, pp. 1866-1871.

Chatters, J. et al., 2014. Late Pleistocene Human Skeleton and mtDNA Link Paleoamericans and Modern Native Americans. *Science*, 16 May, Volume 344, pp. 750-754.

Dillehay, T. et al., 2015. Archaeological Evidence for an Early Human Presence at Monte Verde, Chile. *PLoS One*, 10(11).

Fagundes, N., Kanitz, R. & Bonatto, S., 2008. A Reevaluation of the Native American MtDNA Genome Diversity and Its Bearing on the Models of Early Colonization of Beringia. *PLoS One*, September.3(9).

Fagundes, N. et al., 2008. Mitochondrial Population Genomics Supports a Single Pre-Clovis Origin with a Coastal Route for the Peopling of the Americas. *American Journal of Human Genetics*, March, Volume 82, pp. 583-592.

Gonzalez-Jose, R., Bortolini, M., Santos, F. & Bonatto, S., 2008. The Peopling of America: Craniofacial Shape Variation on a Continental Scale and its Interpretation From an Interdisciplinary View. *American Journal of Physical Anthropology*, Volume 137, pp. 175-187.

Greenberg, J., Turner, C. & Zegura, S., 1986. The Settlement of the Americas: A Comparison of the Linguistic, Dental, and Genetic Evidence. *Current Anthropology*, December, 27(5), pp. 477-497.

Guthrie, D., 2001. Origin and causes of the mammoth steppe: a story of cloud cover, woolly mammal tooth pits, buckles, and inside-out Beringia. *Quaternary Science Reviews*, Volume 20, pp. 549-574.

Hamilton, M. & Buchanan, B., 2010. Archaeological Support for the Three-Stage Expansion of Modern Humans across Northeastern Eurasia and into the Americas. *PLoS One*, August.5(8).

Hey, J., 2005. On the Number of New World Founders: A Population Genetic Portrait of the Peopling of the Americas. *PLoS One*, June, 3(6), pp. 965-975.

Hoffecker, J., Powers, R. & Goebel, T., 1993. The Colonization of Beringia and the Peopling of the New World. *Science*, 1 January, Volume 259, pp. 46-53.

Holden, C., 2004. Scientists Hope Ruling Will Lead Them to Bones. *Science*, 13 February, 303(5660), p. 943.

Hubbe, M., Neves, W. & Harvati, K., 2010. Testing Evolutionary and Dispersion Scenarios for the Settlement of the New World. *PLoS One*, June.5(6).

Jantz, R. & Owsley, D., 2001. Variation Among Early North American Crania. *American Journal of Physical Anthropology*, Volume 114, pp. 144-156.

Kitchen, A., Miyamoto, M. & Mulligan, C., 2008. A Three-Stage Colonization Model for the Peopling of the Americas. *PLoS One*, February.3(2).

Mulligan, C., Kitchen, A. & Miyamoto, M., 2008. Updated Three-Stage Model for the Peopling of the Americas. *PLoS One*, September.3(9).

Oppenheimer, S., 2003. *Out of Eden*. London: Constable & Robinson Ltd.

Perez, I. et al., 2009. Discrepancy between Cranial and DNA Data of Early Americans: Implications for American Peopling. *PLoS One*, May.4(5).

Pitulko, V. et al., 2016. Early human presence in the Arctic: Evidence from 45,000-year-old mammoth remains. *Science*, 16 January, 351(6270), pp. 260-263.

Raghavan, M. et al., 2014. The genetic prehistory of the New World Arctic. *Science*, 29 August, 345(620), pp. 1020,1255832.

Rasmussen, M. et al., 2014. The genome of a Late Pleistocene human from a Clovis burial site in western Montana. *Nature*, 13 Feb, Volume 506, pp. 225-229.

Rasmussen, M. et al., 2015. The ancestry and affiliations of Kennewick Man. *Nature*, 23 July, Volume 523, pp. 455-458.

Reich, D. et al., 2012. Reconstructing Native American population history. *Nature*, 16 August, Volume 488, pp. 370-374.

Waters, M. & Stafford, T., 2007. Redefining the Age of Clovis: Implications for the Peopling of the Americas. *Science*, 23 February, Volume 315, pp. 1122-1126.

Zazula, G. et al., 2006. Vegetation buried under Dawson tephra (25,300 14C years BP) and locally diverse late Pleistocene paleoenvironments of Goldbottom Creek, Yukon, Canada. *Palaeogeography, Palaeoclimatology, Palaeoecology*, Volume 242, pp. 253-286.

# 30: No place like home

Davis, S., 2005. Why domesticate food animals? Some zoo-archaeological evidence from the Levant. *Journal of Archaeological Science*, Volume 32, pp. 1408-1416.

Hershkovitz, L. et al., 1993. Ohalo II man - unusual findings in the anterior rib cage and shoulder girdle of a 19000-year-old specimen. *International Journal of Osteoarchaeology*, September, 3(3), pp. 177-188.

Hershkovitz, L. et al., 1995. Ohalo II H2: A 19,000-Year-Old Skeleton From a Water-Logged Site at the Sea of Galilee, Israel. *American Journal of Physical Anthropology*, Volume 96, pp. 215-234.

Kislev, M., Nadel, D. & Carmi, I., 1992. Epipalaeolithic (19,000 BP) cereal and fruit diet at Ohalo II, Sea of Galilee, Israel. *Review of Palaeobotany and Palynology*, 30 September, 73(1-4), pp. 161-166.

Lieberman, D., 1993. The rise and fall of seasonal mobility among hunter-gatherers. *Current Anthropology*, 34(5), pp. 599-631.

Mithen, S., 2003. *After the Ice: A Global Human History 20,000 - 5,000 BC.* London: Weidenfield & Nicholson.

Nadel, D., 1994. Levantine Upper Palaeolithic - Early Epipalaeolithic Burial Customs: Ohalo II as a case study. *Paléorient*, 20(1), pp. 113-121.

Nadel, D. et al., 2001. New Dates From Submerged Late Pleistocene Sediments in the Southern Sea of Galilee, Israel. *Radiocarbon*, 43(3), pp. 1167-1178.

Nadel, D. et al., 2004. Stone Age hut in Israel yields world's oldest evidence of bedding. *PNAS*, 27 April, 101(17), pp. 6821-6826.

Nadel, D. & Werker, E., 1999. The oldest ever brush hut plant remains from Ohalo II, Jordan Valley, Israel. *Antiquity*, December, 73(282), pp. 755-764.

Piperno, D., Weiss, E., Holst, I. & Nadel, D., 2004. Processing of wild cereal grains in the Upper Palaeolithic revealed by starch grain analysis. *Nature*, 5 August, Volume 450, pp. 670-673.

Simmons, T. & Nadel, D., 1998. The avifauna of the early Epipalaeolithic site of Ohalo II (19,400 BP), Israel: species diversity, habitat and seasonality,. *International Journal of Osteoarchaeology*, 8(2), pp. 79-96.

Snir, A., Nadel, D. & Weiss, E., 2015. Plant-food preparation on two consecutive floors at Upper Paleolithic Ohalo II, Israel. *Journal of Archaeological Science*, Volume 53, pp. 61-71.

Weiss, E. et al., 2008. Plant-food preparation area on an Upper Paleolithic brush hut floor at Ohalo II, Israel. *Journal of Archaeological Science*, Volume 35, pp. 2400-2414.

Weiss, E., Wetterstrom, W., Nadel, D. & Bar-Yosef, O., 2004. The broad spectrum revisited: Evidence from plant remains. *PNAS*, 29 June, 101(26), pp. 9551-9555.

# 31: Prime suspect

Barnosky, A., 2008. Megafauna biomass tradeoff as a driver of Quaternary and future extinctions. *PNAS*, 12 August, 105(Suppl. 1), pp. 11543-11548.

Bartlett, L. et al., 2015. Robustness despite uncertainty: regional climate data reveal the dominant role of humans in explaining global extinctions of Late Quaternary megafauna. *Ecography*.

Cohen, T. et al., 2011. Continental aridification and the vanishing of Australia's megalakes. *Geology*, 5 January, 39(2), pp. 167-170.

Cooper, A. et al., 2015. Abrupt warming events drove Late Pleistocene Holarctic megafaunal turnover. *Science*, 7 August, Volume 349, pp. 602-606.

Faith, T. & Surovell, T., 2009. Synchronous extinction of North America's Pleistocene mammals. *PNAS*, 8 December, 106(49), pp. 20641-20645.

Field, J., 2012. *Australia's Megafauna Extinctions: Cause and Effect*. [Online] Available at: http://www.australasianscience.com.au/article/issue-may-2012/australias-megafauna-extinctions-cause-and-effect.html [Accessed 17 May 2013].

Flannery, T., 1990. Pleistocene faunal loss: implications of the aftershock for Australia's past and future. *Archaeology in Oceania*, pp. 45-67.

Gill, J. et al., 2009. Pleistocene Megafaunal Collapse, Novel Plant Communities, and Enhanced Fire Regimes in North America. *Science*, 20 November, Volume 326, pp. 1100-1103.

Grayson, D., 1984. Nineteenth-Century Explanations. In: P. Martin & R. Klein, eds. *Quaternary Extinctions: A Prehistoric Revolution*. Tucson, AZ: University of Arizona Press, pp. 5-39.

Haub, C., 2002. How Many People Have Ever Lived?. *Population Today*, November/December, 38(8), pp. 3-4.

Martin, P., 1984. Prehistoric Overkill: The Global Model. In: P. Martin & R. Klein, eds. *Quaternary Extinctions: A Prehistoric Revolution*. Tucson, AZ: University of Arizona Press, pp. 354-403.

Roberts, R. et al., 2001. New Ages for the Last Australian Megafauna: Continent-Wide Extinction About 46,000 Years Ago. *Science*, 8 June, Volume 292, pp. 1888-1892.

Rule, S. et al., 2012. The Aftermath of Megafaunal Extinction: Ecosystem Transformation in Pleistocene Australia. *Science*, 23 March, Volume 335, pp. 1483-1486.

# 32: The Radiocarbon Revolution

Renfrew, C., 1973. *Before Civilization*. London: Jonathon Cape.

# 33: First farmers

Barker, G., 2006. The Agricultural Revolution in Prehistory: Why did Foragers become Farmers. Oxford: Oxford University Press.

Bar-Yosef, O., 1998. The Natufian Culture in the Levant,Threshold to the Origins of Agriculture. Evolutionary Anthropology, 6(5), pp. 159-177.

Bellwood, P., 2005. First Farmers. Oxford: Blackwell Publishing.

Binford, L., 1968. Post-Pleistocene adaptations. In: S. Binford & L. Binford, eds. New Perspectives in Archaeology. Chicago: Aldine, pp. 313-341.

Burgess, C. & Shennan, S., 1976. The beaker phenomemon, some suggestions. In: C. Burgess & R. Miket, eds. Settlement and Economy in the Third and Second Millennia B.C. (B. A. R. 33). Oxford: British Archaeological Reports, pp. 309-326.

Cohen, M., 1977. The Food Crisis in Prehistory: Overpopulation and the Origins of Agriculture. New Haven, CT: Yale University Press.

Diamond, J., 1991. The Third Chimpanzee. London: Random.

Diamond, J., 2002. Evolution, consequences and future of plant and animal domestication. Nature, 8 August, Volume 418, pp. 700-707.

Flannery, K., 1969. Origin and ecological effects of early domestication in Iran and the Near East. In: P. Ucko & G. Dimbleby, eds. The Domestication and Exploitation of Plants and Animals. London: Duckworth, pp. 73-100.

Hayden, B., 1992. Models of Domestication. In: A. Gebauer & T. Price, eds. Transitions to Agriculture in Prehistory. Madison, WI: Prehistory Press, pp. 11-19.

Hillman, G., 1996. Late Pleistocene changes in wild plant-foods availble to hunter-gatherers of the Fertile Crescent: possible preludes to cereal cultivation. In: D. Harris, ed. The Origins and Spread of Agriculture and Pastoralism in Eurasia. London: Routledge, pp. 159-201.

Hillman, G. & Davies, S., 1990. Domestication rates in wild-type wheats and barley under primitive cultivation. Journal of the Linnaean Society, Volume 39, pp. 39-78.

Hillman, G. et al., 2001. New evidence of Lateglacial cereal cultivation at Abu Hureyra on the Euphrates. The Holocene, 11(4), pp. 382-393.

Kuijt, I. & Finlayson, B., 2009. Evidence for food storage and predomestication granaries 11,000 years ago in the Jordan Valley. PNAS, 7 July, 106(27), pp. 10966-10970.

Lee, R., 1968. What hunters do for a living, or how to make out on scarce resources. In: R. Lee & I. de Vere, eds. Man the Hunter. Chicago: Aldine, pp. 30-48.

Richerson, P., Boyd, R. & Bettinger, R., 2001. Was agriculture impossible during the Pleistocene but mandatory during the Holocene: a climate change hypothesis. American Antiquity, 6(3), pp. 387-411.

Scarre, C., 2005. The World Transformed:from Foragers and Farmers to States and Empires. In: C. Scarre, ed. The Human Past. London: Thames & Hudson, pp. 176-199.

Scarre, C., 2005. The Study of the Human Past. In: C. Scarre, ed. The Human Past. London: Thames & Hudson, pp. 25-43.

Smith, B., 2001. Low-Level Food Production. Journal of Archaeological Research, 9(1), pp. 1-43.

Weiss, E., Kislev, M. & Hartmann, A., 2006. Autonomous Cultivation Before Domestication. Science, 16 June, Volume 312, pp. 1608-1610.

Willcox, G., 1996. Evidence for plant exploitation and vegetation history from three Early Neolithic pre-pottery sites on the Euphrates (Syria). Vegetation History and Archaeobotany, Volume 5, pp. 143-152.

Wood, J., Milner, G., Harpending, H. & Weiss, K., 1992. The Osteological Paradox: Problems of Inferring Prehistoric Health from Skeletal Samples. Current Anthropology, Aug-Oct, 33(4), pp. 343-370.

Zeder, M., 2006. Central Questions in the Domestication of Plants and Animals. Evolutionary Anthropology, Volume 15, pp. 105-117.

Zeder, M., 2011. The Origins of Agriculture in the Near East. Current Anthropology, Octorber.52(S4).

# 34: First came the temple

Kromer, B. & Schmidt, K., 1998. Two Radiocarbon Dates from Göbekli Tepe, South Eastern Turkey. *Neo-Lithics*, Issue 3/98, pp. 8-9.

Kuijt, I., 2000. People and Space in Early Agricultural Villages: Exploring Daily Lives, Community Size, and Architecture in the Late Pre-Pottery Neolithic. *Journal of Anthropological Archaeology*, Volume 19, pp. 75-102.

Lewis-Williams, D. & Pearce, D., 2005. *Inside the Neolithic Mind*. London: Thames & Hudson.

Peters, J. & Schmidt, K., 2004. Animals in the symbolic world of Pre-Pottery Neolithic Göbekli Tepe, south-eastern Turkey: a preliminary assessment. *Anthropozoologica*, 39(1), pp. 179-218.

Pustovoytov, K., 2002. 14 C Dating of Pedogenic Carbonate Coatings on Wall Stones at Göbekli Tepe (Southeastern Turkey). *Neo-Lithics*, Issue 2/02, pp. 3-4.

Schmidt, K., 1995. Investigations in the early Meospotamian Neolithic: Göbekli Tepe and Gürcütepe. *Neo-Lithics*, Issue 2/95, pp. 9-10.

Schmidt, K., 1998. Beyond Daily Bread: Evidence of Early Neolithic Ritual from Göbekli Tepe. *Neo-Lithics*, Issue 2/98, pp. 1-5.

Schmidt, K., 2000. Göbekli Tepe, Southeastern Turkey A Preliminary Report on the 1995-1999 Excavations. *Paléorient*, 26(1), pp. 45-54.

Schmidt, K., 2003. The 2003 Campaign at Göbekli Tepe (Southeastern Turkey). *Neo-Lithics*, Issue 2/03, pp. 3-8.

# 35: Unlikely partners

Driscoll, C., Macdonald, D. & O'Brien, S., 2009. From wild animals to domestic pets, an evolutionary view of domestication. *PNAS*, 16 June, Volume 106, pp. 9971-9978.

Driscoll, C. et al., 2007. The Near Eastern Origin of Cat Domestication. *Science*, 27 July, Volume 317, pp. 519-523.

Hu, Y. et al., 2014. Earliest evidence for commensal processes of cat domestication. *PNAS*, 7 January, 111(1), pp. 116-120.

Tchernov, E., 1991. Biological evidence for human sedentism in southwest Asia during the Natufian. In: O. Bar-Yosef & F. Valla, eds. *The Natufian Culture in the Levant*. Ann Arbor, MI: International Monographs in Prehistory, pp. 315-340.

Tchernov, E., 1991. Of mice and men. Biological markers for long-term sedentism : a reply. *Paléorient*, 17(1), pp. 153-160.

Van Neer, W., Linseele, V., Friedman, R. & de Cupere, B., 2014. More evidence for cat taming at the Predynastic elite cemetery of Hierakonpolis (Upper Egypt). *Journal of Archaeological Science*, Volume 45, pp. 103-111.

Vigne, J., Carrère, I., Briois, F. & Guilaine, J., 2011. The Early Process of Mammal Domestication in the Near East New Evidence from the Pre-Neolithic and Pre-Pottery Neolithic in Cyprus. *Current Anthropology*, October, 52(S4), pp. 255-271.

Vigne, J. et al., 2016. Earliest "Domestic" Cats in China Identified as Leopard Cat (Prionailurus bengalensis). *PLoS One*, 22 January.11(1).

Vigne, J. et al., 2004. Early Taming of the Cat in Cyprus. *Science*, 9 April, Volume 304, p. 259.

# 36: Best friends

Axelsson, E. et al., 2013. The genomic signature of dog domestication reveals adaptation to a starch-rich diet. *Nature*, 21 March, Volume 495, pp. 360-365.

Ding, Z. et al., 2012. Origins of domestic dog in Southern East Asia is supported by analysis of Y-chromosome DNA. *Heredity*, Volume 108, pp. 507-514.

Driscoll, C., Macdonald, D. & O'Brien, S., 2009. From wild animals to domestic pets, an evolutionary view of domestication. *PNAS*, 16 June, Volume 106, pp. 9971-9978.

Freedman, A. et al., 2014. Genome Sequencing Highlights the Dynamic Early History of Dogs. *PLoS genetics*, January, 10(1), p. e1004016.

Germonpré, M., Lázničková-Galetová, M. & Sablin, M., 2012. Palaeolithic dog skulls at the Gravettian Předmostí site, the Czech Republic. *Journal of Archaeological Science*, January, 39(1), pp. 184-202.

Germonpré, M. et al., 2009. Fossil dogs and wolves from Palaeolithic sites in Belgium, the Ukraine and Russia: osteometry, ancient DNA and stable isotopes. *Journal of Archaeological Science*, February, 36(2), pp. 473-490 .

Larson, G. et al., 2012. Rethinking dog domestication by integrating genetics, archeology, and biogeography. *PNAS*, 5 June, 109(23), pp. 8878-8883.

Leonard, J. et al., 2002. Ancient DNA Evidence for Old World Origin of New World Dogs. *Science*, 22 November, Volume 298, pp. 1613-1616.

Ovodov, N. et al., 2011. A 33,000-Year-Old Incipient Dog from the Altai Mountains of Siberia: Evidence of the Earliest Domestication Disrupted by the Last Glacial Maximum. *PLoS One*, July, 6(7), p. e22821.

Pang, J. et al., 2009. mtDNA Data Indicate a Single Origin for Dogs South of Yangtze River, Less Than 16,300 Years Ago, from Numerous Wolves. *Molecular Biology and Evolution*, 26(12), pp. 2849-2864.

Savolainen, P. et al., 2004. A detailed picture of the origin of the Australian dingo, obtained from the study of mitochondrial DNA. *PNAS*, 17 August, 101(33), pp. 12387-12390.

Skoglund, P., Ersmark, E., Palkopoulou, E. & Dalen, L., 2015. Ancient Wolf Genome Reveals an Early Divergence of Domestic Dog Ancestors and Admixture into High-Latitude Breeds. *Current Biology*, 1 June, Volume 25, pp. 1-5.

Tchernov, E. & Valla, F., 1997. Two New Dogs, and Other Natufian Dogs, from the Southern Levant. *Journal of Archaeological Science*, January, 24(1), pp. 65-95.

Thalmann, O. et al., 2013. Complete Mitochondrial Genomes of Ancient Canids Suggest a European Origin of Domestic Dogs. *Science*, 15 November, Volume 342, pp. 871-874.

Vila, C. et al., 1997. Multiple and Ancient Origins of the Domestic Dog. *Science*, 13 June, Volume 276, pp. 1687-1689.

VonHoldt, B. et al., 2010. Genome-wide SNP and haplotype analyses reveal a rich history underlying dog domestication. *Nature*, 8 April, Volume 464, pp. 898-903.

Wang, G. et al., 2016. Out of southern East Asia: the natural history of domestic dogs across the world. *Cell Research*, Volume 26, pp. 21-33.

# 37: The forked mound

Goring-Morris, N. & Belfer-Cohen, A., 2011. Neolithization Processes in the Levant The Outer Envelope. *Current Anthropology*, October.52(S4).

Hodder, I., 2006. *Çatalhöyük the Leopard's Tale*. London: Thames & Hudson.

Lewis-Williams, D. & Pearce, D., 2005. *Inside the Neolithic Mind*. London: Thames & Hudson.

Mithen, S., 2003. *After the Ice: A Global Human History 20,000 - 5,000 BC*. London: Weidenfeld & Nicholson.

Schmitt, A. et al., 2014. Identifying the Volcanic Eruption Depicted in a Neolithic Painting at Çatalhöyük, Central Anatolia, Turkey. *PLoS One*, January, 9(1), p. e84711.

# 38: A tale of three cemeteries

Mithen, S., 1994. The Mesolithic Age. In: B. Cunliffe, ed. *Prehistoric Europe*. Oxford: Oxford University Press, pp. 79-135.

Mithen, S., 2003. *After the Ice: A Global Human History 20,000 - 5,000 BC*. London: Weidenfield & Nicholson.

O'Shea, J. & Zvelebil, M., 1984. Oleneostrovski Mogilnik: Reconstructing the Social and Economic Organization of Prehistoric Foragers in Northern Russia. *Journal of Anthropological Archaeology*, Volume 3, pp. 1-40.

Rowley-Conwy, P., 1998. Cemeteries, Seasonality and Complexity in the Ertebolle of Southern Scandinavia. In: M. Zvelebil, L. Domańska & R. Dennell, eds. *Harvesting the sea, farming the forest: the emergence of Neolithic societies*. Sheffield: Sheffield Academic Press, pp. 193-202.

Scarre, C., 2005. Holocene Europe. In: C. Scarre, ed. *The human past*. London: Thames & Hudson, pp. 392-431.

Schulting, R., 1996. Antlers, bone pins and flint blades: the Mesolithic cemeteries of Téviec and Hoëdic, Brittany. *Antiquity*, June, 70(268), pp. 335-350.

# 39: Doggerland: a prehistoric Atlantis

Coles, B., 1998. Doggerland: a Speculative Survey. *Proceedings of the Prehistoric Society*, January, Volume 64, pp. 45-81.

Finch, S., Gaffney, V. & Thomson, K., 2007. In Sight of Doggerland: From speculative survey to landscape exploration. *Internet Archaeology*, Volume 22.

Mithen, S., 2003. *After the Ice: A Global Human History 20,000 - 5,000 BC*. London: Weidenfield & Nicholson.

# 40: Lurches and longhouses

Ammerman, A. & Cavalli-Sforza, L., 1973. A population model for the diffusion of farming in Europe. In: C. Renfrew, ed. *The Explanation of Culture Change: Models in Prehistory*. London: Duckworth, pp. 343-358.

Ammerman, A. & Cavalli-Sforza, L., 1984. *The Neolithic Transition and the Genetics of Populations in Europe*. Princeton, NJ: Princeton University Press.

Bentley, A. et al., 2002. Prehistoric Migration in Europe: Strontium Isotope Analysis of Early Neolithic Skeletons. *Current Anthropology*, 43(5), pp. 799-804.

Bentley, R., Krause, R., Price, T. & Kaufmann, B., 2003. Human mobility at the Early Neolithic settlement of Vaihingen, Germany: evidence from strontium isotope analysis. *Archaeometry*, Volume 45, pp. 471-486.

Bollongino, R. et al., 2013. 2000 Years of Parallel Societies in Stone Age Central Europe. *Science*, 25 October, Volume 342, pp. 479-481.

Gkiasta, M., Russell, T., Shennan, S. & Steele, J., 2003. Neolithic transition in Europe: the radiocarbon record revisited. *Antiquity*, Volume 77, pp. 45-62.

Meyer, C., Lohr, C., Gronenborn, D. & Alt, K., 2015. The massacre mass grave of Schöneck-Kilianstädten reveals new insights into collective violence in Early

Neolithic Central Europe. *PNAS*, 8 October, Volume 112(36), pp. 11217-11222.

Rowley-Conwy, P., 2004. How the West Was Lost: A Reconsideration of Agricultural Origins in Britain,Ireland, and Southern Scandinavia. *Current Anthropology*, 45(Supplement, August-October), pp. S83-S113.

Rowley-Conwy, P., 2011. Westward ho!. *Current Anthropology*, October.52(S4).

Scarre, C., 2002. Pioneer Farmers?. In: P. Bellwood & C. Renfrew, eds. *Examining the farming/language dispersal hypothesis*. Cambridge: McDonald Institute, pp. 395-407.

Scarre, C., 2005. Holocene Europe. In: C. Scarre, ed. *The human past*. London: Thames & Hudson, pp. 392-431.

# 41: Drawing down the Moon

Henty, E., 2014. The Archaeoastronomy of Tomnaverie Recumbent Stone Circle: A Comparison of Methodologies. *Papers from the Institute of Archaeology,*, 24(1).

Ruggles, C., 1999. *Astronomy in Prehistoric Britain and Ireland*. New Haven, CT: Yale University Press.

Scarre, C., 2005. Holocene Europe. In: C. Scarre, ed. *The human past*. London: Thames & Hudson, pp. 392-431.

# 42: Of rice and men

Cohen, D., 2011. The Beginnings of Agriculture in China: A Multiregional View. *Current Anthropology*, October, 52(S4), pp. S273-S293.

Fuller, D. & Qin, L., 2009. Water management and labour in the origins and dispersal of Asian rice. *World Archaeology*, 1 March, 41(1), pp. 88-111.

Fuller, D., Qin, L. & Harvey, E., 2008. A critical assessment of early agriculture in East Asia, with emphasis on Lower Yangtze rice domestication. *Pradghara (Journal of the Uttar Pradesh State Archaeology Department)*, Volume 18, pp. 17-52.

Fuller, D. et al., 2009. The Domestication Process and Domestication Rate in Rice: Spikelet Bases from the Lower Yangtze. *Science*, 20 March, Volume 323, pp. 1607-1610.

Gao, L. & Innan, H., 2008. Nonindependent Domestication of the Two Rice Subspecies, Oryza sativa ssp. indica and ssp. japonica, Demonstrated by Multilocus Microsatellites. *Genetics*, June, Volume 179, pp. 965-976.

Huang, X. et al., 2012. A map of rice genome variation reveals the origin of cultivated rice. *Nature*, 25 October, Volume 490, pp. 497-502.

Jiejun, H., 1999. Excavations at Chengtoushan in Li County, Hunan Province, China. *Bulletin of the Indo-Pacific Prehistory Association*, Volume 18, pp. 101-103.

Liu, L., Lee, G., Jiang, L. & Zhang, J., 2007. The earliest rice domestication in China. *Antiquity*, September.81(313).

Molina, J. et al., 2011. Molecular evidence for a single evolutionary origin of domesticated rice. *PNAS*, 17 May, 108(20), pp. 8351-8356.

Zhao, Z., 2011. New Archaeobotanic Data for the Study of the Origins of Agriculture in China. *Current Anthropology*, October.52(S4).

Zheng, Y. et al., 2009. Rice fields and modes of rice cultivation between 5000 and 2500 BC in East China. *Journal of Archaeological Science*, Volume 36, pp. 2609-2616.

Zheng, Y., Guoping, S. & Xugao, C., 2007. Characteristics of the short rachillae of rice from archaeological sites dating to 7000 years ago. *China Science Bulletin (English edition)*, 52(12), pp. 1654-1660.

# 43: An unlikely success story

Beadle, G., 1980. The Ancestry of Corn. *Scientific American*, January, 241(1), pp. 96-103.

Benz, B., 2001. Archaeological evidence of teosinte domestication from Guila Naquitz, Oaxaca. *PNAS*, 13 February, 98(4), pp. 2104-2106.

Dickau, R., Ranere, A. & Cooke, R., 2007. Starch grain evidence for the preceramic dispersals of maize and root crops into tropical dry and humid forests of Panama. 27 February, 104(9), pp. 3651-3656.

Doebley, J., 1990. Molecular Evidence and the Evolution of Maize. *Economic Botany*, 44(3 Supplement), pp. 6-27.

Iriarte, J. et al., 2004. Evidence for cultivar adoption and emerging complexity during the mid-Holocene in the La Plata basin. *Nature*, 2 December, Volume 432, pp. 614-617.

Jaenicke-Després, V. et al., 2003. Early Allelic Selection in Maize as Revealed by Ancient DNA. *Science*, 14 November, Volume 302, pp. 1206-1208.

Long, A. et al., 1989. First Direct Ams Dates On Early Maize From Tehuacan, Mexico. *Radiocarbon*, 31(3), pp. 1035-1040.

Matsuoka, Y. et al., 2002. A single domestication for maize shown by multilocus microsatellite genotyping. *PNAS*, 30 April, 99(9), pp. 6080-6084.

Merrill, W. et al., 2009. The diffusion of maize to the southwestern United States and its impact. *PNAS*, 15 December, 106(50), pp. 21019-21026.

Pearsall, D., 2002. Maize is Still Ancient in Prehistoric Ecuador: The View from Real Alto, with Comments on Staller and Thompson. *Journal of Archaeological Science*, January, 29(1), pp. 51-55.

Perry, L. et al., 2006. Early maize agriculture and interzonal interaction in southern Peru. *Nature*, 2 March, Volume 440, pp. 76-79.

Piperno, D. & Flannery, K., 2001. The earliest archaeological maize (Zea mays L.) from highland Mexico: New accelerator mass spectrometry dates and their implications. *PNAS*, 13 February, 98(4), pp. 2101-2103.

Piperno, D. et al., 2009. Starch grain and phytolith evidence for early ninth millennium B.P. maize from the Central Balsas River Valley, Mexico. *PNAS*, 31 March, 106(13), pp. 5019-5024.

Pohl, M. et al., 1996. Early Agriculture in the Maya Lowlands. *Latin American Antiquity*, December, 7(4), pp. 355-372.

Pope, K. et al., 2001. Origin and Environmental Setting of Ancient Agriculture in the Lowlands of Mesoamerica. *Science*, 18 May, Volume 292, pp. 1370-1373.

Ranere, A. et al., 2009. The cultural and chronological context of early Holocene maize and squash domestication in the Central Balsas River Valley, Mexico. *PNAS*, 13 March, 106(13), pp. 5014-5018.

Smalley, J. & Blake, M., 2003. Sweet Beginnings Stalk Sugar and the Domestication of Maize. *Current Anthropology*, December, 44(5), pp. 675-703.

Staller, J., 2003. An Examination of the Palaeobotanical and Chronological Evidence for an Early Introduction of Maize (Zea mays L.) into South America: A Response to Pearsall. *Journal of Archaeological Science*, March, 30(3), pp. 373-380.

Wang, R. et al., 1999. The limits of selection during maize domestication. *Nature*, 18 March, Volume 398, pp. 236-239.

Zarrillo, S. et al., 2008. Directly dated starch residues document early formative maize (Zea mays L.) in tropical Ecuador. *PNAS*, 1 April, 105(13), pp. 5006-5011.

# 44: Spreading the word

Bouckaert, R. et al., 2012. Mapping the Origins and Expansion of the Indo-European Language Family. *Science*, 24 August, Volume 337, pp. 957-960.

Diamond, J., 1991. *The Third Chimpanzee*. London: Random.

Gimbutas, M., 1997. The Kurgan Culture and the Indo-Europeanization of Europe. In: M. Dexter & K. Jones-Bley, eds. *Journal of Indo-European Studies Monographs No. 18*. Washington, DC: Institute of the Study of Man.

Gimbutas, M. & Dexter, M., 1999. *The Living Goddesses*. Berkeley & Los Angeles, CA: University of California Press.

Gray, R. & Atkinson, Q., 2003. Language-tree divergence times support the Anatolian theory of Indo-European origin. *Nature*, 27 November, Volume 426, pp. 435-439.

Mallory, J., 1989. *In Search of the Indo-Europeans: Language, Archaeology and Myth*. London: Thames & Hudson.

Mallory, J. & Adams, D., 2006. *The Oxford Introduction to Proto-Indo-European and the Proto-Indo-European world*. New York, NY: Oxford University Press.

McWhorter, J., 2002. *The Power of Babel: a Natural History of Language*. London: William Heinemann.

Renfrew, C., 1987. *Archaeology & Language*. London: Jonathon Cape.

Renfrew, C., 2004. Time Depth, Convergence Theory, and Innovation in Proto-Indo-European: 'Old Europe' as a PIE Linguistic Area. In: A. Bammesberger & T. Vennemann, eds. *Languages in Prehistoric Europe*. 2nd ed. Heidelberg: Universitätsverlag Winter, pp. 17-48.

# 45: The copper awl

Craddock, P., 2000. From hearth to furnace : evidences for the earliest metal smelting technologies in the Eastern Mediterranean From hearth to furnace : evidences for the earliest metal smelting technologies in the Eastern Mediterranean. *Paléorient*, 26(2), pp. 151-165.

Garfinkel, Y., Klimscha, F., Shalev, S. & Rosenberg, D., 2014. The Beginning of Metallurgy in the Southern Levant: A Late 6th Millennium CalBC Copper Awl from Tel Tsaf, Israel. *PLoS One*, March, 9(3), p. e92591.

Radivojevic, M. et al., 2010. On the origins of extractive metallurgy: new evidence from Europe. *Journal of Archaeological Science*, Volume 37, pp. 2775-2787.

Roberts, B., Thornton, C. & Pigott, V., 2009. Development of metallurgy in Eurasia. *Antiquity*, Volume 83, pp. 1012-1022.

# 46: Ötzi the Iceman

Bonani, G. et al., 1994. AMS 14C determinations of tissue, bone and grass samples from the Otztal ice man. *Radiocarbon*, 36(2), pp. 247-250.

Dorfer, L. et al., 1999. A medical report from the stone age?. *The Lancet*, Volume 354, pp. 1023-1025.

Endicott, P. et al., 2009. Genotyping human ancient mtDNA control and coding region polymorphisms with a multiplexed Single-Base-Extension assay: the singular maternal history of the Tyrolean Iceman. *BMC Genetics*, 10(29).

Ermini, L. et al., 2009. Complete Mitochondrial Genome Sequence of the Tyrolean Iceman. *Current Biology*, 11 November, 18(21), pp. 1687-1693.

Evershed, R. et al., 2008. Earliest date for milk use in the Near East and southeastern Europe linked to cattle herding. *Nature*, 25 September, Volume 455, pp. 528-531.

Keller, A. et al., 2012. New insights into the Tyrolean Iceaman's origin and phenotype as inferred by whole-genome sequencing. *Nature Communications*, 29 Feb.

Maixner, F. et al., 2016. The 5300-year-old Helicobacter pylori genome of the Iceman. *Science*, 8 January, 351(6269), pp. 162-165.

Muller, W. et al., 2003. Origin and Migration of the Alpine Iceman. *Science*, 31 October, Volume 302, pp. 862-866.

Rollo, F., Ubaldi, M., Ermini, L. & Marota, I., 2002. Otzi's last meals: DNA analysis of the intestinal content of the Neolithic glacier mummy from the Alps. *PNAS*, 1 October, 99(20), pp. 12594-12599.

# 47: The Nebra Sky disc

Meller, H. & Garrett, K., 2004. Star search: Relic thieves, a 3600-year-old disk of the heavens, and an intrepid archaeologist add up to a real-life thriller. *National Geographic*, Volume 205.

Saxony-Anhalt State Museum of Prehistory, 2013. *The Nebra Sky Disk*. [Online]
Available at: http://www.lda-lsa.de/en/nebra_sky_disc/
[Accessed July 2015].

# 48: The Egtved Girl

Frei, K. et al., 2015. Tracing the dynamic life story of a Bronze Age Female. *Scientific Reports*, 21 May.

# 49: Early adopters

Algaze, G., 1993. Expansionary dynamics of some early pristine states. *American Anthropologist*, Volume 95, pp. 304-333.

Childe, G., 1936. *Man Makes Himself*. London: Watts and Co..

Childe, G., 1950. The Urban Revolution. *The Town Planning Review*, April, 21(1), pp. 3-17.

Connah, G., 2005. Holocene Africa. In: C. Scarre, ed. *The human past*. London: Thames & Hudson, pp. 350-391.

Matthews, R., 2005. The Rise of Civilization in Southwest Asia. In: C. Scarre, ed. *The Human Past*. London: Thames & Hudson, pp. 432-471.

McIntosh, J., 2005. *Ancient Mesopotamia: New perspectives*. Santa Barbara, CA: ABC-CLIO.

Smith, M., 2009. V. Gordon Childe and the Urban Revolution: a historical perspective on a revolution in urban studies. *Town Planning Review*, 80(1), pp. 3-29.

Spencer, C., 1998. A Mathematical Model of Primary State Formation. *Cultural Dynamics*, 10(1), pp. 5-20.

Spencer, C., 2010. Territorial expansion and primary state formation. *PNAS*, 20 April, 107(16), pp. 7119-7126.

Trigger, B., 2003. *Understanding early civilizations*. New York, NY: Cambridge University Press.

Wright, H., 1977. Recent research on the origin of the state. *Annual Review of Anthropology*, Volume 6, pp. 379-397.

Wright, H. & Johnson, G., 1975. Population, exchange, and early state formation in Southwestern Iran. *American Anthropologist*, Volume 77, pp. 267-289.

# 50: Writing

Akkermans, P. & Duistermaat, K., 1997. Of storage and nomads: the sealings from Late Neolithic Sabi Abyad, Syria. *Paléorient*, 22(2), pp. 17-44.

Powell, B., 2009. *Writing: Theory and History of the Technology of Civilization*. Chichester/Malden, MA: Wiley-Blackwell.

Schmandt-Besserat, D., 1992. *Before Writing (2 vols.)*. Austin, TX: University of Texas Press.

# Index

Jebel Irhoud, 116

Jebel Qafzeh, 116, 119

Jerf el-Ahmar, 156

Jericho, 156

Jiahu, 196

Jones, Sir William, 204

Jwalapuram, 118

Kabwe skull, 66

Katanda, 107, 108

Kebara Cave, 138

Kebaran, 138, 140

Keith, Sir Arthur, 19

Kennewick Man, 133, 136

*Kenyanthropus platyops*, 30, 35

Kenyon, Kathleen, 156

Kuahuqiao culture, 196

Kurgan hypothesis of Indo-European origins, 208-10

Lake Mungo remains, 123-6

Lake Turkana, 34

languages, 13, 30, 41, 65-7, 96, 101, 129, 135, 199, 204-7, 209-10

Langweiler, 185

Lascaux cave, 127-29, 131-2

Last Common Ancestor (LCA), 19, 27

Last Glacial Maximum (LGM), 129, 134, 138, 154, 168, 217

Leakey, Louis, 32

legumes, 139, 152

Levallois method, 70

Lewis-Williams, David, 130-2, 175

Liang Bua, 86

Linearbandkeramik culture (LBK), 185-90

Linnaeus, Carl, 14-7

logograms, 236

Lovejoy, Owen, 25-7, 29

Lucy (*Australopithecus afarensis*), 28-31, 35

Lyell, Sir Charles, 11

maize, 153, 155, 199-203

manioc, 203

Manis, 135

Martin. Paul, 142

Mellars, Sir Paul, 74-6

metallurgy, 211-4

microliths, 107, 109-10, 154, 177

Mithen, Steven, 107, 175

Mitochondrial Eve, 103, 105-6, 116

modern human (*Homo sapiens*), 6-9, 15-6, 19-20, 26, 29, 40, 44, 56, 61, 65-6, 68-70, 72, 74-83, 85, 87-88, 90-96, 99-101, 103, 105-7, 110, 114-23, 125-7, 134, 142-3, 146, 152, 168, 177

rituals, 67, 73-4, 98, 124, 129-30, 132, 160-1, 165, 175, 178-9, 184-5, 192-4, 219, 223

Rowley-Conwy, Peter, 187

rye, 155-6

Sahara, 62, 115

*Sahelanthropus tchadensis*, 8, 22

Sahul, 92, 123, 126

San Andrés, 202

Sarich, Vincent, 22, 104

Schmidt, Klaus, 159-60

seafood, 117, 121, 133, 158, 227

sedentism, 140, 158

sexual dimorphism, 25-6

shamanism, 130-32, 160, 175, 223

Shangshan culture, 196

Shanidar Cave, 73, 81-3, 139

sheep, 40, 138, 152, 157, 159, 163, 174, 206, 227, 234-5

Sibudan tool industry, 110

sickles, 153-4

Sierra de Atapuerca, 57

Sima de los Huesos, 73-4, 81, 93, 98

Sinai, 115, 120

Skateholm, 177-9

social brain hypothesis, 42

Solutrean, 109

*Sporormiella*, 143, 145

squashes, 202-3

St. Césaire 1 (Neanderthal), 82

stable isotope and isotope ratio analysis, 37-8, 45-6, 125, 133, 149, 165, 168, 175, 187-90, 215, 220, 223, 226-8

Star Carr, 182

Stillbay tool industry, 108-10, 112, 114

Stonehenge, 148, 150-51, 159-61, 191-2

Stoneking, Mark, 104

Stringer, Chris, 71

Swan Point, 134-5

Swartkrans Cave, 54, 95

symbols, 65, 127, 129, 159, 221, 236

taro, 197

Téviec, 177-80

Thorne, Alan, 123-24

Three Sisters, the (maize, beans, squashes), 203

Toba supervolcano eruption, 118, 122

Trægtbægerkultur (TRB), 185

Trinil, 44, 51-2

tubers, 36, 60, 197

Ubaid culture, 230, 232

52828422R10153

Made in the USA
San Bernardino, CA
10 September 2019